D0229477

THE MOVIE DOCTORS

THE MOVIE DOCTORS

SIMON MAYO + MARK KERMODE

with additional material by
Martin Toseland + Simon Toseland

CANONGATE
Edinburgh · London

First published in Great Britain in 2015 by Canongate Books Ltd
14 High Street, Edinburgh EH1 1TE

www.canongate.tv

Copyright © Simon Mayo and Mark Kermode, 2015
The moral rights of the authors have been asserted
For permissions acknowledgements, please see p.333

British Library Cataloguing-in-Publication Data
A catalogue record for this book is available on
request from the British Library

ISBN 978 1 78211 662 2

Art Direction by **Rafaela Romaya**
Design by **Hüman After All**™
Picture Research by **Hedda Archbold**

Printed and bound in Italy by Lego S.p.A

To the ushers and projectionists of the world

CONTENTS

Welcome to the Hospital

ENTRANCE

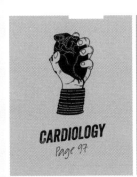

OCCUPATIONAL THERAPY
Page 143

OPHTHALMOLOGY
Page 157

PAEDIATRICS
Page 175

ISOLATION CLINIC
Page 189

PHYSIOTHERAPY
Page 207

GENERAL SURGERY
Page 215

COSMETIC SURGERY
Page 229

GERIATRICS
Page 243

TRANSPLANTS
Page 255

MORGUE
Page 269

INDEX
Page 317

CHAPEL
Page 285

**OUTPATIENTS'
CLINIC**
Page 299

**PATIENT
TRANSPORT**
Page 309

IMAGE PERMISSIONS
Page 333

ACKNOWLEDGEMENTS
Page 336

EXIT

INTRODUCTION

Simon & Mark

Dr Mayo: So, we're the Movie Doctors?

Dr Kermode: Well strictly speaking only one of us *earned* our title. Yours is an honorary doctorate. Mine was earned by actually writing a thesis on modern horror fiction.

Dr M: Well mine was earned by *actually* looking so fabulous in a gown, they decided to give me another one. So we are both, strictly speaking, doctors.

Dr K: Yes but neither of us is a medical doctor. However as 'movie doctors' we are well aware that some movies need medical attention . . .

Dr M: And also how other movies can make you feel happier, make you nicer and well . . . weller?

Dr K: I think you mean healthier.

Dr M: I think you're right, I do. And have we constructed a rather fine conceit around this?

Dr K: Indeed. So. Imagine you're a movie in need of medical attention – you might be far too long, or unnecessarily upbeat, or be in need of a live organ transplant . . .

Dr M: . . . or you might be an actual human patient in need of a cure for a broken heart, tinnitus or . . .

Dr K: Celluloid or humanoid, the Movie Doctors' Clinic will help.

Dr M: Films will be referred to the relevant department, depending on whether they need a bit of cosmetic surgery or something more drastic.

Dr K: You can find Michael Bay's films in the recovery room.

Dr M: And patients?

Dr K: Unlike in a real hospital, waiting times for patients' clinics is minimal.

Dr M: From the moment you arrive at our doors, we'll diagnose you and suggest cures for your problems. We've colour coded everything so you don't get lost —

Dr K: Or find yourself accidentally incorporated into a Human Centipede.

Dr M: So sit back, dip your hand into your bucket of corn-based snack and enjoy this beautifully designed, elegantly written and strikingly affordable movie concept book. Nurse, the screens . . .

ACCIDENT & EMERGENCY

Have you ever found yourself in A & E late on a Friday night? If so, you'll know that it can be quite a sweary, violent and unpleasant place. Rest assured that the Movie Doctors' A & E is nothing like that. True, our clinic is full of **action**, **drama**, **glamour** and **movie magic**: **car chases**, **heroes who survive ridiculous injuries**, **real-life accidents on set.** But ours is safe – you could watch the goriest, most violent scenes in our clinic and it wouldn't add up to an hour spent in an actual A & E. Go on, collect a ticket at reception. **The Movie Doctors will attend to you shortly.**

ON-SET A & E

A Clinical Examination

Film sets are really dangerous places to work. In August 2014, the *Independent* newspaper reported that gruff-voiced action star Jason Statham (of whom both the Doctors are huge fans) had 'narrowly avoided death on the set of *The Expendables 3*'. According to the story, 'the actor was forced to leap from a truck he was driving before it plunged 60ft into the sea after a stunt went horribly wrong'. 'He faced death,' declared *Expendables* co-star Sylvester Stallone with a straight face (or at least a face as 'straight' as Sly can actually manage). 'He was test driving a three-ton truck and the brakes run out. It went down 60ft into the Black Sea and was impaled.'

For anyone else, it would have been catastrophic – but not for The Stath. Luckily, before becoming everyone's favourite shirtless, oil-wrestling screen star, Jason was a champion diver (he competed for England at the Auckland Commonwealth Games in 1990) and was thus able to leap nimbly from the crashing vehicle, presumably performing a perfectly executed pike en route, before swimming briskly to safety. 'If anyone else had been in that truck he would have been dead,' Stallone told the *Indie*. 'But because Jason is an Olympic quality diver he got out of it.' As for The Stath himself, he proved as cool as his on-screen persona, playing down the allegedly life-threatening incident, and insisting that the worst thing that happened to him during the shoot of *The Expendables 3* was the fact that 'I snapped a shoelace in the very first scene.' You can see why we love him.

Jason's on-set accident made for acres of lively news coverage, all of which helped to publicise the movie. But the fact remains that (if the story is true) Statham had a very lucky escape. Others have been less fortunate. Indeed, over its hundred-year-plus history, the art of moviemaking has often proved injurious and occasionally lethal, with cast and crew risking life and limb in pursuit of a good shot.

Michael Curtiz's disaster epic *Noah's Ark* (1928) was billed as 'The spectacle of the ages!', using a reported 600,000 gallons of water to bring the image of a massive biblical flood crashing onto cinema screens. Audiences were awestruck by the results, but few contemporary viewers knew that such overwhelming spectacle had been achieved at an extremely high human cost. According to popular folklore, three extras drowned during the climactic flood sequences, while another lost a leg from injuries incurred on the set. Indeed, so high was the casualty rate on *Noah's Ark* that Hollywood promptly instigated new stunt-safety regulations with the specific aim of minimising the risks which had become an everyday part of moviemaking. Yet even with such apparent safeguards in place, lives have continued to be lost while making movies.

Glancing back over the last forty years of film-making, we find a litany of tragic accidents which demonstrate just how perilous the profession can be. Most distressingly, in the early eighties seasoned performer Vic Morrow and youngsters My-ca Dinh Le and Renee Shin-Yi Chen were killed on the set of *Twilight Zone: The Movie* (1983) when an action sequence involving a helicopter went horrifyingly wrong (the ensuing scandal and lawsuits would last a decade). In the nineties, rising star Brandon Lee died of a gunshot wound during the making of *The Crow* (1994), an accident blamed by many upon cost-cutting measures which led to a breakdown in standard safety procedures (a props master, rather than a weapons expert, was left in charge of the gun). In 2007, set dresser David Ritchie was killed when 'a frozen piece of sand and gravel' fell from the wall of an outdoor set during the making of the sci-fi thriller *Jumper* (2008). As recently as 2015, Randall Miller became the first film-maker to be jailed for an on-set fatality in the US. Miller pleaded guilty to the involuntary manslaughter of camera operator Sarah Jones, who died when a train hit a metal-frame bed during the filming of a dream sequence on the Gregg Allman biopic *Midnight Rider* (the film has since been abandoned).

While such horrendous cases become headline-grabbing news, far more common are the stories of everyday injuries which have long been a part of the moviemaking process. Back in the late 1920s, screen icon Louise Brooks was warned by friends and colleagues that *Beggars of Life* director William Wellman was 'a madman' who would try to get her to take part in dangerous stunts from which she should steer well clear. Yet, true to form, Brooks merely saw the warnings as a challenge, and opted to do several potentially lethal scenes herself, including a sequence in which she jumps a freight train with co-star Richard Arlen. Apparently, the rule of thumb for hobos at the time was that if you couldn't count the lug nuts on the wheels of a train, it was moving too fast to board. Just try counting the lug nuts on the train onto which Brooks jumps in *Beggars of Life.* Even allowing for a degree of photographic ingenuity, that train is clearly moving fast enough to present a very real danger to the famously fearless actress, who miraculously completed the shoot without needing to be carted off to the local hospital.

In those days, such fortitude was business as usual for screen performers. Leading players Lillian Gish and Richard Barthelmess performed their own stunts for D.W. Griffith's masterpiece *Way Down East* (1920), including the celebrated river sequence in which Gish drifts on a slab of floating ice toward a waterfall while Barthelmess leaps to her death-defying rescue. Filmed at White River Junction in Vermont, the sequence opened with Gish – wearing only a thin dress and a shawl – running out into sub-zero temperatures, the shock of which famously caused her to faint. A nurse was on hand to tend to Gish, but the medical ministrations seem to have amounted to little more than taking the actress indoors to warm up a bit before being sending her outside to do it again. Next, Gish was required to fall face down onto a slab of ice (*real* ice, as opposed to prop ice) which breaks free and floats off down the river. With her hair and a hand trailing in the icy water, Gish promptly found her face frozen (you can see the ice forming on her skin) and lost the feeling in several fingers. Years later she would note that the hand in question still caused her pain. Meanwhile, Griffith (whose face also froze) kept his camera warm by lighting a small fire beneath it to prevent the machine from grinding to a standstill. To this day, the fact that both Gish and Barthelmess appear to be in genuine peril remains a key part of this legendary sequence's appeal – an alluring mix of dramatic invention and documentary endangerment.

At around the same time that Gish was having her fingers frozen off on *Way Down East*, comedian Harold Lloyd was having two fingers blown off his right hand when a prop bomb exploded during the making of *Haunted Spooks* (1920). Meanwhile Buster Keaton fractured his neck while filming *Sherlock Jr.* (1924), but continued filming the scene in question, his injury not being detected until it showed up on an X-ray eleven years later! Dancers had a hard time of it too. While shooting a celebrated number for *Swing Time* (1936), Ginger Rogers was left with bleeding feet, prompting the famous quote that 'Rogers did everything Fred Astaire did, except backwards and in high heels'. As for Astaire, he got whacked in the face by Rogers' 'flying sleeve' while filming 'Let's Face the Music and Dance' for *Follow the Fleet* (also 1936) but 'kept on dancing, although somewhat maimed'. The smack made it into the movie.

Other minor on-set accidents which have been caught on camera include Charles McGraw suffering a broken jaw as his head is forced into a vat of soup by Kirk Douglas in *Spartacus* (1960); Ellen Burstyn ricking her back while being hoisted off her feet by unseen ropes in *The Exorcist* (1973); Viggo Mortensen breaking two toes while kicking a helmet in frustration in Peter Jackson's *Lord of the Rings: The Two Towers* (2002); Robert Downey Jr. breaking Halle Berry's arm as he attempts to restrain her character in *Gothika* (2003); and

Leonardo DiCaprio accidentally smashing a glass with his hand in 2012's *Django Unchained* ('Blood was dripping down his hand [but] he never broke character,' recalled producer Stacey Sher admiringly). Meanwhile, Brad Pitt spent a large portion of *Se7en* (1995) with a heavily bandaged arm after accidentally putting his hand through a car window ('we worked his injury into the storyline'), and during the filming of *Troy* (2004), in which he plays hunky Achilles, managed to tear – guess what? – his Achilles tendon!

Afflictions such as these are all part of the rough and tumble of moviemaking, and there can be few performers whose screen careers have passed without a work-related visit to A & E. Oddly, audiences seem to rather like the idea of performers suffering actual bodily harm for the sake of their entertainment, provided the injuries remain relatively trivial. Yet the occasional tragedy shows us just how dangerous moviemaking can really be, and reminds us why film-making unions spend so much time banging on unfashionably about 'health and safety'.

Films may be fantasy, but on-set accidents are real, and the Movie Doctors look forward to a future in which cinema is not just spectacular, but – more importantly – *safe*. As executive producer Steven Spielberg observed in the wake of the *Twilight Zone* (1983) tragedy, 'A movie is a fantasy – it's light and shadow flickering on a screen. No movie is worth dying for. I think people are standing up much more now than ever before to producers and directors who ask too much. If something isn't safe, it's the right and responsibility of every actor or crew member to yell, "Cut!"'

CAR CHASES FOR THE CONSTIPATED

Doctors in Discussion

Dr Kermode: So, car chases.

Dr Mayo: I don't really like them.

Dr K: Really?

Dr M: Yes. Apart from the obvious . . .

Dr K: *Bullitt, The French Connection* . . .

Dr M: Sure, those but also the three that spring to my mind: the Minis in *The Italian Job*, the police car pile-up in *The Blues Brothers* and the Moscow chase in *The Bourne Supremacy*. Apart from those . . .

Dr K: You think they're boring.

Dr M: Yes, I mean they should be the thing that makes you gasp in awe, makes you have to wipe the seat in the cinema, but that doesn't really happen, does it?

Dr K: The problem with most movie car chases is that they're too fast.

Dr M: You want a slow chase?

Dr K: In a way. The thing is, car chases are only exciting when they have a sense of danger – for example, when the streets are crowded. Look at *The French Connection*. That film was produced by Philip D'Antoni, who produced *Bullitt*. He and director William Friedkin specifically set out to top the car chase from *Bullitt* . . .

Dr M: A pretty tough call given there's the Steve McQueen effect in *Bullitt*.

Dr K: . . . and the most memorable thing about *The French Connection* chase is the sheer amount of traffic. Indeed, for certain sequences, rather than getting the necessary permissions, and getting the streets properly cleared, they just went ahead and filmed some sequences *in the middle of normal traffic*.

Dr M: What, with real people, real cars and everything?

Dr K: Yes.

Dr M: And speed bumps?

Dr K: And speed bumps. So Gene Hackman's car – which stuntman Bill Hickman was driving – does actually bang into a city bus at one point, for real.

Dr M: Ouch. Lawsuit.

Dr K: Oddly, no. The point is that one of the reasons the car chase in *The French Connection* really is a thrill ride is because it genuinely appears to be dangerous.

Dr M: So, you're saying, contrary to popular belief, that it's not how fast and furious the chase is, it's how overcrowded it is.

Dr K: I am. That's exactly what I'm saying.

Dr M: But still, they're usually boring, aren't they?

Dr K: Well a lot of them are because they're too inconsequential. You're supposed not to care that fifty-six people have just been shunted off the freeway in a frenzy of twisted metal and squealing brakes because, hey, they're not the stars of the movie!

Dr M: Well you should toughen up a bit. Be like the guy who wins the chase. You crash through the streets of San Francisco or Las Vegas or Rome at 150 mph pursued by an evil assassin in some souped-up, off-road supercar and you emerge with nothing more than a rather sexy cut on the right edge of your forehead. That's class.

Dr K: Precisely. 'Whiplash' becomes merely the title of a film about a drummer (which, incidentally, isn't really about a drummer).

Dr M: So we agree. Unless there are actual people, in actual cars, with speed bumps, we're not advocating a car chase to get your pulse racing?

Dr K: Yes, I think that's medically sound.

BEYOND BELIEF

Movie Heroes Who Defy Medical Science

JAMES BOND

SKYFALL (2012)

Shot with a depleted uranium shell, plummeting into a river from a racing train and fighting under water so cold it would make the surface of Mars feel like the Seychelles counted as a mildly hectic afternoon for 007 who, we submit, would have been as dead as an unnamed extra within the first seven minutes of the film.

How dead? ☠☠☠☠☠☠☠☠☠

FRODO BAGGINS

THE LORD OF THE RINGS: THE RETURN OF THE KING (2003)

The Movie Doctors – despite our lack of detailed medical knowledge – can happily confirm that anyone who stands that close to a lake of molten rock bubbling nicely at 1200°C (in the accurately named Mount Doom) would simply self-combust. Unless you are a geothermal miracle and have magma running through your veins, you're having a lava.

How dead? ☠☠☠☠☠☠☠☠

JOHN RAMBO

RAMBO (2008)

Most of the gunshots in *Rambo* seem to either sever their targets around the midriff (Dr M: Medically speaking, 'the abdomen') or produce a gory collage of brain and blood from a direct head shot. Rambo himself is made of sterner American steel. Plugged on the shoulder by a cannon, yes an actual Burmese military cannon mounted on a gunboat, he screams in pain a bit, and then carries on with the carnage. Proof that moral certainty based on a superior political system can perform biological miracles.

How dead? ☠☠☠☠☠☠☠☠☠

VINCENT

COLLATERAL (2004)

When Jamie Foxx decides he's had enough of Tom Cruise in the back of his cab (and who amongst us hasn't thought that), he takes action. Instead of pulling over and asking him to leave, he turns the car over multiple times amid much metal-sparking, screeching of tyres and smashing of glass. The car finally comes to an upside-down halt and Tom shakes his head, dusts down his attractive suit and continues on foot. We don't even think he was wearing a seatbelt...

How dead? ☠☠☠☠☠☠☠

JOHN McCLANE

DIE HARD WITH A VENGEANCE (1995)

Tom the cat in *Tom and Jerry* has nothing on John McClane in the *Die Hard* franchise – he can dust himself down having fallen fifty feet, survive a hailstorm of machine-gun fire and, in a scene the Movie Doctors particularly like for its medical accuracy, can throw a massive explosive device out of the back of a subway train and survive unscathed – always armed with a pithy one-liner and a winning grimace. And our favourite vest, ever.

How dead? ☠☠☠☠

DOCTOR IN THE HOUSE

Essential First Aid in the Cinema

The Movie Doctors recommend that each and every cinemagoer undertakes at least a basic course in first aid because the cinema can be a physically and psychologically challenging experience. For example, say your movie companion is sucking on a chili dog (like John Mellencamp said) and a piece lodges itself in his/her throat, how do you rescue the situation while still maintaining focus on the action? Or, say, during *Diana* your buddy experiences an existential crisis of identity brought on by the mind-numbing awfulness of everything, how do you lead him/her back to tranquillity and self-respect? Part first-aid kit, part instruction manual, our guide to essential first aid in the cinema is an invaluable resource.

ANTI-NAUSEA PILLS

For 3D films. Designed to reduce the headaches and eyestrain which cause a feeling of sickness while squinting at the screen through badly designed polarised glasses.

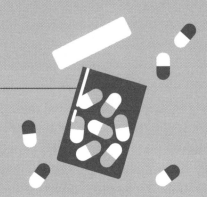

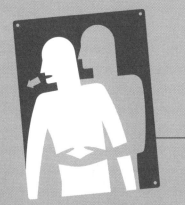

THE HEIMLICH MANOEUVRE

For stuck snacks and plot twists impossible to swallow, press one fist, thumb side in, just above the belly button and grab with the other fist. Pull your fists upwards and inward to force the trapped object out. Pick up the ejected object and hand to the patient – these things are too expensive to waste.

COUGH SYRUP

There's nothing more annoying than a good movie ruined by a persistent hacking cough. If you are a cougher – don't go to the movies. Stay at home and annoy your family. But if you insist on acting selfishly, we, the rest of the cinema audience, assert our right to force-feed you Benylin.

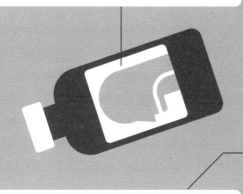

NIGHT-AND-BAY CREAM

A protective emollient to condition your skin against overexposure to vast amounts of fiery explosions. Also reduces wrinkles due to wincing at excruciating dialogue.

EARPLUGS

There is a risk here that you will look like Prince Charles at a Meat Loaf concert. But if you put that to one side, as HRH did during 'Bat Out of Hell', then you should know we only have your future movie enjoyment as our concern. When even *Cinderella* is turned up to *Fast and Furious*, it's time to wear protection, kids.

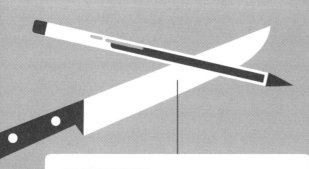

TRACHEOTOMY

Having trouble breathing while watching one of Noah Baumbach's stifling early works? A steak knife and a biro will open the airwaves nicely.

PHARMACY

Everyone needs a little balance in their lives, but try telling that to the average Hollywood executive, panicked by the latest test screenings which show their sure-fire summer blockbuster is sinking faster than the *Lusitania*. **Luckily, the Movie Doctors are here with their bag of totally legal, mood-altering movies** to bring you up or down a notch, on demand. We also have a cure for the needle-phobic. Just tell us what the problem seems to be, and the Movie Doctors can fix it.

UPPERS AND DOWNERS

Movies to Lighten or Darken Your Soul

Working in the media, we see many wrecked and ruined lives. Talented men and women who started so full of hope and promise but who then got sucked into the downward spiral of *Big Brother*, *Keeping Up with the Kardashians* and *The Week in Westminster*.

Occasionally, however, we encounter those happy folk who are too enthusiastic, too keen to progress, too optimistic about their inevitable career path. They smile and bellow from all corners of the building about how their latest idea has been commissioned without even a budget, a presenter or a title. We all come to the reassuring conclusion that there is something very wrong here, some darkness they are dying to conceal.

Whether we are meeting the cheerful or the sad, the Movie Doctors always carry an emergency pack of mood-altering films to bring the desperate and needy back to normality. Here we share them with you so that you too can be prepared to meet life's ups and downs with equanimity. Let's start with gloom . . .

DOWNERS 💀

If you suspect that you are being a little too positive at work, if your pay rise was slightly on the generous side and your colleagues admire you just a bit too much, here are some movies to take you down a peg or two. These are depressing films not because they are cheap, badly made or poorly acted, but because they are *bleak*. Because just reading about them fills your heart with darkness and makes you stare,

along with Mr Herzog, into the abyss. Use sparingly and always in a light, airy, well-ventilated room.

ANGELA'S ASHES *(1999)*

A miserable, poor, wet, sick, violent, cruel Catholic childhood in Limerick becomes slightly less miserable in New York.

Measure of gloom 💀💀💀💀💀💀💀

RING OF BRIGHT WATER *(1969)*

It's a pet movie. A pet movie set on the west coast of Scotland starring the *Born Free* pairing of Bill Travers and Virginia McKenna. We know how this will play out. Bachelor Bill buys an otter called Mij, finds it's too much of a handful for his small London flat and they move to an idyllic, remote cottage. Virginal Virginia who lives next door falls for them both, and the course of true love is set: man, woman and otter in perfect harmony.

This all works beautifully until Mij is chopped in two by a ditch digger with a spade. It is sudden, brutal and shocking. There has been no build-up, no hint of illness, the otter never coughs or looks depressed. One minute he's running happily through the peaty bog, the next he's been dispatched to that otter holt in the sky.

For a U-certificate film, this wretched vision will hit viewers hard. And with Val Doonican singing the title track, this more than deserves its place as a top downer.

Measure of gloom ☠☠☠☠☠☠☠☠

THE MIST *(2007)*

No one does misery quite like Stephen King (indeed no one did *Misery* quite like Stephen King), but the real scaremonger here is screenwriter/director Frank Darabont. If it's terror, slaughter and hopelessness you need, then *The Mist* is your film. Some are misled by the fact that the King/Darabont combo produced *The Shawshank Redemption*, concluding that while there may well be some tough scenes to endure here, ultimately there'll be an ending to cheer. Maybe even a boat-polishing beach scene to send us home happy. Well, think again. After a storm-induced shopping trip to the local mall, the titular mist rolls in. (Meteorological NB: as the visibility is less than one kilometre, this is not a mist but a fog. But as that would make it *The Fog* and John Carpenter has already done that, everyone has to call it 'a mist'. As none of our protagonists mentions a fear of ghostly lepers, we conclude none of them can have seen this 1980 horror film.) Surfing in on the wave of condensed water droplets are spiders, bugs, a many-tentacled thing – and more than a suggestion that our friends in the military are to blame.

King's novella has an inconclusive ending, but Darabont's movie is something else. Just when you think the final reel has got as grim as it could possibly get, he delivers a final scene so devoid of hope that you'll pop back to *The Road* for some light relief (see p.305).

Measure of gloom ☠☠☠☠☠☠☠☠☠

WINTER LIGHT *(1963)*

If you have worked out the meaning of life and your place in the celestial order, make an appointment to see Pastor Tomas Ericsson. He might have the church and all the right clothes, but that turns out to be misleading. Here's a priest who, if asked to present 'Pause For Thought', would just tell us to end it all now. He can't stop an anguished fisherman from committing suicide, he can't take the affection on offer from young Marta and he can't believe in God any more. The stunning photography and brilliant performances offer some brief consolation before we reflect on the utter meaninglessness of life.

Measure of gloom ☠☠☠☠☠☠

WHEN THE WIND BLOWS *(1986)*

Just because it's a cartoon doesn't mean it won't fill you with despair. Raymond Briggs produced this story when we were still (just about) worried about the pesky Soviets and the cowboy in the White House. Jim and Hilda Bloggs are preparing for the coming nuclear attack with the guidance of leaflets from the government. The voices of John Mills and Peggy Ashcroft reassure us briefly before they both die of radiation poisoning. The only consolation for the modern viewer is that this was all a long time ago, when Russia was thought of as a dangerous country with a crazed leader who had designs on its neighbours. So that's all right, then . . .

Measure of gloom ☠☠☠☠☠☠☠

UPPERS ☀

Yes, please. The combined effect of all those downers has made the Movie Doctors look more pasty-faced than ever. It is time to prescribe some films that will *brighten your life*. Films that we are sure will make you feel better about yourself, your neighbour and *the world in general* (see also 'Patient Transport', p.308). Unlike the downers, you may watch as many as you like, as often as you like.

OIL CITY CONFIDENTIAL (2009)

It's time for some *feel-good* movies. And for our first choice, an actual, real-life *feel-good* movie. This Julian Temple documentary about Dr Feelgood has been unfairly pigeonholed as being only for yearning, nostalgic men in their fifties who wish they could still fit the shiny suits they wore in the seventies. Not so. This movie we prescribe for everyone. There is something irresistibly joyous about *OCC* which demands its inclusion.

It is the story of four guys from Canvey Island, Essex, making music that will lift your soul. The joke was always that a storm had blown through Canvey Island causing millions of pounds' worth of improvements, but here Temple runs with the gag that the Thames Estuary is linked with the Mississippi Delta. Thus we have the Thames Delta – our very own swampland. This is an upper for all because it is a *proper film*. Even if you've never heard of Dr Feelgood, never been to Canvey Island and never worn a shiny suit, you will leave this movie dancing your way to the nearest oil terminal.

Feel-good factor **ALL THE FEELGOODS**

THE SHAWSHANK REDEMPTION (1994)

And this, Mr Darabont, is the sort of Stephen King story that we like you working on. Topping endless lists of 'Best Movie Evs!' (Dr K wrote a book, made a documentary, and still whinges on endlessly about the 'tacked-on ending'), *The Shawshank Redemption* had to make our uppers list. For much of this prison drama you may be wondering why we are prescribing it; as we have observed before, you have to get through a lot of Shawshank before you get any redemption. But there is something so noble about Andy Dufresne and Red (Tim Robbins and Morgan Freeman) that even when the baton-wielding, Bible-preaching redneck guards are a-clubbin' and a-beatin', we are so warmed by this story of hope that we stay with it. When justice finally rains down on the vile prison warden Norton (Bob Gunton) we are more than ready to whoop and holler.

Red says, 'You either get busy livin' or you get busy dyin',' and whether you get grumpy at the ending or you just love it as it is, you'll finish this movie with hope in your heart and the desire to go varnish someone's boat (not a euphemism).

Feel-good factor ☀☀☀☀☀☀☀

THE COLLECTED WORKS OF RICHARD CURTIS APART FROM THE BOAT THAT ROCKED

If you are walking through town and something lovely happens, that's Richard Curtis. If your partner says, it's OK, he forgives you, that's Richard Curtis. And if as you drive along the A303 you notice a wavy-haired man on his knees proposing to his flaxen-haired girlfriend in the middle of Stonehenge while a boy band mime an Elvis Costello song, that too is Richard Curtis. There is not a single writer, producer or director anywhere who has devoted

more time to warm-heartedness than Richard Whalley Anthony Curtis.

This does not mean soppy. This does not mean sugar-coated pap with horrible characters who make you vomit with their nauseating sincerity and po-faced moralising. It just means that he wants to make films about love (yes, actually). *Four Weddings and a Funeral*, *Notting Hill*, *About Time*, *Bridget Jones* and even *Trash* are all movies that will make the world a brighter, less threatening place. Charles gets Carrie and Anna gets William, though Harry messes things up with Karen (careful with that elaborately wrapped necklace).

Feel-good factor ☀-☀-☀-☀-☀-☀-☀-☀-☀-☀

MAMMA MIA! *(2008)*

My, my, how can we resist you? Is it the best movie in the world? Er, no. Is it the best musical movie in the world? No again. Do any of the cast (Meryl Streep, Pierce Brosnan, Amanda Seyfried, Colin Firth et al) get to deliver career-best performances? We think not. *However*, this film – made in 2008 when the Greeks still had money (even if, as we learned later, it was all ours) – is so bad it is strangely wonderful.

In summary: on a Greek island, Meryl Streep sings the Abba catalogue like it's Ibsen, Colin Firth can't dance, Pierce Brosnan can't sing and Stellan Skarsgård looks like he's accidentally wandered in from a completely different movie. Fortunately for us, the songs are bombproof and somehow turn this sow's ear into a celluloid silk purse. Before you know it you are dancing in the aisles and giving money to tramps. Don't argue, just surrender to your inner dancing queen. Couldn't escape if you wanted to.

Feel-good factor ☀-☀-☀-☀-☀-☀-☀-☀-☀

SULLIVAN'S TRAVELS *(1941)*

If you want an 'upper' that will impress passing film students, then start here. Written and directed by

Preston Sturges, it tells the story of a successful, if shallow, film director John Sullivan (Joel McCrae) who wants to make a film that *means something*. He worries that maybe all that froth and silliness (*Hey Hey in the Hayloft*) won't count for much when the final tally is being calculated. So, much to the horror of his studio bosses who don't think such a spoiled lightweight like Sullivan can make an 'issues' picture, he sets off dressed as a tramp to 'get real' (as they never said in 1941). He finds The Girl (Veronica Lake), and together they set off to understand what poor folk are really like.

He is robbed, beaten up, arrested and sentenced to a labour camp. This, as you might realise, is the downer section of the film. But while in the camp he watches a screening of Walt Disney's *Playful Pluto*, a 1934 animation noted for a sequence where Pluto gets stuck on some flypaper. The crowd around Sullivan lap it up and he realises that comedy does, after all, have a purpose. He ditches his planned social epic *O Brother, Where Art Thou?* (yes, this is where it all started) and promises to stick to comedy. He also gets The Girl. As one of the best satires on the morals of Hollywood, your laughs are righteous, intellectual laughs, and so count double. Your recovery is assured.

Feel-good factor ☀ ☀ ☀ ☀ ☀ ☀ ☀

GROUNDHOG DAY *(1993)*

The Movie Doctors believe that being what some people call 'grumpy' is actually just *having standards*. You're no longer a child, you barely remember teenage angst and now, with a certain maturity, you find that standards, everywhere, are slipping. You might have put up with it once – when you knew no better – but not now.

The Danes invented the word (*grum* means cruel) but it's an American who leads the field here. Few movie stars do 'grumpy' better than Bill Murray. He doesn't even have to say anything, his *face* is grumpy. One stare at the camera and you know

that he's just very disappointed. With everything. And he has a lot to be disappointed about. He's a bored weatherman stuck repeating the same day over and over again; a day that starts with the clock radio playing 'I Got You Babe' by Sonny and Cher (a trick repeated hilariously by Dr Mayo one fab Radio 1 morn). He's in love with Andie MacDowell. She thinks he's a jerk. But as the groundhog in question – 'Punxsutawney Phil' – works his magic, Murray uses his time to do good works and compile a list of MacDowell's favourite things: poems, ice cream flavours, songs etc. She falls for this stuff completely, he toasts world peace and they 'retire' for the evening.

You'll wake up tomorrow happy with your lot, keen to do good deeds and to avoid rodent-based weather forecasting.

Feel-good factor ☀ ☀ ☀ ☀ ☀ ☀

DIE HARD *(1988)*

A man in a vest takes on not just mercenaries with mullets (studios take note: that's a new franchise right there) but a snarling German anarchist (is there any other kind?). There is no doubt that this action movie is a hoot – a feel-good film full of jokes and memorable one-liners. True, there are a quite few deaths, falling bodies, explosions and scenes of general peril, but we never for one second doubt that Bruce Willis's moral compass is pointed firmly at Righteous North.

Plus! You can luxuriate in an era of outdated terrorists. This is a time where the threat came from the 'New Provo Front', 'Liberté de Quebec' and 'Asian Dawn', who Alan Rickman's Hans Gruber has just read about in *Time* magazine (he's only pretending to be a terrorist in order to get the FBI to cut off the power). One viewing of *Die Hard* and you'll be bouncing from your bed, hiding your detonators and yelling 'Yippie-ki-yay, melon farmers!' You'll be back at work by morning.

Feel-good factor ☀ ☀ ☀ ☀ ☀ ☀ ☀ ☀

KEEP TAKING THE HAPPY PILLS

A Clinical Examination

There's an old showbiz adage which states that the key to success is to leave an audience wanting more. In movie circles, this has been refined to read 'leave the audience wanting *nothing* more' – to satiate their desires so thoroughly that viewers will leave the cinema on a euphoric high, ready to tell all their friends how *fabulous* the movie they just saw made them feel. In practical terms, this means 'leave 'em smiling' – no matter how grim or downbeat the preceding drama may have been, all will be well if the final reel closes with a life-affirming hug or a pulse-quickening freeze-frame.

The idea that what audiences really want from movies is to make them feel happy, positive, and upbeat is as old as the hills. There's also nothing new about film-makers giving their audiences exactly what they think they want; as the racy compendium *The Good Old Naughty Days* (2002) proves, the birth of moving pictures predates the birth of moving pornography by about five minutes – a clear example of early 'market driven' movie-making. Yet the idea that the only guarantee of success is to leave viewers 'feeling good' has long been a bone of contention, with directors and

producers regularly butting heads over the benefits (or otherwise) of ensuring that everything ends happily ever after.

As a case study, let's look at Ridley Scott's *Blade Runner* (1982), now widely considered to be one of the most important and innovative science fiction movies of the late twentieth century. Based on a short novel by Philip K. Dick (*Do Androids Dream of Electric Sheep?*) *Blade Runner* portrays a dystopian future in which 'replicants' rebel against their human creators and demand 'more life' when faced with inbuilt obsolescence. The screenplay,

written (separately, initially) by Hampton Fancher and David Webb Peoples, casts android-hunter Rick Deckard as a noirish assassin despatched to track down and eliminate rogue replicants, one of whom he falls in love with. In a classic *Romeo and Juliet*-style twist, Deckard becomes besotted with the android Rachael, despite knowing that her existence is terminal, and her future finite. As an associate tauntingly tells him, 'It's too bad she won't live, but then again, who does?'

As originally conceived by director Scott, who had previously scored both critical and financial success with his stylish sci-fi shocker *Alien* (1979), the film was a dark parable about forthcoming 'dangerous days' – a discussion of the nature of so-called 'artificial' intelligence, and a foreboding look at the potential obsolescence of humanity itself. Unsurprisingly, the story was low on feel-good laughs; set in a desolate near-future besieged by acid rain and advertisements for 'Off-World' colonies (an alternative to the misery of Earth), *Blade Runner* was designed to unsettle its audience, to leave them pondering the mysteries of their humanity while dazzling them with all-too-believable snapshots of a disturbingly plausible future.

For the title role of Deckard, Scott cast Harrison Ford, still hot from the sci-fi success of *Star Wars* (1977), which had introduced a new generation of viewers to the crowd-pleasing thrills of a *Buck Rogers* serial. From the outset, Scott and Ford were at loggerheads, the actor believing that his director was more interested in lighting a shot than in engaging with his cast. In 2000, Scott explained to Dr Kermode that 'I was not given then to spending a lot of time on explanation and stroking. I've got too much to do to get what I want, because I have a performance as well.' Indeed, it wasn't until the days of *Thelma & Louise* (1991) that Scott would begin to be considered an 'actor's director', the visual style of his early films apparently taking precedence over his interaction with the performers.

One of the key disagreements between Scott and Ford was the true nature of Deckard's character. Although it was never made explicit in the original script, Scott had become obsessed with the idea that Deckard was himself an android, a replicant hunting his own kind, with no knowledge of his own artificial nature.

This tantalising idea is not quite as groundbreaking as it sounds. A robot hater turns out to be a robot himself at the end of *The Creation of the Humanoids* (1962), and many other stories, films and TV episodes have the same twist – including 'Demon With a Glass Hand' (*The Outer Limits*, 1964), which was filmed in the Bradbury Building, just like *Blade Runner*. In fact, the theme of Deckard's artificiality (which is not present in Dick's source) had been introduced accidentally by the screenwriters, who had misunderstood each other's rewrites – both have credited the other with coming up with the idea, as is evidenced in Dr Kermode's 2000 documentary, *On the Edge of Blade Runner*. For Scott, this was a eureka moment, a way to crack the enigma of Dick's source and cut to the heart of the story's central man-vs.-machine dichotomy. Indeed, it proved a talismanic riddle in his original cut of *Blade Runner*, which ended with Deckard and Rachael (Sean Young) exiting into the darkness of an uncertain future, her death assured, his implied . . .

Artistically, this ending made perfect sense. But having spent tens of millions of dollars funding Scott's ever-expanding epic, financiers wanted to be certain that the finished film would go down well with the same audiences who had whooped and cheered at Harrison's Han Solo role in *Star Wars*. Test cards from early preview screenings, however, revealed that viewers were both depressed and confused; depressed by the downbeat nature of the story, and confused by the twists and turns of the plot, which seemed to them utterly incomprehensible.

Worried that the movie was going to sink, the film-makers embarked upon hasty recuts, adding an explanatory voice-over (a generic concession which had its roots in early script drafts), removing Deckard's inhuman origins, and – most ridiculously – concocting an utterly stupid happy ending in which Rachael is granted a new lease of life and the lovers escape into unpolluted nature to live happily ever after. Calling upon the assistance of Stanley Kubrick, Scott used out-take footage from the opening sequence of *The Shining* (1980) to conjure up an entirely new finale featuring shots of rolling hills, over which Deckard and Rachael's triumph over all odds could be played. In this new version, *Blade Runner* ends on an unambiguously upbeat note, the lovers united for ever despite the previous action which had made absolutely clear that no such resolution could ever be reached.

The new ending was utter baloney, but as far as the test cards were concerned it was what the audience wanted, and that was that.

As it turned out, most audiences *didn't* want *Blade Runner*, with or without its new happy ending. During its first-run theatrical release the movie spectacularly failed to recoup its extravagant costs, leaving its financiers in the red, and leaving Scott with the stigma of having helmed an expensive flop.

It wasn't until some years later, when an earlier cut of *Blade Runner* was screened (almost by accident) to an adoring audience, that Scott's prophetic instincts were proved right. Reissued in variously recut forms (the 'Director's Cut' and so-called 'Final Cut') *Blade Runner* became a belated cult hit, praised by fans for its bleak, uncompromising tone and hailed by critics as one of the most important genre movies of the decade. Today, it is almost impossible to watch a big-budget sci-fi movie without seeing Scott's trademark fingerprints everywhere you look. Just as *2001* changed the look and feel of sci-fi for a generation, so *Blade Runner* became the creative font from which all future fantasies would draw.

The fact that giving *Blade Runner* a happy ending didn't make it a hit would seem to prove

once and for all that Hollywood's infatuation with an upbeat finale is at best misplaced, and at worst plain bonkers. Yet the history of modern cinema is littered with examples of producers attempting to make movies 'better' (and in the process making them much, much worse) by slapping a happy face onto the end of the final reel.

Take the case of Terry Gilliam's *Brazil* (1985). A tragicomic vision of an Orwellian future (the film was once saddled with the potential alternative title *Nineteen Eighty-Four and a Half*), Gilliam's masterpiece was centrally concerned with the triumph of imagination over reality. Its anti-hero Sam Lowry (Jonathan Pryce) is a near-future office worker who falls in love with the rebellious Jill Layton (Kim Greist) only to be crushed by the forces of a faceless totalitarian authority which tramples individual human emotion under a mountain of bureaucratic red tape. While the script boasted a celebration of the liberating power of artifice and invention, the plot follows an inexorable path toward physical imprisonment; the body suffering while the mind is set free.

A graduate of the hugely successful Monty Python team, Gilliam had already racked up directing credits on *Monty Python and the Holy Grail* (1975), *Jabberwocky* (1977) and *Time Bandits* (1981), the last of which had taken over $40 million in the US – a handsome return on its $5 million budget. Viewed by executives at Universal as a maverick talent with crossover potential, Gilliam had received the green light to go ahead with *Brazil* despite the dark undertones of its uncompromising script. But when production was completed, executive Sid Sheinberg declared that *Brazil* required savage re-editing and (most importantly) a new, happy ending.

As per Gilliam's version (released internationally by Fox), *Brazil* ends with the bound and tortured Sam Lowry escaping the horrors of the real world by drifting into a fantastical reverie. Imagining an action-packed jailbreak led by Robert De Niro's anarchic heating engineer Harry Tuttle, the film's

.

Dear Sid Sheinberg

When are you going to
release my film, 'BRAZIL'?

Terry Gilliam

final movement sees Sam and Jill break out of the stifling confines of the city into the lush greenery of the countryside – only to cut back suddenly to Sam still in the clutches of the authorities, a catatonic smile on his face, humming the film's recurrent theme 'Aquarela do Brasil'. 'He's got away from us,' observes Deputy Minister Mr Helpmann (Peter Vaughan), the camera pulling back to show Sam in the vast and terrifying surroundings of the 'Information Retrieval' room (Croydon B Power Station providing an ominous location), his body bound, his mind ... broken?

It's an extremely powerful ending, which can be read either as a stark celebration of the liberating power of imagination, or as a bleak admission that the forces of evil will always prevail in the 'real' world. In this version of the film, Jill has in fact been 'killed resisting arrest' ('the odd thing is it appears to have happened twice ...') and Sam is once again alone in a cold and uncaring world, defeated by bureaucracy, corruption and incompetence. Only in his dreams can he prevail over the forces of darkness, while on Earth chaos reigns.

Sheinberg, who had problems with the whole film, absolutely *hated* this ending. As far as he was concerned, no audience would want to watch a movie which concluded that the real world was a nightmare in which lovers are crushed by jackbooted authoritarianism. For Sheinberg, it was essential that Sam and Jill wind up together, that their 'happy ending' be *real* rather than *imaginary*.

What followed is now known in popular movie parlance as *The Battle of Brazil*, the title of an utterly engrossing tome by Jack Matthews documenting in forensic detail Gilliam's fight to get his version of the film released in America. Breaking the movie business code of '*omertà*' which decrees that disagreements between film-makers and financiers shall be kept behind closed doors (for fear of damaging a movie's potential profitability), Gilliam organised unauthorised screenings of his cut of *Brazil* for critics, causing the influential Los Angeles Film Critics Association to honour it with their award for Best Picture, even as Universal dithered about its US opening. While Sheinberg continued to fiddle away with his own cut of *Brazil* (now known as the 'Love Conquers All' cut), Gilliam took out a full-page advert in the influential trade publication *Variety* which read simply:

Dear Sid Sheinberg
When are you going to release my film, 'BRAZIL'?
Terry Gilliam

In the end, Sheinberg was forced to back down, and *Brazil* went on to become one of the most enduring cult movies of the late twentieth century (although it performed poorly at the US box office on initial release). As for Sheinberg's 'Love Conquers All' cut, it finally found its way onto US TV before becoming something of a curio amongst Gilliam completists, an 'additional feature' on laserdisc, DVD and Blu-ray releases, interesting primarily for its wide-eyed awfulness.

Of course, there's nothing new about studios' desire to give their movies a happy ending. Back in 1942, the makers of *Casablanca* tied themselves up in knots trying to figure out a way in which Rick and Ilsa could end up together, rather than have Humphrey Bogart put Ingrid Bergman on a plane with the assurance that 'we'll always have Paris'. Throughout the production, the writers wrestled with possible solutions, which ranged from Ilsa's husband Victor being conveniently killed in the third act, to Ilsa simply declaring, 'Ah to hell with it, I'm *staying*' and running back down the runway into Rick's waiting arms. The problem back in the censorious forties was that the idea of an adulterous woman deciding to leave her husband and shack up with a seedy bar owner was simply intolerable. So, despite the fact that everyone *wanted* the lovers to end up together, decorum decreed that they had to part. Today, no such moral squeamishness exists; if someone remade *Casablanca* in the twenty-first century, the

final shot would probably be Rick and Ilsa sharing a post-coital cigarette while Victor made goo-goo eyes at the stewardess on his departing plane.

Fast-forward to 1990, and the rewards of keeping the audience happy, happy, happy are perfectly demonstrated by the case of *Pretty Woman*. In its original inception, this feel-good hit (which took close to half a billion dollars in cinemas worldwide on a production budget of $14 million) was a rather darker tale of drugs and prostitution. J.F. Lawton's screenplay was written under the working title *3000* – the amount of money rich businessman Edward Lewis pays hooker Vivian Ward to pose as his girlfriend for a week – and ended with the couple going their separate ways, each back to their own very different worlds.

Rising star Julia Roberts was famously unimpressed by Lawton's original script. According to her, it was 'a really dark and depressing, horrible, terrible story about two horrible people, and my character was this drug addict, a bad-tempered, foulmouthed, ill-humored, poorly educated hooker who had this weeklong experience with a foulmouthed, ill-tempered, bad-humored, very wealthy, handsome but horrible man, and it was just a grisly, ugly story about these two people.'

Sounds like fun, huh?

It was movie mogul Jeffrey Katzenberg who insisted that Lawton's script be rewritten as a romantic comedy, a modern retelling of the Pygmalion myth which had inspired George Bernard Shaw's play, and in turn the hit musical (both stage and screen) *My Fair Lady* (1964). Out-takes from the shoot suggest that Vivian's character was sweetened ever further in the edit (a scene in which she tells Edward, 'I could just pop ya good and be on my way' hit the floor), producer Laura Ziskin pushing for both protagonists to be made more sympathetic, more likeable, more . . . fun! As for the ending, while Lawton had written a bittersweet pay-off which found Vivian taking the bus to Disneyland with her sex-worker best friend,

the laws of profitability demanded something altogether more upbeat. Thus, the movie now ends with Richard Gere climbing up a fire escape (significantly overcoming his fear of heights – see 'Phobias', p.84) to wrap Vivian in his arms and sweep her off to a new life of wealth, privilege and everlasting love.

This fairy-tale ending makes no dramatic sense whatsoever, but audiences swooned to its 'Love Conquers All' message, turning the movie into a global phenomenon. In the wake of *Pretty Woman*'s extraordinary box office success, studios suddenly started throwing money at the romcom genre in the hope of repeating its magical winning formula. Indeed, it's arguable that the resurgence of romcoms as one of the most reliably lucrative staples of modern cinema was down to *Pretty Woman* – and its happy, sappy ending.

Other examples of producers wanting to leave the audience smiling are rather more subtle. In 1997, British director Iain Softley filmed a brilliant adaptation of Henry James's *The Wings of the Dove* which drew critical plaudits for its strong performances, insightful screenwriting and outstanding production values. The film follows an increasingly embittered early twentieth-century love triangle between the scheming Kate Croy (Helena Bonham Carter), the terminally ill Milly Theale (Alison Elliott) and the morally wavering Merton Densher (Linus Roache). Holidaying together in a ravishingly picturesque Venice, Kate persuades long-time suitor Merton to seduce Milly in order to secure a place in her will. But when left alone with the goodhearted Milly, Merton finds his affections unexpectedly engaged. By the time Kate and Merton finally get what they thought they wanted, their dreams have melted into dust.

Intelligently scripted by Hossein Amini, Softley's film finished on a boldly nihilistic note: a scene of lovemaking notable for its sense of desperation and darkness, a daring and provocative finale to a richly insightful adaptation.

Miramax mainstay Harvey Weinstein loved the film, and thought it had Oscar potential. But he was also anxious about the whole 'desperation and darkness' thing – particularly since it was the film's parting shot. Working on the basis that audiences leaving a theatre can only remember the very last thing they saw (a maxim which has proved surprisingly enduring in Hollywood), Weinstein thought that it would be a good idea to remind viewers what a lovely, scenic time they had had in Venice before everything turned to moral torpor and desolation back in Blighty; to get them talking about the ravishing costumes and eye-catchingly romantic settings which he believed to be one of the film's major selling points.

Thus, Hands-on Harvey 'suggested' to Softley that instead of the final fade to black which currently ended his movie, the screen should return once more to an image of Venice, leaving the audience with a vision of the beautiful Milly in a shimmering gondola while an out-of-context voice-over spoke of love from beyond the grave. Softley resisted, knowing that such a coda was hardly in keeping with his carefully constructed vision. But Weinstein pushed the matter, insisting that unless moviegoers left the theatre with thoughts of upbeat romance (rather than downbeat moral squalor) the all-important 'word of mouth' would suffer. Eventually, Softley relented and devised a way of including the Venetian footage without spoiling his otherwise flawless film. Duly appeased, Weinstein threw his far-from-inconsiderable weight behind *The Wings of the Dove*, which went on to bag four Oscar nominations and five BAFTA nods.

Of course, the problem with artificially enhancing a film's happy-quotient is that, like antidepressants, the effects can be short lived. Would *Love Story* (1970) have stood the weepy test of time if Ali McGraw's Jenny had been miraculously cured of her illness at the end? Would teenage girls have flocked to see *Titanic* (1997) time and time again if Kate Winslet's Rose had found a piece of wood big enough for two, and Leo hadn't sunk like a stone to the bottom of the ocean? Would *Butch Cassidy and the Sundance Kid* (1969) have achieved its classic status if our heroes had managed to give the Bolivians the slip? (In fact, the famous freeze-frame ending of George Roy Hill's much-loved Western was already a concession to positivity, replacing the brutal, bloody death scenes which were originally planned.)

Perhaps the most celebrated case of a nonsensically changed ending is that of Adrian Lyne's *Fatal Attraction* (1987), which got a whole new third act after preview audiences decided that they couldn't be doing with Glenn Close's bunny-boiler taking her own life and then framing Michael Douglas's philandering husband from beyond the grave – which is what happened in James Dearden's original script. Already tweaked prior to filming (he's arrested, but then his wife finds evidence proving his innocence), *Fatal Attraction* dismayed test viewers who wanted to see Anne Archer 'Kill the bitch!' before closing on a reassuring close-up of a happy family photo (group hug, everyone!). The revised ending is terrible, but proved horribly effective, helping *Fatal Attraction* to become a box office smash around the world. Except in Japan, where they got the *original* (and better) ending, on the grounds of enhanced 'cultural compatibility' . . .

Really.

In the end, we are left with the question of whether it's always better to be happy, or whether there is a time and a place for good honest misery. Should movie doctors prescribe antidepressants willy-nilly just because they *may* improve a film's box office potential, even if doing so means effectively lobotomising the movie? Do we really want our entertainment to arrive with the rictus grin of enforced jollity, or should directors be able to claim that it's their party and they'll cry if they want to?

Frankly, when it comes to cinema, happiness is overrated.

THIS WON'T HURT A BIT

We Need to Talk About Needles

Come in. Nice to see you. Do sit down. Roll up your sleeve. It's just a brief exchange in your local surgery, but you know what's coming next. *You'll just feel a little prick . . .* And that's precisely the point at which you run kicking and screaming through the waiting room. Or you stamp on the hypodermic needle, breaking it in two. Or maybe fight the nurse for the syringe before plunging it deep into her neck . . .

This is why we need to talk about needles. We know you aren't one of those crazed anti-vaxxers – that would be ridiculous. There are many who suffer from trypanophobia and have no one to turn to for comfort and treatment; you have the Movie Doctors. We have hit upon a rather extreme treatment which may well not be to everyone's taste, but we believe it works. We have found three of the most extreme needle-related movie scenes. If you can survive these, then the next time you need a vaccination you won't be so weedy. Watch with the lights on, the sound low and holding hands with your honey.

PULP FICTION *(1994)*

You've just snorted something that wasn't a nasal spray (you being Uma Thurman, by the way). Turns out it wasn't cocaine either, but heroin. You are a class A chump. When your friend realises what you've done (he's John Travolta, obviously), he whips out a syringe and (after an excruciating delay while he indulges in some typical Tarantino dialogue) stabs you in the heart. He then injects you with Adrenalin and you instantly recover. The science here is dodgy to say the least, but the fact that you'd actually be dead is not our main concern (you weren't really in any shape to point out that there is no treatment in modern medicine that requires a medic to stick a needle in your heart). What you need to focus on here is the lingering, loving close-ups of the super-sized, 6-inch needle dripping with 'Adrenalin' (it's actually Epinephrine, but could be 7 Up for all you care).

LESSON LEARNED When you are next in the surgery, your experience will not be like this. You won't be on the floor unconscious, you won't be stabbed in the chest, you won't come round with the hypodermic still deep in your rib cage. Time to move on.

DEAD AND BURIED *(1981)*

So you've survived the heartache of *Pulp Fiction*, now you're ready for the next step in your desensitising. Keeping the lights on (actually turn them up, maybe plug in some more), let's try the 1981 horror film *Dead and Buried*. A number of gruesome murders have taken place in a small town called Potters Bluff. General nastiness is the order of the day as a series of grisly scenes play out (stabbing, poking, very large rocks) but the scene we need is (inevitably) in the hospital. Our poor patient has suffered terribly and is covered with bandages. The only part of them exposed is the left eye. When a sweet-looking nurse arrives, momentarily we think all will be well. But when she says 'Just lie still. I'm going to give you something to make you feel even better' and produces the mega-syringe, we know what's about to happen.

LESSON LEARNED Being stabbed in the eye by a crazed nurse with a 9cm needle is a rare occurrence these days. The American healthcare reforms have largely eliminated homicidal maniacs pretending to be medics. Rest easy.

FIRE IN THE SKY *(1993)*

Last one. You've done *so* well. The final test comes with the last fifteen minutes of this 1993 science fiction horror yarn based on an alleged true story. It's Arizona, there are loggers and there's a UFO. Main logger guy is abducted but released after apparently undergoing a session with the aliens that makes Potters Bluff look like Notting Hill. Abattoir-loving spacemen with tortoise heads cover him with a membrane, then reach for their handyman selection of clamps, drills and chisels. Just as logger guy is thinking he might get away with a little extra-terrestrial Botox, the galaxy's biggest drill descends from the ceiling. It is mounted with – you guessed it – an enormous needle, and it is heading straight for his right eye. There's a deafening clanging that fills the room and logger guy gets his Gloucester-in-*King-Lear* moment.

LESSON LEARNED All things considered, it isn't that different to flying Ryanair.

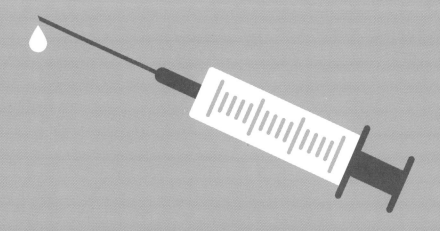

LAUGHING GAS

Movies to Tickle the Funny Bone

ownbeat endings may be 'artistically valid', but there are times when an audience just wants to laugh. On those occasions when only Dr Giggles will do (though not *Dr Giggles*, the terrible slasher movie), Doctors Kermode and Mayo prescribe . . .

LAUREL AND HARDY IN THE MUSIC BOX *(1932)*

'Get that piano out of that box!'

BUSTER KEATON IN THE GENERAL *(1926)*

Keaton loads a cannon which promptly takes aim at him in one of silent cinema's most celebrated runaway train gags.

GENE WILDER'S 'FRONKENSTEEN' AND MARTY FELDMAN'S IGOR IN YOUNG FRANKENSTEIN *(1974)*

'Tonight we shall ascend into the heavens, we shall mock the earthquake, we shall command the thunders, and penetrate into the very womb of impervious nature herself!'

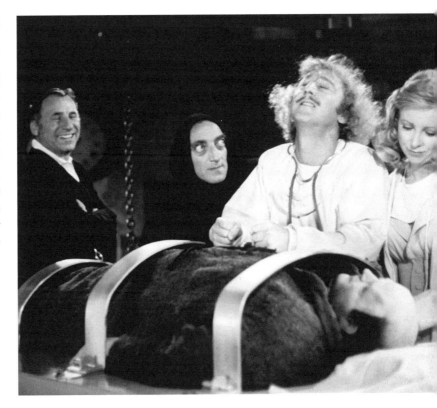

WOODY ALLEN AND DIANE KEATON IN ANNIE HALL *(1977)*

'I think what we got on our hands is a dead shark.'

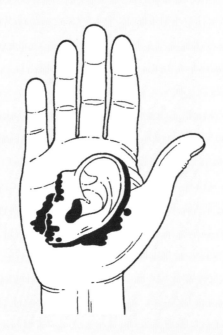

EAR, NOSE & THROAT

Anyone who has been to a multiplex in recent years will know that two things have gone up: **ticket prices and volume.** Going to see a major blockbuster in a big cinema is now as loud as going to a Motörhead concert – *Mad Max: Fury Road* cleaned most of the wax out of the Movie Doctors' ears. In our own version of an ENT clinic, we offer **advice about tinnitus**, **nose jobs** and **how to choose a good dentist**. No need to thank us – it's all part of the service.

EARACHE

How the Movies Can Cure Your Tinnitus

Strictly speaking, tinnitus is not an illness, it's a *condition*. There are no measurable symptoms but the constant ringing in the ears – a pulsing, never-ending, clangorous, nerve-shredding interference – should be familiar to cinemagoers who have experienced the aural sensation of any Michael Bay film. The effects can vary from mild (*The Lionel Ritchie Collection*, 2003) to total-pain-in-the-ass (*Transformers*, 2007).

As a youth you may have strayed too close to the front of a concert and stood unnervingly near to the speaker stack – you paid the price. Later you may have turned your headphones up beyond the European recommended limits – you coped with the consequences of your foolishness. You may have witnessed a party of five-year-old boys just after the Haribo kicked in and just before the entertainer (not to be confused with *The Entertainer*, the 1960 Laurence Olivier movie or 'The Entertainer' from the soundtrack to *The Sting* (1973)). The aftermath was with you for days.

Prescribing films for tinnitus is a tricky task. Silent movies are a disaster (although, as Dr Kermode is constantly reminding us, 'silent cinema was *never* silent – actually, it was quite noisy'). Gentle, softly spoken movies won't work either, as everything will take place with the seemingly incessant chirruping of a thousand crickets in the background.

What is needed is a big, thumping, flamboyant film to distract and console. This might appear counter-intuitive: why go see a noisy movie if tinnitus is your problem?

Here's the answer: YOLO. There is no cure for tinnitus so you might as well forget it for a while and take in some meaningful noise instead. There is good noise and bad noise. The Movie Doctors have selected these films for having *the right kind of noise*. The coolest headphones are noise-cancelling headphones. These films are head noise-cancelling films.

INTERSTELLAR (2014)

A film you don't hear with your ears. Bypassing that buzzing in your head, you hear *Interstellar* with your chest. You feel it in your diaphragm (this won't work if you're watching it on a phone. Or if you are using any fewer than the 1,000 speakers per channel system recommended by your local IMAX/THX/Dolby dealer.

When it was first released, some viewers complained about the sound, arguing that they couldn't hear the dialogue above all the effects and Hans Zimmer's score. This isn't tinnitus, this is idiocy (see 'Films for Idiots' below). Director Christopher Nolan has said that he and sound designer Richard King mixed the movie over a six-month period, using dialogue as a sound effect. You are not *supposed* to hear what Matthew McConaughey is saying. It's the Tom Waits school of enunciation. And anyway, what's a little ringing in the ears compared with the time-warping bedlam of inter-universe space travel?

ALADDIN (1992)

A riot of flamboyant distraction which will quieten your infuriating, roaring head for all of its ninety minutes' running time. Magic carpets, silk pantaloons, palaces, jewellery, curly slippers, treasure, the world's grumpiest parrot, the Sphinx, singing, bazaars and dastardly moustaches – what more does your tired and noisy brain need?

The big, dazzling, fabulous star is of course the genie, as played by Robin Williams. It doesn't really matter that the other characters seem a bit feeble, the story a little ho-hum and the Arab characterisation somewhat lazy. This genie has been silent for ten millennia, and he has a lot of catching up to do.

'I'm kinda fond of you, kid,' he tells Aladdin. 'Not that I want to pick out curtains or anything . . .'

The movies sometimes struggled to capture Williams's comic genius (though Dr Mayo still maintains he enjoyed *Patch Adams*) so maybe it was always going to be an animation that could keep up with the speed of his character changes. By the end, Williams's performance, taking in his Nicholson, his De Niro, Groucho Marx, Arnie and so many others, will leave you exhausted. And your head, for the moment at least, quiet.

SCHOOL OF ROCK (2003)

Of course, *School of Rock*. Jack Black playing accidental music teacher Dewey Finn is an irresistible (if obvious) choice to cure your tinnitus. Loud rock gives you tinnitus! A loud rock movie takes it away again!

'Immigrant Song', 'Sunshine of Your Love' and 'Substitute' have caused millions of ears to ring for decades, so we might as well put them to good use now. The research into laughter's curative properties in this area is admittedly in its early days. Just about to get going, in actual fact. But it is true that exercise increases the blood flow to the different parts of the ear (genuine medical fact) and this is a good thing. Therefore, the more you laugh, the better the karma flows and the biorhythms of healing will flood your body (less factual). For example, here's Dewey's new, improved school timetable: '8.15 to 10, Rock History. 10 till 11, Rock Appreciation and Theory. And then Band Practice till the end of the day.' Here he is addressing his class: 'It's gonna be a tough project. You're gonna have to use your head, your brain and your mind too.' And the staff: 'Those who can, do. Those who can't, teach. Those that can't teach, teach gym' (a great line, albeit lifted from Woody Allen).

The thing is, we all know that Jack Black's rocking Gareth Malone figure will have tinnitus and have it a whole lot worse than you. And because Jack plays for real with his band Tenacious D, he understands and feels your pain. Does it stop him raising his goblet of rock? Of course it doesn't.

THE RAID *(2012)*

A really rather useful feel-better-all-round film. Whatever your pain, watch *The Raid* and feel your aches just melt away. Over the course of its 101 minutes, whichever part of your body is afflicted, you will see it punched, stabbed or kicked (maybe all three at once) so often, that you realise you have nothing to complain about.

A new member of a SWAT team finds himself in a fifteen-floor block full of ruffians. He and his noble band of bobbies need to arrest the head ruffian, but wouldn't you know it, the cad won't come quietly. So everyone has to be killed. There are many hi-tech, high-powered weapons lying around, but why use them when fists and feet are so much more *wholesome*? So much more *balletic*? We prescribe this movie for tinnitus because the way Gareth Evans directs,

each crunched skull and smashed spine is like a small explosion going off in your head. This has the pleasing effect of extinguishing the rather feeble ringing in your ears. And don't worry about the dialogue. There's barely five minutes' worth (all in subtitled Indonesian), and who wants to talk (or indeed read) when there is another groin to kick?

DISTRICT 9 *(2009)*

Nothing pleases the ear more than the sound of an extra-terrestrial bug getting splattered. There's something about the yuckyness of it all that leaves a fevered head calmed and reassured. And it's a relief to know you aren't a prawn from outer space.

That might be hard on the prawns in Neill Blomkamp's South African movie, as they turn out to be considerably brighter than many of their Uzi-waving tormentors, most of whom work for an outfit called Multi-National United. With a name like that, it's not difficult to work out that these guys aren't going to be on the side of motherhood and bobotie pie. And in their alien killer-in-chief Koobus, they have a man who is definitely on the side of DEATH AND FLAME THROWERS.

Spaceships, disgusting eating habits (cat food, mainly) and a good old-fashioned shoot-out make this a feast of fabulous noise. An aural jacuzzi for your tired head.

So we learn that The Tremeloes got it so wrong with their 1967 hit 'Silence Is Golden'. Silence is *not* golden. For the tinnitari, silence is a nightmare. Go see a movie.

DR DAVE NORRIS'S HEARING TEST

Dr Mayo: Dr Dave Norris knows all about sound and vision at the movies – see p.110 for his guide to all things 'aspect ratio'. Here he sets a quick quiz about how the speakers should work in a cinema.

Dr Kermode: And if you have one of those home cinema surround-sound thingummys, it works for those as well. Who said this book had no practical use whatsoever?

Dr Mayo: You? Take it away, Dr Dave.

Dr Dave Norris: Sound design is an increasingly important element in any production. An incorrectly set-up sound system and sound level in the cinema can ruin a film. See if you can match the correct speaker to the correct element of a movie soundtrack.

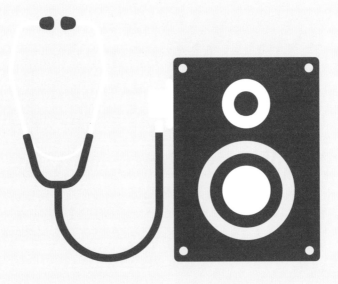

IDENTIFY WHICH SPEAKER SHOULD HANDLE WHICH KIND OF SOUND AT THE CINEMA

TYPES OF SOUND

- Dialogue
- Explosions, rumbles
- Ambient noises – dogs barking, birds singing etc
- On screen sound effects, music

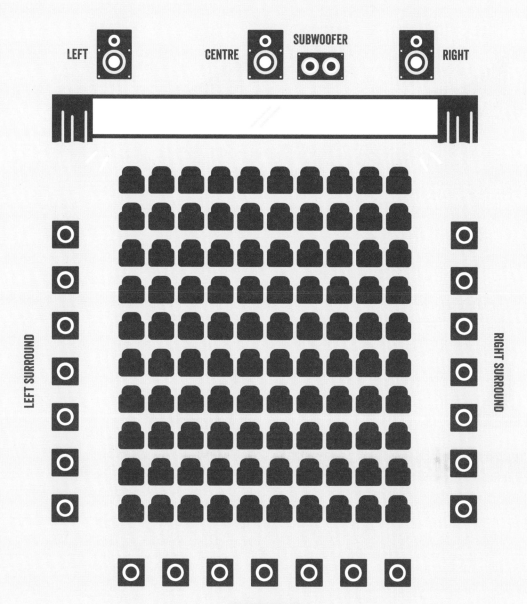

LEFT   CENTRE   SUBWOOFER   RIGHT

LEFT SURROUND

RIGHT SURROUND

REAR SURROUND

SOLUTION Dialogue: *centre* • Explosions, rumbles: *subwoofer* • Ambient noises – dogs barking, birds singing etc: *left, rear and right surround* • On screen sound effects, music: *left and right*

NOSE JOBS

Some Movies Just Stick Out . . .

THE CHILD CATCHER
CHITTY CHITTY BANG BANG *(1968)*

Once seen, never forgotten. Like all the best children's films, there is something distinctly sinister about *Chitty Chitty Bang Bang*, and Sir Robert Helpmann's Child Catcher, with his long, child-sniffing nose, was mostly responsible: 'There are children here somewhere. I can smell them.'

GERARD DEPARDIEU
CYRANO DE BERGERAC *(1990)*

Another Oscar (and BAFTA) nominee for the man attached to 'Cyranose'. Depardieu plays the bashful, swashbuckling poet who, embarrassed by his hooter, romances the beautiful Roxane by proxy, assisting the dashing, tongue-tied Christian de Neuvillette in his wooing of her.

NICOLE KIDMAN
THE HOURS *(2002)*

This notorious prosthetic proboscis gained almost as much publicity for *The Hours* as the entire cast put together. Denzel Washington presented the 2003 Oscar for Best Actress in a Leading Role, saying, '. . . and the winner, by a nose, is Nicole Kidman.'

STEVE MARTIN
ROXANNE *(1987)*

'Laugh and the world laughs with you; sneeze and it's goodbye Seattle.' Steve Martin stars in Fred Schepisi's Cyrano update, most famous for the fabulous string of nose-ist gags which the impressively proboscissed Martin recites.

PINOCCHIO *(1940)*

The real giant of movie snouts, Pinocchio's extending schnozzle has had generations of children going cross-eyed as they test out the 'tell me lies and your nose will grow' theory.

DAN AYKROYD
NOTHING BUT TROUBLE *(1991)*

Writer/director Dan Aykroyd plays a 106-year-old judge with – and there's no other way of putting this – a penis for a nose. Sadly, that's the most interesting thing that can be said about this 'adventure comedy horror' romp. Really.

EMMA THOMPSON
NANNY MCPHEE *(2005)*

The Reverse Pinocchio – Nanny McPhee's appearance is a bellwether for the behaviour of the seven unruly Brown children. Her nose starts off as a bulbous, warty potato, but with every step in the right direction Cedric Brown's seven children not only transform their family's fortunes, but turn their hideous nanny into Emma Thompson – and what could be better than that?

RALPH FIENNES
HARRY POTTER AND
THE DEATHLY HALLOWS
PART 1 *(2010)* AND PART 2 *(2011)*

Harry Potter: My nemesis's got no nose.
Dumbledore: How does he smell?
Harry Potter: Horful!

SQUEAKY CLEAN

The Good Dentist Guide

A tricky area. We assume that if you find yourself in this section of our ENT Clinic, your dental check-ups to date may not been entirely regular. You may, like Dr Mayo, have had a school dentist. And you may think that surely only the sweetest, most compassionate of dental practitioners would have been allowed to practise on the nation's youth? You would be *wrong*.

In fact, testifies Dr Mayo, the opposite seems to have been the case. All dental treatment was to be dispensed as swiftly as possible. Anaesthetics were far too costly (three shillings and fourpence per dose) so despite these being the druggy sixties, no medication was available to small boys who needed pain relief in Croydon.

This association of dentists with misery is commonplace, both in real life and in the movies. You need look no further than *Marathon Man* (1976) for proof. Dr Mayo grew up thinking all dentists were Nazis anyway, so the idea of Laurence Olivier playing one for real was no surprise. The famous 'I'm now going to drill your whole mouth away' sequence is, rightly, regarded as one of the most horrific ever filmed (see p.102).

So the cinematic tradition here is that teeth = pain (except for the 2007 movie *Teeth*, which, like its 2004 Japanese predecessor *Sexual Parasite: Killer Pussy*, is about castration anxiety). The Movie Doctors therefore have tried to change this for you. We have managed the impossible; we have found five movies where – get this – dentists

are portrayed as *good people*. That's right. Not sadists, not idiots, not even morally dubious, but good, decent folk you'd hang out with. If there was really no other option.

EVERSMILE, NEW JERSEY *(1989)*

Would you trust Daniel Day-Lewis if he was your dentist? Would your mind fill with the random acts of violence he has performed on screen over the years? Beatings, scalpings, that kind of thing? Well, this obscure offering (maybe the least viewed Day-Lewis picture ever) offers us our hero as Dr Fergus O'Connell, an Irish dental missionary pounding the back roads of Patagonia. They don't want to trust him either. Despite being on a mission to improve the nation's oral health, he ends up getting beaten up or shunned by most of his would-be patients. You see, he may be a *good* man but Dr O'Connell is definitely a bit *weird* too.

But DDL still smiles that anti-bacterial, teeth-whitening smile, and so all is well. The next time you find a gaucho with a rotting molar, you'll know who to call.

THUMBSUCKER *(2005)*

If Dr Day-Lewis can't see you, why not sign on with Dr Keanu Reeves? He seems just your sort. Young, floppy-haired and prone to saying things like 'the trick . . . is living without an answer' – he is either a guru, a visionary or just deeply annoying. But if he's a great dentist, who cares if he mumbles his way through the Van Morrison phrase book?

In *Thumbsucker* he plays Perry Lyman, an orthodontist who shows how cool he is by smoking in his surgery. Seventeen-year-old Justin, who needs a new approach, is impressed. He is the titular thumbsucker and, having fallen for beautiful Rebecca, is finding the habit rather embarrassing. His real problem, however, turns out to be his parents Audrey and Mike, played by Tilda Swinton and Vincent D'Onofrio. The issue is not Tilda's suspect record as an on-screen parent (*We Need to Talk About Kevin* (2011) didn't end too well for anyone) the issue is this: he calls them Audrey and Mike. Science shows us that any child who calls his or her parents by their first names will grow up to be *problematic*.

But at least he has found a mentor in Keanu Reeves, one of the few on-screen dentists not wanted for trial at the International Court of Human Rights.

GHOST TOWN *(2008)*

If Daniel Day-Lewis is action man dentist and Keanu Reeves is spiritual dentist, Ricky Gervais is spectrum dentist. He plays Bertram Pincus, an uptight, misanthropic, Scrooge-like Brit (surprise!) who likes dentistry but hates his patients. He is never happier than when filling their mouths with cotton wool and dental equipment, just to shut them up.

Nervous readers might query our selection of such a film as being uncomfortably true to their own experience. But salvation, maybe for the first time, comes in the form of a colonoscopy. While undergoing this simple medical procedure, Pincus 'dies' for seven minutes. He subsequently finds he can see dead people, who turn out to be more needy than the living.

But just hang on a minute – there's a girl who is neither a hygienist nor Tilda Swinton, so his road to redemption becomes clear. An almost-cuddly, funny and skilful dentist emerges and we can chalk up another orthodontist who isn't going to hell.

FINDING NEMO *(2003)*

Yes, we are reduced to finding comfort in cartoon characters. In Pixar's acclaimed story of the timid clown fish, not enough praise has gone to dentist Philip Sherman. He has been unfairly lambasted for his role in taking Nemo from the ocean and putting him in the compulsory dentist's fish tank. He then wants to hand Nemo to his hideous niece Darla who, we know, is so terrifying she must have come straight from the Barney the Dinosaur school for nauseating children (see p.120 for other pupils from said school to avoid).

However, we need to prescribe *Finding Nemo* to you because P. Sherman (like 'fisherman' obvs) is a *good* man with a *bad* niece. He only takes Nemo from the sea because he thinks he will get eaten. He only plans to give Nemo to Darla because he is blind to the sadistic glint in the devil-girl's eye. He is only motivated by compassion, generosity and fish rights. Not sadism, greed or an overpowering need to impose himself on the helpless.

Thank you, Pixar.

LITTLE SHOP OF HORRORS *(1986)*

We know what you are thinking. We have lost the plot and are prescribing *precisely* the sort of film that has caused your dentophobia in the first place. This is an understandable, if misguided, reaction. It is true that Steve Martin's sadistic dentist (following John Shaner's Dr Farb in the original 1960 Roger Corman film) appears to enjoy inflicting pain on puppies, fish, cats, dental assistants and his patients. He drills, injects and abuses his nitrous oxide. He smashes doors into faces. He thinks he's Elvis and seems obsessed with his hair (imagine that!).

However, but and nevertheless . . . After we see the full range of his ghastliness, Martin's dentist asphyxiates, is chopped up and fed to a plant. We cheer, we applaud and punch the air, realising that this is what happens to bad dentists. They face their judgement. They cannot rule with impunity. *Little Shop of Horrors* is a morality tale which states that over-billing and over-filling will be punished by dismemberment. This alone should put a spring in your step and a sparkle in your smile.

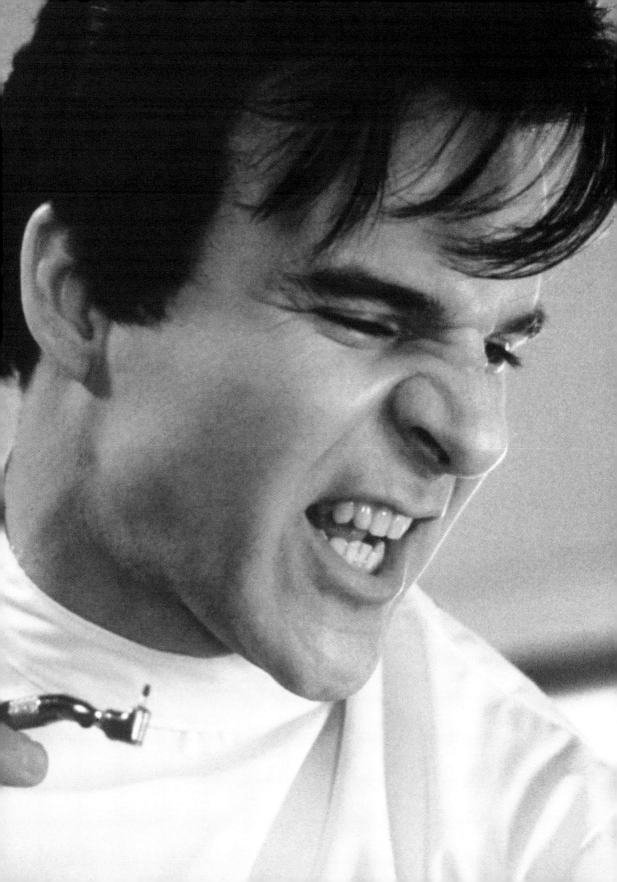

SLEEP
CLINIC

Sleep. One of those things that everyone seems to get too much or too little of. Thankfully, the Movie Doctors are on hand to prescribe a **cure for the insomniacs** amongst us, and also to let you know which directors' films are best for catching up on much-needed **zzzz's . . .**

AVOID WATCHING WHEN DROWSY

How the Movies Can Cure Your Insomnia

I t's 4 a.m. You've been awake since forever. Your other half is happily snoring away despite your nudging, kicking and harrumphing. You've tried the radio but that appears to be running endless features on misery around the world and how it is actually all your fault. You've switched stations but the phone-in host seems as idiotic as his listeners. You'd try your favourite podcast but that is way too stimulating. What you really need is a movie.

Not just any movie. You don't want stimulation (if you do, you're in the wrong clinic – see 'Cardiology', p.96). You daren't risk a film that will excite you in any way. You can do without shouting, merriment or disrobing. What you need is the cinematic alternative to counting sheep. We can prescribe a few. These aren't bad films; these are films that you can tune out from and it won't actually matter that much. Films that give you permission to drift away, safe in the knowledge that when you wake up, *nothing much will have changed.*

Medical NB: this is not to be confused with anaesthesia. See below

THE PIANO *(1993)*

Welcome to New Zealand, where it is raining. It's been like this since the 1850s, and by now everyone is really pretty muddy. Remember your dampest, dreariest holiday when you spent the entire time shivering, drinking soup in a beach hut and wondering how wet your towel had to be before it was heavier than lead? Well *The Piano* is like that, only bleaker.

As your lids grow heavy, part of your brain might remember that Anna Paquin, Holly Hunter and Harvey Keitel got awards and great reviews for their performances, but that need not concern you now. In the same way that the sound of rain on your tent or caravan roof can lull you to sleep, here the deluge that starts at the beginning of Jane Campion's movie, and continues for two waterlogged hours, contains miraculous, soporific qualities. Go ahead, nod off, you won't miss a thing.

PLAYTIME *(1967)*

The one thing that might keep you from sleeping is a good *story*. What happens next? Will she escape? Will the out-of-control combine harvester miss the sleeping farmer? And so on. But if we could prescribe a movie with *no story at all*, that could well be just the ticket.

So step forward Jacques Tati. When he made *Playtime* it was the most expensive film in French history. It had a huge cast, a huge set and it bankrupted him. It won a Best European Film award in 1969. It was the inspiration behind the Spielberg/Hanks film *The Terminal*. Terry Jones loves it. David Lynch loves it. Even Dr Kermode loves it. When you're feeling better you need to come back and watch it properly.

But for now, all you need to know is that it has no story. Instead, Tati – as Monsieur Hulot – wanders around a maze of modern Parisian architecture, getting lost and hanging out with American tourists. It has a surreal, dream-like quality which is perfect for us – even the traffic and roundabout action becomes hypnotic.

And here's the killer. *It has an intermission.* It's most complete presentation includes a twenty-minute break. So even if you have been drawn into Tati's world, your sleep time has been built into the structure of the film. Your dreams could well be the most avant-garde and stylishly outré you have ever had. Left Bank Insomnia may even be a more pretentious strain of your condition that others will aspire to once they have tired of their boring UK version.

EMPIRE *(1964)*

How long would you like to sleep for? Is six hours enough? Would you settle for seven? Well here is a movie that can run for all of that and still be going when you wake up. Clocking in at eight extraordinary hours, this is Andy Warhol's single-shot take of the Empire State Building from early evening until 3 a.m. the following day. This clearly trumps Tati's *Playtime*, as not only has it no story, it has no action and no actors either.

Just.

The.

Empire.

State.

Building.

For.

Ever.

You could fly to New York to see the Empire State Building itself in the time it takes for nothing to actually happen. In fact Warhol intentionally slowed the whole thing down – it was shot at twenty-four frames a second and projected at sixteen – just in case it was all zipping along too fast for the hardcore art crowd. And just in case you're awake at the wrong bit (spoiler alert), there are three reels where you can see Warhol and cinematographer Jonas Mekas reflected in the window they're shooting through. Not exactly worth hanging around for, but when you've been looking at one building all day, pretty much anything counts as excitement.

The *New York Times* maintains that because it has no script and elevates the mundane, *Empire* is actually a precursor to reality TV. If the choice is five minutes watching Kim Kardashian or 480 minutes watching concrete, we'll take the concrete every time.

SLEEP INTERMISSION

Length of Nap Possible During Directors' Films

QUENTIN TARANTINO

WOODY ALLEN

PETER JACKSON

STANLEY KUBRICK   0   *Exception Eyes Wide Shut:*

PAUL THOMAS ANDERSON   *Exception Punch Drunk Love:*   0

OLIVER STONE

ERICH VON STROHEIM

 = 10 minutes

IN DREAMS

Doctors in Discussion

Dr Kermode: There's a line in *A Nightmare on Elm Street*: 'Whatever you do, don't fall asleep.'

Dr Mayo: That could prove tricky; though not, admittedly, during *A Nightmare on Elm Street*.

Dr K: I love the central idea of that film: you fall asleep, and the thing that scares you most – in this case, Freddy Krueger – comes for you in your dreams. It's absolutely terrifying.

Dr M: And is that a metaphor for the way cinema works overall?

Dr K: Well, David Lynch has always said that we live inside a dream – that life itself is like watching a movie, or dreaming a reality.

Dr M: Yes, but they don't actually mean anything, dreams, do they? They're just a load of random stuff your brain chucks at you during your daily period of repose.

Dr K: If you say so.

Dr M: I mean if I dream that, I don't know, say, Mahatma Gandhi delivers a pizza while I'm having a chat with Lord Palmerston, it doesn't have any significance beyond the fact that I've probably eaten a bit too much cheese late at night.

Dr K: Is that the kind of thing you dream about? Most people dream that they're turning into an eagle or something.

Dr M: That would be great. I'd be Don Henley, definitely, but the point is dreams don't mean anything.

Dr K: Perhaps. But watching a movie should be like living in a dream. The very best movie experiences are immersive – they drag you into the world they create.

Dr M: Even if Mahatma Gandhi rides around on a moped with a pizza-shaped box on the back.

Dr K: Even if that happens. And here's another thing about dreams and the movies – when someone's in the middle of a dream, or if they're sleepwalking, they say that you should *not* wake them up. Apparently, the shock of being jolted out of the immersive experience can be very distressing. I find it's the same if you come out of the cinema or out of a screening room after a particularly powerful movie experience and someone immediately asks you, 'How was that? What did you think?' It's like being woken up too quickly . . .

Dr M: Particularly if you're a Movie Doctor.

Dr K: Yes, particularly then, although I think most people want to be allowed to emerge gently and slowly from a powerful movie experience.

Dr M: So, are we saying that good movies are as immersive an experience as good dreams – of the non-violent-resistance pizza delivery or eagle-metamorphosing kind – and that you shouldn't disturb anyone whether they're in a dream or in their own post-movie dream sequence because the shock is too great?

Dr K: Pretty much. Unless there is a psychopath roaming around your head – in which case, just don't fall asleep. Ever.

PSYCHIATRY

Doctors have had a raw deal at the movies. At best they tend to be portrayed as one scalpel short of a successful operation, at worst, well, take your pick. The same goes for phobia-sufferers, rarely offered even a pipette's worth of **tea and sympathy** by film-makers. The good news is that whatever the anxiety, real or imagined, the Movie Doctors are here to help. Nurse Ratched, please show the next patient in, **mwah ha ha . . .**

MAD DOCTORS IN THE MOVIES

A Clinical Examination

The poster for the 1981 rock musical *Shock Treatment* tells us much about cinema's essentially suspicious attitude toward medicine: a still of a crazed-looking Richard O'Brien leering at us through bottle-top glasses, with the tag line, 'Trust me, I'm a doctor.' O'Brien plays Dr Cosmo McKinley, an utterly unscrupulous (and very likely unqualified) physician who, along with his equally dubious sister Dr Nation McKinley, is engaged in a scam to send poor Brad Majors to their own private funny farm. Duped, drugged and duly 'diagnosed', Brad is summarily strapped into a straitjacket and thrown, bound and gagged, into an isolated cell, while fast food tycoon Farley Flavors conspires to steal away his life, his identity and (most importantly) his wife.

The film is a very modern comedy (it pretty much predicted the rise of reality TV), but like its predecessor, *The Rocky Horror Picture Show* (1975), it pays cine-literate homage to a grand heritage of cinema – a heritage in which movie doctors (as opposed to 'The Movie Doctors') have been repeatedly portrayed on screen as little more than licensed psychos.

One source of inspiration for *Shock Treatment* was Robert Wiene's 1920 chiller *The Cabinet of Dr. Caligari*, which used expressionist sets and shadowy lighting to conjure a vision of a sinister sideshow hypnotist who sends his somnambulist patient out into the world to do his darkest bidding. In a surprise twist, Caligari turns out to be an inmate's imagined evil version of the director of the asylum wherein he is confined, and the film ends with the director announcing that he can now cure his delusional patient. Yet more often than not, movie doctors are anything but curative. In *The Mad Doctor* (1940), Basil Rathbone plays a medic who murders his wives. In *The Abominable Doctor Phibes* (1971), Vincent Price is a music and theology specialist who murders the medical doctors he blames for killing his wife. Starting to see a pattern here?

MEDICAL TOP TRUMPS

Who Would You Like to See by Your Bedside?

DR HANNIBAL LECTER

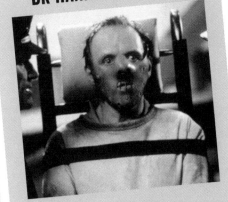

Movie: *The Silence of the Lambs*

Year:	1991	SPECIALITY:
TC:	10	Liver specialist
FF:	10	
PT:	10	

DR EMMETT LATHROP 'DOC' BROWN

Movie: *Back to the Future*

Year:	1985	SPECIALITY:
TC:	0	Fabulously stiff hair
FF:	0	
PT:	6	

DR HAWKEYE PIERCE

Movie: *MASH*

Year:	1970	
TC:		SPECIALITY:
FF:	5	Chemist/alcohol distiller
PT:	1	
	0	

KEY

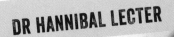

TC = Technical competence

FF = Fear factor

PT = Psychotic tendencies

DR ORLANDO WATT

Movie: *Carry on Screaming*

Year:	1966	SPECIALITY:
TC:	1	Not being struck off
FF:	5	
PT:	3	

DR JACK STARTZ

Movie: *Behind the Candelabra*

Year:	2013	SPECIALITY:
TC:	3	'Smile, though your heart is breaking . . .'
FF:	0	
PT:	2	

NURSE RATCHED

Movie: *One Flew Over the Cuckoo's Nest*

Year:	1975	SPECIALITY:
TC:	0	Relaxing musical therapy; hairstyling; telling your mum
FF:	10	
PT:	10	

Think about it: if someone asks you to name a famous screen physician, you're more likely to come up with the murder suspects of *Doctor X*'s medical academy than the jovially roguish interns of *Doctor in the House* (1954). This is true across a wide range of medical disciplines. Is cinema's most famous nurse Barbara Windsor's lovable Nurse Sandra May from *Carry on Doctor* (1967), or Louise Fletcher's sadistic Nurse Ratched from *One Flew Over the Cuckoo's Nest* (1975)? Cinema's favourite dentist? No contest – Laurence Olivier as escaped Nazi Dr Christian Szell who tortures Dustin Hoffman with an assortment of whirring drills while asking, 'Is it safe? Is it safe?' As for cinema's best psychiatrist, look no further than Anthony Hopkins as Dr Hannibal Lecter in *The Silence of the Lambs* (1991, and its various sequels/prequels), the doctor who decided to stop treating his patients and start eating them instead. (We'll overlook the fact that Brian Cox actually originated the Hannibal the Cannibal role in Michael Mann's *Manhunter* (1986), a film which remains the best adaption of any Thomas Harris novel.)

Everywhere you look, the movies are full of terrible medical role models doing things no doctor should, from Vincent Price's pathologist Dr Warren Chapin accidentally setting a centipede-like terror-parasite loose in 1959's 'Percepto'-enhanced shocker *The Tingler* ('When the screen screams, you'll scream too . . . if you value your life!') to Jeffrey Combs's medical student Herbert West messing around with undead decapitated heads in Stuart Gordon's disgustingly scrungy *Re-Animator* (1985). Even when portrayed sympathetically on screen, medics usually have a touch of madness about them. Perhaps the most heroic doctors of modern movies are Donald Sutherland's 'Hawkeye' Pierce and Elliott Gould's 'Trapper John' McIntyre in *MASH*, both of whom spend most of the movie battling to retain their sanity by indulging in ever crazier acts of war-torn madness, spiced up by 'Suicide is Painless' singalongs.

Meanwhile, Donald Pleasence's Dr Sam Loomis may be the nominal 'good guy' in John Carpenter's 1978 stalk-and-slash smash *Halloween*, but his character somehow manages to be the creepiest thing on screen. No wonder they kept bringing him back for the sequels.

There are, of course, examples of charming, attractive and basically decent doctors in cinema: think of Lew Ayres as dashing Dr Kildare in a string of movies from the thirties and forties (*Calling Dr Kildare*, *The Secret of Dr Kildare*, *Dr Kildare's Strange Case*, *Dr Kildare Goes Home* etc); of Omar Sharif as Doctor Zhivago in David Lean's timelessly sweeping 1965 historical romance; or even of Robin Williams as the loveable Patch Adams, merrily waving his bottom at the medical establishment as he proves that laughter can be a cure for almost anything (the Movie Doctors concur on this point – see 'Laughing Gas', p.46). Sometimes the casting can be a little credibility-stretching. Did anybody really buy Meg Ryan as a heart surgeon communing with heavenly creatures in the syrupy *City of Angels* (1998)? Or Keanu Reeves as a dashing doctor with the hots for Diane Keaton in *Something's Gotta Give* (2003)? Or Gael García Bernal making white-coated goo-goo eyes at Kate Hudson in *A Little Bit of Heaven* (2011), a 'romantic fantasy' which included the unforgettable valentine card greeting 'Roses are Red, Violets are Blue, I've Got Ass Cancer . . .'? These doctors were unconvincing, but also unthreatening. Yet since the birth of the moving image, we've been more than ready to see doctors as little more than mad scientists, with patients their (often unwilling) test tubes.

Two key texts underwrite cinema's long-standing nervousness about bad science and even worse medicine: Robert Louis Stevenson's *Strange Case of Dr Jekyll and Mr Hyde* and Mary Shelley's *Frankenstein: or, The Modern Prometheus*. Both proved terrifyingly popular novels, and have been endlessly adapted and reinterpreted on screen, striking a chilling chord with cinema audiences. As early as 1908, Otis Turner's production of *Dr Jekyll and Mr Hyde* established the figure of the physician who fails to heal himself (in the book he's actually a research chemist) as a beastly cinema staple. Umpteen adaptations followed, with John Barrymore famously taking the title role in John S. Robertson's 1920 silent, Fredric March winning an Oscar for his portrayal of the mad doctor in Rouben Mamoulian's 1931 version, and Spencer Tracy co-starring alongside Ingrid Bergman and Lana Turner in the 1941 remake of Mamoulian's hit, which again drew heavily on Thomas Russell Sullivan's stage play. As the movie adaptations multiplied, so Hyde's crimes worsened, his character becoming weirdly conflated (as it had been in theatrical productions) with the legend of Jack the Ripper, cementing the cinematic archetype of the monstrous doctor.

As for *Frankenstein*, an early screen version produced by the Edison company saw director J. Searle Dawley laying the template for the bubbling cauldrons and magical hocus-pocus that would define mad screen doctors and scientists for decades to come. Other famous adaptations of Shelley's text included James Whale's legendary 1931 production in which Colin Clive memorably screams 'It's alive!'; Hammer's studio-defining 1957 shocker *The Curse of Frankenstein* with Peter Cushing as Victor and Christopher Lee as his ungodly creation; and Kenneth Branagh's much-maligned 1994 reboot of *Mary Shelley's Frankenstein* which proved that being a mad doctor hell-bent on resurrecting deceased body parts didn't mean you couldn't be ripped. The movie bombed after director/star Branagh was berated by critics for making Victor a hunk who spent a lot of time running around with his shirt off. In fact, Ken's youthful portrayal was closer to Shelley's source than the ageing, tweedy weirdos who had become the stock-in-trade of cinema adaptations.

Of course, these early screen 'doctors' were often more mad scientists than medics, the confusion and conflation of the two being an integral part of cinema's approach to both professions. As far as cinema audiences were concerned, there was a very thin line between 'making people better' and attempting to 'play God', and turn-of-the-century advances in both science and medicine merely added to this sense of unease. It's no coincidence that the birth of cinema itself was tied up with the growing use of electricity, a mysterious power of which everyone was aware but few understood. With its roots in the phantasmagorical magic lantern displays of the carnival sideshow, early cinema exploited its audience's fascination with (and fear of) electricity, with Doctors Frankenstein and Rotwang employing spectacular electrostatic arcs to breathe unnatural life into their respective creations.

Other medical developments which have inspired some freakishly disturbing films include the transplantation of organs, research into which flourished in the bloody aftermath of the First World War. In 1924, Robert Wiene's Austrian gem *The Hands of Orlac* attached the fingers of a murderer onto the body of Conrad Veidt's formerly peaceful pianist, setting in motion a string of transplant-based horrors which would flourish throughout the twentieth century. Several adaptations and re-imaginings of Maurice Renard's 1920 potboiler *Les Mains d'Orlac* followed, most famously Karl Freund's *Mad Love* (1935), in which former Frankenstein Colin Clive played Stephen Orlac, while Peter Lorre leered menacingly as a lovestruck Doctor Gogol. ('Suitable Only for Adults' declared the poster for *Mad Love*, in which Lorre's staring eyes epitomised the cinematic spectre of the ever-so-slightly deranged doctor.) In 1960, an Anglo-French production of *The Hands of Orlac* was shot simultaneously in French and English, co-stars Mel Ferrer and Christopher

Lee taking great pride in their ability to perform their roles in both languages, while the 1962 American horror *Hands of a Stranger* told this now familiar story once again under the lurid tag line: *'The surgeon's scalpel writes a thriller!'*

The early seventies saw a spate of Orlac-inspired transplant shockers such as *The Incredible 2-Headed Transplant*, in which a child-like man has the head of a psycho killer grafted onto his body, and *The Thing With Two Heads*, in which a dying white racist wakes up with his severed head attached to the body of a black death-row convict. Most bizarrely, the 1970 sexploiter *The Amazing Transplant* attributed the sudden rapist urges of its central character to the attachment of a brand new penis, which apparently had a mind of its own. A similar scenario resurfaced in the 1971 British film *Percy*, which proudly boasted 'music by The Kinks!'

In Michael Crichton's 1978 thriller *Coma*, patients at an apparently caring hospital would be drugged into a state of suspended animation and then harvested for body parts to be sold to the highest bidder, a paranoid fantasy which struck a nerve with a public becoming increasingly disturbed by urban myths about organ theft (a myth that was still going strong when Stephen Frears made the black-market body-parts thriller *Dirty Pretty Things* in 2002).

Just as cinema has always been innately suspicious of organ transplants, so film-makers would also leap upon genetic engineering as a way of getting under their audience's skin. The key text here is Erle C. Kenton's *Island of Lost Souls*, adapted from H.G. Wells's nineteenth-century novel *The Island of Doctor Moreau* in 1932, and long refused a certificate by the BBFC on the grounds that its subject matter was 'against nature' (it has since been reclassified as an uncut 'PG' – how times change. See p.196). Charles Laughton excelled as the bad doctor who dreams of cross-breeding animals and humans, while Kathleen Burke's animal charms graced eye-catching posters which promised that 'THE PANTHER WOMAN lured men on – only to destroy them body and soul!' Despite the censors' anxieties, the figure of Dr Moreau has proven another popular cinematic staple, resurfacing regularly as the embodiment of twisted medical madness, played by such stars as Burt Lancaster in Don Taylor's 1977 adaptation, and Marlon Brando in John Frankenheimer's 1996 version. If you look hard enough, you can just about spot the ghost of Dr Moreau in the figure of Dieter Laser's Dr Heiter from Tom Six's repulsive *The Human Centipede (First Sequence)* (2009), a movie which reminds us that even in the twenty-first-century, doctors are viewed as twisted madmen by the cinemagoing public.

So, have the movies been bad for medicine? Well, not entirely. In his terrific 2005 book *Mad, Bad or Dangerous? The Scientist and the Cinema*, Professor Sir Christopher Frayling points out that 'Horror films have had some very unexpected social consequences, just like the research they are depicting, even within the scientific community.' In particular, Frayling points to the legacy of the 1931 *Frankenstein*, which unexpectedly inspired a medical breakthrough by Dr Jean B. Rosenbaum of New Mexico. According to Frayling, 'the idea of the first cardiac pacemaker came to him in 1951 when he recalled being scared out of his wits as a child by the laboratory scene in James Whale's *Frankenstein* . . . The memory of electricity stimulating Karloff's body as he twitched into life on the slab led directly to his invention of the pacemaker.'

All of which means that if you are one of the many people whose lives have been immeasurably improved by the insertion of a small but effective heart regulator, then you owe your good health to the healing power of cinema in general, and horror movies in particular!

As the Movie Doctors like to say: It's alive!

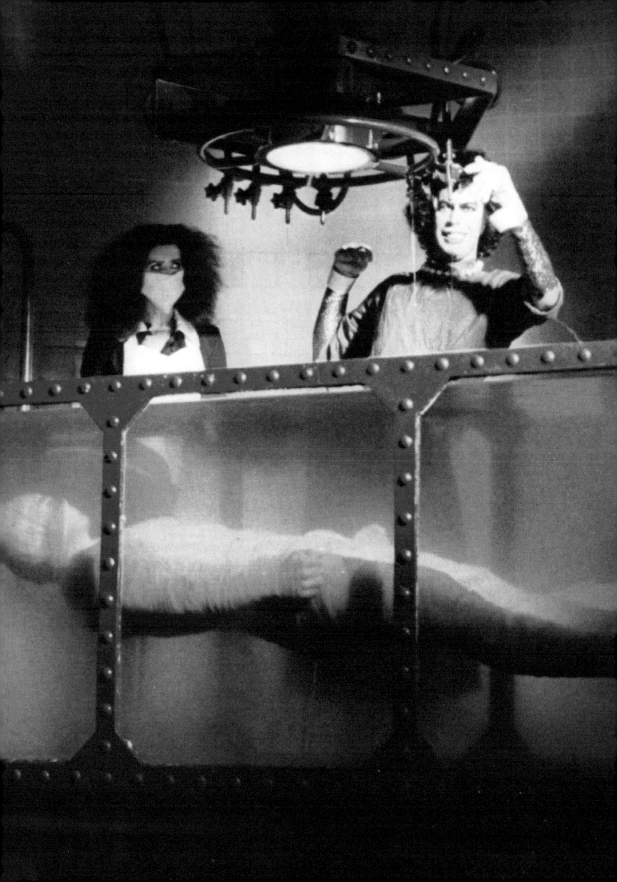

AND RELAX

How the Movies Can Relieve Stress and Anxiety

Modern Life, so Blur taught us, is rubbish. If that is taking it a little too far, modern life is certainly stressful. Your job prospects, your bank balance, your parents, your housemates, your deadlines, your kids and your ailments are just the start of it. Then there's the government, other governments, terror threats, international financial insecurity, global warming and films shown in the wrong aspect ratio (see p.110). Life is so complicated.

Many turn to alcohol, drugs and decadence. This is understandable – there are times when the Movie Doctors have been known to seek solace in the adult beverage cupboard. This section exists to point to a road less travelled. When those anxious moments take hold, when the burden of the day seems off the scale, watch a movie. Watch the right movie. Here are some stress-busters we can prescribe that should have the desired effect. Lie back, breathe deeply, press play.

84 CHARING CROSS ROAD *(1987)*

(Includes spoilers, on the sound basis that you really don't want any surprises.)

The only way this won't work is if you find the idea of two old people reading letters aloud to each other for 100 minutes a bit too racy. Then you might struggle. For everyone else, welcome to the world of antique books. Usually you might expect the cinematic treatment of ancient, dusty tomes

to include at least a murdered thirteenth-century monk hell bent on revenge on the first modern reader it can find (usually a blousy woman up to no good). But not here. Anne Bancroft stars – and we all know she can blouse if she wants to – but in David Jones's film of Helene Hanff's bestseller (via James Roose-Evans's play), all she wants is books. Not just any books, but rare books, the kind of books that Anthony Hopkins sells. She writes to him. He replies. She thanks him for his reply, he sends more books. They never meet. He dies.

Bancroft and Hopkins are, of course, wonderful. She is a struggling writer and therefore difficult and feisty. He is the manager of the bookshop and therefore studious and quiet. Very few actors do stillness like Sir Anthony, and his portrayal of Frank Doe is a study in self-containment.

A transatlantic love story where the protagonists don't share a single scene is a gentle, warming, noble experience. Maybe *your* relationships would have been easier if you'd never actually met anyone, just experienced the whole thing – as here – in voice-over? Cleaner and neater all round.

(Medical PS: If you're tempted to continue

the Anthony Hopkins theme and pick, say, *The Remains of the Day*, be warned. You might expect the whole Merchant Ivory deal to be perfect for the stressed twenty-first-century consumer, but you'd be wrong. The business with Nazi appeasement and an anti-Semitic lord is bad enough without the 'just kiss Emma Thompson and get on with it' storyline. This on its own is enough to drive you crazy. It is almost worth the raised blood pressure just to hear Hopkins's butler Stevens say to Thompson's housekeeper Kenton, 'Do you know what I'm doing Miss Kenton? I'm placing my thoughts elsewhere while you chatter away.' But then Hugh Grant appears and it's game over.)

THE BIG LEBOWSKI *(1998)*

We'll start with a medical NB. There's a whole lot of toking going on here. Jeff Bridges is never more than a few moments away from another joint. Don't give in to temptation. Hold fast.

Briefly. Bridges is a Lebowski but he is the wrong Lebowski. He is Jeffrey Lebowski the stoner, not Jeffrey Lebowski the multi-millionaire. So when some hoodlums urinate on his rug (it's the wrong rug, too) as a means of making him pay a debt that isn't his in the first place, he decides to do something about it. The Coen brothers give us a whole bunch of plot and an impressive cast of characters. But it isn't the inclusion of John Goodman, Julianne Moore and Philip Seymour Hoffman that will calm your fast-beating heart. Nor is it the bowling scenes, which look wonderful and will have you yearning for those weedy bowling shoes they insist you wear (by the way, spraying that stuff inside the shoe doesn't stop them smelling of damp pants). And it isn't even the film's soundtrack with its splendid John Fogerty/Mozart/Eagles combo. No, the reason we prescribe some Lebowski for the overly anxious is that *nothing really seems to bother him that much.* He is the 'laziest man in Los Angeles County', a hippy layabout, a wastrel, someone who goes shopping in his pyjamas and writes a cheque (ask your parents) for 69 cents. His car is stolen and burned. He thinks he's getting a stack of cash, then doesn't. He gets his head shoved down a toilet. He's offered oral pleasures by a trophy wife though nothing is forthcoming. But through it all he remains (and this is referred to 133 times) 'The Dude'.

Now you might, like the Movie Doctors, have an instant dislike of anyone who gives themselves a nickname (indeed, Dr Kermode has often complained that *The Big Lebowski* is 'overrated', to which The Dude would doubtless reply 'Yeah, well, you know, that's just like, er, your opinion man . . .') But there's just no way this guy could be a Jeffrey. Or even a Mr Lebowski. He is The Dude. And because he is The Dude, he takes what comes his way. He keeps calm and carries on. 'Dudeism' is now an official religious movement, with adherents attending the Church of the Latter-Day Dude. The Dude abides. Take a bath. Take it easy.

DOUGAL AND THE BLUE CAT *(1972)*

It is fair to say that the Movie Doctors are divided as to the merits of this feature-length spin-off from the original TV series. It is either a wonderful work, which Dr Kermode genuinely believes to be one of the greatest movies ever made. Or (as Dr Mayo would have it) it's a rather overblown stoner movie. Great if you had the original album and are still in love with Fenella Fielding (who does a mysterious voice-over), a little dreary for everyone else.

However. Where we agree is that it is totally bonkers. This is the world of the 1960s and '70s children's TV animation *The Magic Roundabout*, which was French in origin but totally anglicised by the fabulous Eric Thompson, who wrote and performed his own scripts, largely ignoring whatever the original Gallic story had been (way to go, Eric). The TV shows were five minutes long and featured Dougal the sarcastic, Tony Hancock-inspired dog, Dylan the hippy, drug-addled rabbit and Zebedee the jack-in-a-box whose catchphrase 'Time for bed' would usually close the show. And if your stress and anxiety need dealing with, just spend eighty-two mind-altering minutes in their weirdly colourful world. The normally gentle TV storylines have been replaced by the arrival of a megalomaniacal blue cat called Buxton. One by one he wins over and then imprisons the other characters, spurred on by Fielding's sultry voice calling, 'Blue is beautiful, blue is best.' It may well be that some form of psychedelic hypnosis is at work here, but you will find your cares slide away as you follow our fabulous friends, even when they blast off into space. Some may wish to download the cruder Jasper Carrott 1975 homage for some better jokes to use as a playout sequence, but until then, *Dougal and the Blue Cat* will certainly take your fevered mind on a well-earned magical mystery tour.

DRIVING MISS DAISY *(1989)*

If all these de-stressing movies haven't helped, then there is nothing for it but a drive in a 1949 Hudson Commodore. It's a beautiful car and a fabulous ride. The upholstery is luxurious, the drive is smooth. Ideally – for maximum chill – get a chauffeur to do the driving. If that could possibly be a wise, patient and graceful chauffeur then so much the better. And in case you are an ageing, rich white Southern lady who despite her self-proclaimed liberalism is really quite a racist, this is essential.

You will need – obviously – to find your way to the Atlanta roads of somewhere between 1948 and 1973, when genteel living was only occasionally interrupted by racist, anti-Semitic cops. By all means teach your chauffeur to read and become friends, but always remember the car. Feel the leather. Relax into the power of the gasoline engine managing 0–60 mph in sixteen seconds, 95.5kW/128hp/130PS, torque:269Nm/198kb-ft (all these stats are accurate. Say them fast, no one will question you. It works for Dr Kermode).

(*Top Gear*-style NB: if offered, don't accept a 1948 Chrysler Packard. These have a tendency to reverse into your neighbour's yard and demolish walls. Especially when you lose control of the accelerator and brake pedals. This may result in your son – who surprisingly seems to be Dan Aykroyd – demanding you stop driving. Awkward.)

PHOBIAS

A Cure for (Nearly) Everything

I f needle phobia is your foible, turn to p.44. For everything else, you're in the right place. Whatever phobia you have, chances are there's a movie just for you. If you like, you can say you're just watching 'for a friend'.

ACROPHOBIA
FEAR OF HEIGHTS

(Medical NB: not vertigo. That is a spinning sensation when you're not actually spinning. James Stewart *does* suffer from vertigo, but Hitchcock's film should really be called *Acrophobia*.) Try repeated screenings of *Man on Wire* where Philippe Petit tightrope walks between the two towers of the World Trade Center in 1974.We see him on Notre Dame (scary), Sydney Harbour Bridge (terrifying) and then the towers (he's French). Follow up with *Cliffhanger*. You're dangling at 4,000 feet, but Sylvester Stallone has grabbed your wrist. He says he has got you and you're not going to fall. He's wrong.

ARACHNOPHOBIA
FEAR OF SPIDERS

There are many genres in moviemaking. Westerns, war films, sci-fi, comedy, horror. And there are also spider movies. Spiders are likely to turn up in any film, anywhere, anytime and always spell disaster, catastrophe and/or death. Try these in measured doses:

TARANTULA *(1955)*
'Horror 100 feet high!'

THE GIANT SPIDER INVASION *(1975)*
'Creeping! Crawling! Crushing!' (though these spiders are only fifty feet across, so therefore feeble).

SPIDERS II: BREEDING GROUND *(2001)*
'They're back and they're breeding mad!'

ARACHNOPHOBIA *(1990)*
It's got Julian Sands in it.

BOTANOPHOBIA
FEAR OF PLANTS

This is not the same as a fear of gardening, which can be more usefully characterised as 'laziness'. And we should be clear – some plants *are* worth being scared of. There are all kinds of spiky, stingy, thorny shrubs out there just waiting for your tender, innocent hands. Thorns, nettles and cacti cannot be trusted, poison ivy can cause anaphylaxis, and as for the seeds from the strychnine tree . . . So before answering the call of your garden, watch the following carefully. Then lay AstroTurf:

THE RUINS *(2008)*

Americans and Germans wander into a Mayan sacrificial garden centre. You know that annoying rash that appeared yesterday? Turns out it's not contact dermatitis, but actually carnivorous vines that eat your flesh and grow inside you. You'll be needing an axe, not antihistamine.

DAY OF THE TRIFFIDS *(1963)*

'Man-eating plants! Spine-tingling terror!' Nothing good ever came from a meteor shower, and here we get worldwide blindness then alien-spawned creepers. And yes, that's Howard Keel leading the resistance; he promises not to sing and the battle is done.

VENUS FLYTRAP *(1970)*

Also known as *Body of the Prey*, *The Revenge of Doctor X* and *Women Wear No Clothes for Absolutely No Reason*. Well it is 1970, after all. You can't have a mad scientist trying to mate sea cucumbers with a Venus flytrap without a few topless beauties lending their unique perspective.

CATOPTROPHOBIA
FEAR OF MIRRORS

Mirrors are such flexible movie props. You can pose in front of them, kill people with them, summon the dead, snort cocaine and see rampaging dinosaurs with them.

It's easy to get the wrong idea about mirrors, of course. In *Oculus* (2013) a rather ornate looking glass seems to be responsible for the deaths of forty-five people. In *Dracula* (1931) it exposes a reflection-less Bela Lugosi as a vampire. In *Candyman* (1992) you only have to mention the name of the titular monster five times in front of a mirror and, lo and behold, he appears. For a generation scarred by Dollar's 1981 hit, the flouncy 'Mirror Mirror', a certain terror when looking for reflections is quite rational. Sometimes, however, they can be used to impart vital information. If you are actually no longer 'the fairest of them all', who else but a mirror will tell you? If you are writing 'REDRUM' on a door, only a mirror will explain that this isn't about horses. But relief is at hand, and the Movie Doctors always prescribe *Duck Soup* (1933) for our patients. This is the Marx Brothers of course, and we spool to the mirror sequence where Harpo has smashed a huge mirror (ooh – unlucky!) and is pretending to be Groucho's reflection. All thoughts of demons, drugs and debauchery are banished as you watch a comedy masterclass. The shattered mirror lies at their feet. The spell is broken. You are cured.

COULROPHOBIA
FEAR OF CLOWNS

Not a phobia at all, but a well-grounded mistrust of anyone who thinks putting on a wig, a red nose, painting their face white and wearing loon pants *is in any way funny*. The elongated shoes aren't funny. The stupid, back-firing car isn't funny. And no, I don't want a balloon. See these films for proof that *all clowns should be locked up*:

IT *(1990)*

Tim Curry's terrifying Pennywise the Dancing Clown. He could take any form to scare his victims, but the clown is his weapon of choice. He preys on children and lives in the sewers. Case closed.

KILLER KLOWNS FROM OUTER SPACE *(1988)*

As if the use of the letter K wasn't scary enough, now alien clowns are invading Earth! They are rampant, human-eating clowns who use balloons and other clown paraphernalia for general wickedness and death.

ZOMBIELAND *(2009)*

It says a lot that Jesse Eisenberg's character Columbus isn't really afraid of zombies, he's afraid of clowns. When he breaks his rule about not being a hero, it is to hammer a drooling, stitched-together zombie-clown. Bravo, Jesse.

HAEMOPHOBIA
FEAR OF BLOOD

So many films involve blood loss that if you are a sufferer, you might need to stick with *Driving Miss Daisy* (see 'How the Movies Can Relieve Stress and Anxiety', p.80). If you are brave enough to try some shock treatment then look no further than *Braindead* (also known as *Dead Alive*) directed by none other than *Lord of the Rings* genius Peter Jackson. There's a Sumatran rat-monkey, a domineering mother and a whole bunch of zombies – a combo that has never worked out well before and it certainly doesn't here. We single out this 1992 movie because of the notorious lawnmower scene. It features more blood and dismemberment in one sequence than the Movie Doctors can recall seeing anywhere else. Lionel is the man with the hover mower and he walks, blade up, into a corridor full of zombies who seem to relish the whole limb-chopping experience. Pray you're at the shallow end.

CYNOPHOBIA
FEAR OF DOGS

A very understandable condition most of us will have suffered from when young. 'Just keep still!,' we are told, 'and he'll go away!' This is good advice unless you're facing a 90kg St Bernard with rabies (thanks again, Stephen King). You need to see that dogs are your friend, dogs are cuddly and dogs are rarely possessed by the agents of Satan (unlike, say, cats). Try these slobber-tastic, warm-hearted, dog-loving films.

BECAUSE OF WINN-DIXIE *(2005)*

A heart-warming story of a dog named after the local supermarket ('Here, Tesco! Down, Tesco!') 'Discover what happens when you go looking for a miracle and the miracle comes looking for you.'

And you thought loyalty cards were annoying . . .

GOOD BOY *(2003)*

Dogs came from out of space thousands of years ago to colonise earth. 'Rover is about to take over.'

TOP DOG *(1995)*

Director Aaron Norris! Starring Chuck Norris! (how does that happen!) And terrorist-fighting dog, Reno! 'They're Licensed for Action!'

ENTOMOPHOBIA
FEAR OF INSECTS

Bugs in movies are rarely a sign of good things. Hollywood has tended to ignore their complex ecological roles and their vital place in the food chain ('run that insect pollinator storyline past me again...'). Far easier to show us three pairs of jointed, scampering legs, evil non-blinking eyes, quivering antennae, indestructible exoskeletons, millions of eggs and fangs dripping with poison. OK, so we lied about the fangs, but the picture is clear: an insect is a harbinger of doom. An earwig crawling over your bread? Guaranteed there's a swarm of killer locusts on the way. A moth flutters into your bedroom? It'll have laid its eggs in your open mouth before you wake. Get used to our 100-legged friends with these top bug movies.

MIMIC *(1997)*

Everything from New York has to be bigger and noisier, and this applies to its cockroaches too. Guillermo del Toro directs entomologist Mira Sorvino and a mutant breed of DNA-shifting beasties (although del Toro insists that the most frightening thing about *Mimic* was working with Miramax).

THEM! *(1954)*

A thinly disguised CND propaganda movie (even if they hadn't been formed just yet) where the trifle of a nuclear explosion leads to 'Terror! Horror! Excitement! Mystery!' as giant ants run amok. 'No one word ever heralded such a heart-pounding experience' is the claim, but this is the fifties and no one has heard of 'Kardashian'.

BLACK SWARM *(2007)*

Entomophobia plus conspiracy-theory paranoia. Genetically modified, bio-engineered mutant wasps have been developed by the government to keep hard-working families oppressed. The appearance of Robert 'Freddie Krueger' Englund can only be bad news. Speaking of which . . .

SOMNIPHOBIA
FEAR OF SLEEP

If insomnia is your problem, you're in the wrong clinic – see p.62. Somniphobia is far more hardcore. Luckily, we can treat it. Unless of course your address is Elm Street, USA. Here you'll find that if you fall asleep you'll be pursued by a man in a brown hat and stripy jumper with knives for fingernails. Before Wes Craven's *Nightmare on Elm Street* in 1984 there were very few cases of somniphobia reported. Suddenly everyone had it. 'Whatever you do, don't fall asleep . . .'

PTEROMERHANO-PHOBIA
FEAR OF FLYING

Consider this your in-flight movie playlist. More than any other movie genre, all of the plot is in the title.

FREE FALL *(1999)*

A plane free falls.

TURBULENCE *(1997)*

It's bumpy.

TURBULENCE 2: FEAR OF FLYING *(1999)*

It's bumpier.

TURBULENCE 3: HEAVY METAL *(2001)*

It's never been so bumpy.

FLIGHT OF THE LIVING DEAD: OUTBREAK ON A PLANE *(2007)*

Zombies on a plane.

AIRPLANE VS. VOLCANO *(2014)*

A plane gets caught up with a volcano.

HIJACKED: FLIGHT 285 *(1996)*

A plane is hijacked.

CRASH LANDING *(2005)*

A plane crashes.

PANIC IN THE SKIES *(1996)*

There's panic on a plane.

SNAKES ON A PLANE *(2006)*

There's snakes on a plane.

SUBMERGED *(2000)*

Plane sinks.

FEELING DOWN?

The Movie Doctors' Casebook	*The doctors are IN*

INT. MOVIE DOCTORS' SURGERY – DAY

Dr Kermode is wearing a black suit and tie matched with scruffier than usual shoes. Dr Mayo is sporting a rather inappropriate Mental As Anything T-shirt from 1986. Dr Kermode is cursing his computer, Dr Mayo has given up telling him to buy a new one. They are ready to go.

> **DR MAYO**
> Hey.

> **DR KERMODE**
> Hey.

> **DR MAYO**
> You need a proper laptop. A generic, fruit-based one
> would be better.

> **DR KERMODE**
> Thought you'd given up on this.

> **DR MAYO**
> Well, if you're happy . . .

DR KERMODE
I haven't been really happy since Nixon resigned.

DR MAYO
Nice to hear that one again.

DR KERMODE
I've said that before?

DR MAYO
(*sotto voce*) Give me strength.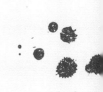

DR KERMODE
Next patient?

DR MAYO
Let's rock.

They stand to welcome a sorrowful student type. He shuffles in and slumps into the chair.

DR MAYO
Is it Michael?

MICHAEL
Yes, it is and I need your help.

DR MAYO
(momentarily taken aback by this fluency) OK, what seems to be the problem?

MICHAEL
I'm feeling a bit gloomy.

DR KERMODE
Well, you should smarten up, buy yourself some top

quality hair wax and all will be well.

MICHAEL
No, that would just make me look like a fifties beatnik who listened to jazz all day. That would be sad.

DR KERMODE
(shifting uncomfortably in his seat) You sound like you might have been listening to too much Coldplay . . .

MICHAEL
Well, I'm down to just a few songs a night now.

DR MAYO
Hmm. Do you know why you're feeling gloomy?

MICHAEL
Oh yes. My marks this term are rubbish, I'm broke, my flatmates think I smell and my girlfriend's left me.

DR MAYO
Gosh. That sucks.

MICHAEL
Thanks for your insight.

DR KERMODE
Well, now I think we can prescribe some movie medicine to make you happier.

MICHAEL
It can't be that simple?

DR MAYO
You'd be surprised. We have some legal mood enhancers here.

DR KERMODE
Are you familiar with *Young Frankenstein*, Mel Brooks's affectionate horror spoof?

MICHAEL
A horror spoof? How lame. I've seen *Scary Movie* 5. If you think Charlie Sheen can make anyone better, I'm in the wrong place . . .

DR MAYO
No, it's not like that. This is from 1974, in black and white. Starring Gene Wilder and Marty Feldman.

DR KERMODE
Wilder plays the grandson of Dr Victor Frankenstein, but as he is a surgeon and fed up with everyone mentioning his notorious ancestor, he pronounces his name Fronkensteen.

MICHAEL
Be still my aching sides.

Dr Kermode raises an eyebrow.

DR MAYO
Let's try a scene. I'm Igor, and Dr Kermode is Inga, a busty blonde, *and* Dr Frankenstein.

MICHAEL
That's Fronkensteen . . .

DR MAYO
Correct.

DR KERMODE
(in high-pitched, busty blonde voice. One of his many

extraordinary impressions.) Werewolf! (now switching brilliantly to Frankenstein) Werewolf?

DR MAYO

(as Igor, who appears to be Cornish) There.

DR KERMODE

(as Frankenstein) What?

DR MAYO

(as Igor) There, wolf. There, castle.

DR KERMODE

(as Frankenstein) Why are you talking like that?

DR MAYO

(as Igor) I thought you wanted to.

DR KERMODE

(as Frankenstein) No I don't want to.

DR MAYO

(as Igor) Suit yourself, I'm easy.

Doctors Kermode and Mayo smile at Michael.

MICHAEL
1974 is a long time ago . . .

The Doctors consult behind their hands.

DR MAYO
Tough one here.

DR KERMODE
Arts student?

DR MAYO

(nodding knowingly) Think we need the station scene.

DR KERMODE

(smiling broadly) They have a plan. The scene is
Transylvania station. Dr Frankenstein is shrouded
in fog. He hears the sound of someone approaching.
Someone who is walking very strangely. It is Igor, his
new assistant.

MICHAEL

Why is he walking strangely?

DR MAYO

He is disfigured, with a pronounced hump.

MICHAEL

(looking uncertain and glancing between the Doctors)
A comedy, you say?

DR KERMODE

Frankenstein offers to remove Igor's hump but he
doesn't think he has one.

DR MAYO

'What hump?' he says!

Both Doctors laugh uncontrollably. They hand Michael a prescription.

DR KERMODE

Watch twice a day until your *schwanzstucker* recovers.

DR MAYO

(anticipating the question) You'll just know. Trust us.
We're the Movie Doctors.

CARDIOLOGY

It goes without saying that you have to **take care of your heart** – whether you're a movie or a patient. Luckily for some, taking care of the heart in the Movie Doctors' clinic doesn't necessarily mean shelling out **thousands of pounds** on **a gym membership** – regular, cardio-tastic exercise can be had watching a **good action** or **horror movie**. After two hours you'll come out feeling like you've been pounding the treadmill. So come on in, we'll help you through those **heart-wrenching break-ups**, too – ensuring you come out a **wiser**, **happier and more confident person**.

AFFAIRS OF THE HEART
Cinematic Cures for the Broken-Hearted

So many patients, so little time. In our Cardiology Clinic the Movie Doctors see a steady stream of the broken-hearted. Self-obsession, needless tears, maudlin fascination with introspective poets and dressing like Bella Swan from the *Twilight* films – all symptoms of those who have suffered the ravages of a relationship gone bad. Some need comfort, some seek revenge, a few of our more enthusiastic patients need to be escorted from the building. (Increasingly Dr Kermode has to fend off the wizened revolutionary veterans of the 1968 student uprisings and Dr Mayo has to be alert to the wiles of the stretch-jeaned, big-haired Brosettes from the St Austell Roadshow of 1988. The old Trots bring their own barricades and the Bros fans still tie Grolsch bottle tops on their shoes; when the two groups meet, the scenes can get ugly.)

The lovelorn sometimes seek solace in entirely inappropriate ways. Alcohol, ice cream and pizza (individually or taken together) offer only *desperation, disaster and destruction*. Don't be tempted. Just say no.

Instead choose the sensible course. Take the movie medicine we prescribe and marvel at your recovery; no queuing, no appointment, no embarrassing scenes of eviction. You may choose one or more movie depending on the severity of your condition.

SHIVERS *(1975)*

David Cronenberg's feature debut (a favourite of Dr Kermode's, who has a soft spot for such scrungy 'body horror') works splendidly as a break-up film.

You don't even have to watch all of it – an hour should be sufficient. You may well never want to touch anyone ever again. Welcome to Starliner Towers! It's a pretty swanky residence on Starliner Island, near Montreal. It has everything a modern community could need: doctors, dentists, shops, a deli, a gym and a new strain of parasite that wants to take over your organs. Over the course of the eighty-seven minutes' running time, it is this last feature that tends to dominate proceedings.

The specially grown parasite turns everyone it infects into a sex zombie. This is not a good thing, but this is where romance gets you. It's an alternative take on the hippy peace and love movement of the sixties.

LESSON LEARNED Live on your own. And if you have to live in a gated community, keep as many orifices closed as is feasible.

FORGETTING SARAH MARSHALL *(2008)*

Any movie which shows you that, just possibly, your ex could end up with Russell Brand should be encouragement in itself. All you need to recover is Mila Kunis and a trip to Hawaii.

LESSON LEARNED Being a preening narcissist doesn't always win the day.

The Movie Doctors' Top Five Rock Stars To Pray To:

1. Slipknot
2. The Singing Nun
3. Kenny Rogers
4. Hank Williams
5. The Tremeloes

HIGH FIDELITY *(2000)*

So you've been dumped. Maybe you did the dumping. Whatever. Doesn't matter. The real question – inspired by this Stephen Frears comedy from Nick Hornby's novel – is where does it register in your top five break-ups? It might be that this kind of thing seems like a ludicrous waste of time. Some guys, however, love this kind of thing, and Rob Gordon, here played by John Cusack, is one enthusiastic 'top five-er'.

Rob's been dumped by Laura. He runs something called a record shop (this is something from a long, long time ago, boys and girls. Ask an adult for more detail). In his break-up chart, Laura, he decides, is in at number five. He discusses this with 'the musical moron twins' he works with (Todd Louiso and Jack Black) but finds he needs much better counsel. Where can this wisdom be obtained? Parents? Priest? Don't be ridiculous! The only trusted source is of course The Boss, and so it is Bruce Springsteen himself who appears to Rob. He tells him it is time to 'move on down the road'. 'Thanks, Boss,' says Rob to his dreamlike rock god.

LESSON LEARNED When you need romantic advice about your next entanglement, try asking whoever your 'Boss' is. Dr Kermode always asks Elvis what he would do (NB: not advisable on dietary or medical matters).

WAR OF THE ROSES *(1989)*

One of our most effective remedies. Michael Douglas and Kathleen Turner are the titular Roses, Oliver and Barbara, and very happy they are too. They met at an auction, bidding for the same lot, had sex, got married, got rich, got bored. She wants out and so begins one of the most bitter divorce battles ever committed to film.

And, make no mistake, this could happen to you. Happily married couples will watch this film and say, *sotto voce*, 'could this happen to us?' You, on the other hand, will say, *fortissimo*, 'Thank heavens I'm not involved in any of this relationship nonsense! Marriage is for losers! Chandeliers are for lighting not throwing!' And so on.

LESSON LEARNED You are on your own. And that's a very good place to be.

SILVER LININGS PLAYBOOK *(2012)*

An inspirational choice for the recently single. *SLP* involves us in a surprising American version of an old British pantomime tradition. While watching *Cinderella/Puss in Boots/Dick Whittington/Ali Baba* (it doesn't matter which) there is always a moment where the main baddie (played by that guy from that soap who had an affair with that woman) appears behind the good guy (played by Christopher Biggins). The audience takes a break from pouring E-numbers down its collective throat to shout, 'He's behind you!'

In *Silver Linings Playbook*, Bradley Cooper's Pat Solatano eventually realises that pursuing his estranged wife Nikki is a waste of time. This is because a) she's not interested and b) the whole audience, having spotted the brilliant Jennifer Lawrence in close attendance, has for some time been yelling, 'She's next to you!' Eventually he realises we are right and they all live happily after.

LESSON LEARNED Your new romantic adventure may be closer than you think.

BOOM, BOOM, BOOM

The Movie Doctors' Cardiovascular Workout

Some movie genres provide a whole fitness routine in themselves.

WARM UP
LET'S GET THE BLOOD PUMPING

NORTH BY NORTHWEST *(1959)*

THE TOWERING INFERNO *(1974)*

MARATHON MAN *(1976)*

DIE HARD *(1988)*

THE BOURNE SUPREMACY *(2004)*

WORKING HARD
IT'S TIME TO GET THE HEART RACING

THE WAGES OF FEAR *(1953)*

DUEL *(1971)*

SPEED *(2004)*

THE HURT LOCKER *(2008)*

RUSH *(2013)*

STARTING TO GET FRIGHTENING
THE SUSPENSE SHOULDN'T KILL YOU

VERTIGO *(1958)*

ONIBABA *(1964)*

DON'T LOOK NOW *(1973)*

JAWS *(1975)*

MAN ON WIRE *(2008)*

HIT THE EMERGENCY STOP BUTTON
THIS WORKOUT IS HORRIFYING!

PSYCHO *(1960)*

THE EXORCIST *(1973)*

THE TEXAS CHAINSAW MASSACRE *(1974)*

THE SHINING *(1980)*

COOL DOWN
LET'S GENTLY CALM THE PULSE

ON GOLDEN POND *(1981)*

BABETTE'S FEAST *(1987)*

THE PIANO *(1993)*

X-RAY DEPARTMENT

The Movie Doctors are all for **technological advances**, so long as they're used to the benefit of the cinemagoer, and respect the expertise of **unsung industry heroes**, like the projectionist. At home, meanwhile, technology has **transformed** movie watching, and generally much for the better– just remember that you are still in Acacia Avenue, not deep undercover in 'Nam, when you press 'pause' and go to make a cup of tea . . .

THE (IN)OPERATING THEATRE

A Clinical Examination

magine that you need to go into hospital for an operation. Nothing life threatening, just something which requires the attention of a highly trained and skilled surgeon. You arrive on the day of your treatment, and you are told that you will be tended to in one of eight operating theatres – this being the kind of big new hospital which has been purpose-built to serve the varying needs of a wide and diverse range of patients. It all sounds jolly convenient, and you're in excellent spirits as you are wheeled into Theatre Number 8, where your grumbling appendix is due to be removed.

As you gaze around the room, you are reminded of that scene from the 1983 Monty Python movie *The Meaning of Life* in which a patient is surrounded by an increasingly vast array of expensive hospital equipment including 'the machine that goes "Ping"!' While the equipment all seems very shiny and impressive, you're a little concerned by the absence of any other people – nurses, surgeons, anaesthetists and so on. You wait a while. Nothing happens. You wait some more. Still nada. After a time, you contemplate getting up off the operating table and going to tell someone that you seem to have been forgotten about. But you don't want to make a fuss.

And surely the hospital knows what's going on . . .

It's at around this point that it dawns on you there isn't going to be a surgeon – at least, not a human one. Because this is one of those new fangled 'multiplex' hospitals in which all the real surgeons have all been replaced by machines which can apparently do the job just as efficiently, and at a fraction of the cost. At which point, the vast array of technology around you suddenly lurches into life and begins to perform the very complicated operation which, only a few years ago, would have been performed by someone who had spent several years learning to do the job properly, but who has recently been fired for being too expensive. Unfortunately, the machines are suffering from an entirely unforeseen programme malfunction and have become confused as to which operation is meant to be taking place in which theatre. Thus, just as you drift into automated anaesthetised unconsciousness, you realise that the machines in your theatre have been instructed to remove your left leg, rather than your appendix, and there's nothing anyone can do about it. Because, simply put, there is nobody around to observe what's going on in Theatre 8, to think, 'I'm pretty sure that patient came in here with a pain in their abdomen rather than a gangrenous left leg, perhaps I should do something about this...'

Indeed, there is only one 'technician' in the entire building, and since their energies are currently being expended dealing with an unforeseen head transplant over in Theatre 2, they can't be on hand to deal with your petty little problems. When you remonstrate with the management several hours (and the odd organ) later, you are told that the mix-up was nobody's fault but was entirely due to a 'technical irregularity' which occurred several thousand miles away at a head office in Beijing. As you are whisked out of the door, you are given a voucher which guarantees you 30 per cent off your next appendix removal, provided you have it done on a Wednesday afternoon.

This nightmare medical scenario may be the stuff of science fiction, but if, like the Movie Doctors, you have visited a fully automated multiplex cinema in the past few years you will recognise immediately the parallels with your own increasingly endangered entertainment experience. Ever since the introduction of 'digital distribution' (no bad thing in itself), more and more cinema chains have decided that they no longer need skilled projectionists to run their ever-multiplying screening rooms. Where once there was an industry maxim that 'In the cinema, only projectionists have final cut', now the screening of movies has been handed over to computers which can't tell the difference between an animated kids' fantasy and a found-footage live-action horror movie. Thus it was that in October 2012, children waiting to enjoy *Madagascar 3* in one of the many screens of Nottingham's Cineworld emporium were forced to run screaming from the theatre as *Paranormal Activity 4* started to unspool before them, replete with non-family-friendly bloodied corpses and worse. 'It was enough to scar the children for life,' said one patron, Natasha Lewis, who had taken her eight-year-old son to the 10 a.m. screening. 'All you could hear were children crying and screaming. Dylan doesn't want to set foot in the cinema again!' According to a Cineworld spokesperson, 'There was a "technical error" with the projector...'

Sadly, such 'technical errors' are increasingly commonplace in a world in which the once-revered art of screening movies properly has been replaced by the click-and-go automation of the modern multiplex. In the spring of 2015, for example, young audiences waiting to see the new U-rated live-action *Cinderella* were treated to a trailer for the 15-rated *Insidious: Chapter 3*, prompting numerous complaints from the parents of traumatised kids. Once again, the 'technical error' apparently occurred because there was nobody in the projection booth to notice that anything was amiss in the first place. More and more, cinema patrons are growing used to seeing films projected in the wrong ratio, through the wrong lens, with the wrong 3D filter etc. And all of these avoidable mistakes go entirely unregistered by the cinema management until some poor patron makes it their business to go and find someone to whom to complain. Indeed, under the current automated regime, the chances of the right film hitting the right screen at the right time in the right ratio are dwindling by the day. No wonder so many former cinemagoers are opting to stay at home and just download movies onto their computers and TVs instead, unimpressed by the prospect of shelling out the best part of £20

so that an overworked cinema manager can press 'Go' by remote control, and hope that the right film appears on screen.

As with medicine, the advance of technology in cinema has not made the human touch any less significant. On the contrary, at a time when machines are being asked to perform more and more complicated (and mission-critical) tasks, it is ever more crucial that experts are on hand to guide and control those machines. In healthcare terms, projectionists are the hands-on experts who nurse a movie on its perilous passage from the womb of the hard drive or celluloid reel, through the birth canal of the projector, to the glorious world of the silver screen. They are the A & E team ready to offer quick responses when accidents happen, and to ensure that the cuts and bruises of everyday life are bandaged and made better with skill and dexterity. They are the radiographers who can see inside the workings of a malfunctioning projector, and the surgeons who can be trusted to delve inside its innermost organs without causing it to shut down in shock. They are the ophthalmologists who know how to replace fading bulbs and faulty lenses to ensure that a film is not dimmed or damaged by light loss or blurred focus. Most important of all, they are the general practitioners who ensure that cinema continues to be healthy and energetic for generations to come, providing regular check-ups, diagnosing ailments as they occur, and offering the kind of specialist care and attention without which movies cannot continue to connect with a mainstream audience.

You wouldn't go to a surgery without doctors, and you wouldn't take health advice from a machine – why should the movies be any different?

If you want to know who the real Movie Doctors are, they're the ones up in the projection booth. Treat them with respect – the good health of cinema should be in their hands.

THE LAST PROJECTIONIST STANDING

Dr Dave Norris's Guide to the Art of Movie Projection

Dr Kermode: As I am fond of pointing out, 'A building without a projectionist isn't a cinema. It's a sweet shop with a video.' Dr Dave Norris is that rare being – someone who understands the art of film projection. He was the West End's longest-serving projectionist until he left to run the screening rooms at Universal Pictures in 2012. Here he offers us his guide to that underrated cinematic art of putting on a show – properly. It's all very well having a billion-dollar budget, the hottest stars in Hollywood and the best special-effects company money can buy working for you, but if the film is casually thrown at the screen by someone who doesn't know their 'flat' from their 'scope', you might as well have shot it on your phone.

Dr Mayo: We asked Dr Dave to help movie-goers understand some aspects of this essential part of the movie-going experience – so that they can diagnose when the local multiplex decides to let the popcorn seller into the projection booth.

Dr Kermode: That's the trailer, now dim the lights. It's all yours, Dave. Roll opening sequence . . .

Dr Dave Norris: The projectionist is (or should be, if your local cinema still employs one) the person who makes sure that the movie is shown the way the director wanted people to see it. In fact, I often say that the projectionist is the last link in the chain of film production: they translate the director's vision onto the screen while you gaze on in rapt admiration. The film-maker decides on the photographic framing of the story which is defined as the aspect ratio, the relationship between the width and height of the image. Over the course of the history of cinema, there have been many different standard ratios. Some of the changes – particularly in the 1950s and '60s – were developed to counter the threat of television while others arose because technological advances allowed for a wider image to be projected.

The ratios are expressed as the proportion of width to height. So the 'Flat' format is 1.85 (width) to 1 (height). Take a look at this graphic – it shows the most commonly used ratios in cinema history.

Dr Dave

1.33:1 FOR SILENT MOVIES

Became 1.37 in 1932 to accommodate sound on film. Commonly known as 'Academy' ratio.

1.85:1 'FLAT'

The common ratio for ads and trailers in the modern age and for features not shot in scope.

2.35:1 CINEMASCOPE

The first film shot in this ratio was *The Robe* in 1953.

2.39:1 THE MODERN DAY 'PANAVISION' EQUIVALENT OF CINEMASCOPE

Commonly referred to as 'scope' and the modern-age standard for features not shot in flat.

Dr Dave in 1.33:1 . . .   . . . and projected in 1.85:1 'Flat'

Dr Dave in 2.39:1 'Scope' . . .   . . . and projected in an
anamorphic squish in 1.33:1

HOW TO SPEAK 'PROJECTIONIST'

As with any profession, projectionists have their own language. If you really want to frighten the management at your local multiplex, try using these loudly as you stand in the queue to buy your tickets and sugary snacks.

ANAMORPHIC FORMAT

An ingenious way of shooting a widescreen picture on standard 35mm film stock with a non-widescreen aspect ratio. The anamorphic lens allows for the image to be 'squeezed' when it is being shot and then 'unsqueezed' (anamorphic derives from the Greek words meaning 'formed again') using an anamorphic lens on the projector in the cinema. It was the basis for the CinemaScope ratio. The anamorphic process also allowed for films that had been shot on 65mm (for 70mm projection) to be printed on 35mm film.

This technique lost some of the scale of the original film but saved a huge amount of money as 35mm film was a fraction of the cost of 70mm.

Take a look at the two stills opposite. The one on the right is from the original stock of *Ben-Hur* (1959). It was filmed in 65mm with a slight anamorphic squeeze, then squished much further for 35mm film.

You can see how squeezed the 35mm image is. The anamorphic lens loaded onto the projector at the cinema would 'unsqueeze' it when it came to be shown.

Of course, in the digital age there isn't actually any film rolling through the camera or projector so the digital camera can simply capture a 2.39 image without having to squeeze it. When the film is shown in the cinema the projector lens just zooms out to fill the 2.39 screen size. The problem of black bars on the screen, or bits of the image missing, only arises when the projectionist/confectionery vendor has set the projector up incorrectly and tries to show a 1.85 picture in 2.39. Sigh. Enough said.

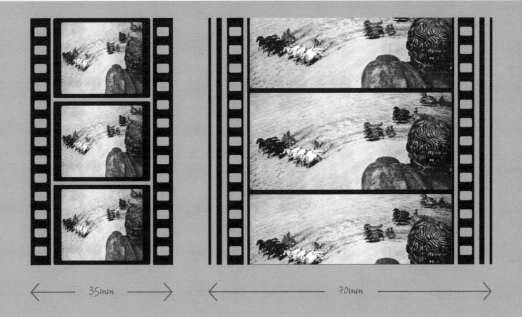

$\longleftarrow$ 35mm $\longrightarrow$ $\longleftarrow$ 70mm $\longrightarrow$

MASKING

The black cloth fixed to a movable motorised rig that frames the 1.85 or 2.39 screen image on the cinema screen. It covers the part of the screen that isn't used. Many modern day multiplexes don't have masking any more, they simply 'mask off' the image electronically in the projector.

RACKING (OR FRAMING)

Each frame of 35mm film stock takes up four perforations of the film. In order to make each frame whole on the screen – and avoid having part of the previous or subsequent frame showing – the film has to be threaded (or 'laced') so that the frame lands perfectly on the film gate (the place where light is shone through the film to project the image). Projectionists also have to be careful when repairing film and joining up reels because misalignment there could also result in a 'rack'. Digital film doesn't need to be laced, so it is less of an issue now.

These days only two aspect ratios are commonly used – 'flat' (1.85:1) and 'scope' (2.39:1) – although you do still get the occasional 'Academy' film like *The Artist* (2011), or 1.66 presentations like *Slow West* (2015). When the screen appears to expand at the end of trailers, the moment you've been waiting forty-five minutes for, that's the projectionist readying the screen for a different aspect ratio – usually moving from 'flat' to 'scope' (see 'Masking' above).

Sometimes it goes wrong and a film is shown in the incorrect aspect ratio and you end up with horrible black bars at the top and bottom of the screen, or the subtitles are missing. When that happens, it's the projectionist's responsibility and you should immediately complain to the popcorn seller-in-chief.

Dr Kermode: Thanks, Dr Dave. So now you know your flat from your scope, your masking from your racking . . .

Dr Mayo: . . . and when to collar the popcorn seller-in-chief and assert loudly 'YOU'RE USING THE WRONG ASPECT RATIO'. I can see a merch line on the horizon . . .

IN-HOME CARE
From A(nalogue) to D(igital)

This is, of course, the future of all treatment. The days of attending an old, uncomfortable building where the staff are trying to sell you unhealthy snacks while you wait for your ministrations are long gone. These days the most exciting therapies are administered *in the home*. Fortunately the Movie Doctors are pioneers when it comes to making house calls and can vouch for their effectiveness.

Whether faced with the sick, the tired or the lazy, the Movie Doctors approach the patient with the same cheery bedside manner. Ailments are assessed and movie prescriptions administered, limited only by your TV and playback facilities. In the old days the choices were bleak. Namely 1) watch what was on the TV *at the time*. Imagine that! Your only choice was to change the channel to where some other half-witted controller will have programmed something equally soul-destroying for you to watch. Or 2) run some of your dad's holiday cine films. These were dark days. Not only was a projector needed, but also an ability to thread plastic film through red-hot machinery. A small portable screen which doubled as a finger-chopper added to the fun.

Then the video cassette player came along and we were in business. Once we got past the slight inconvenience of the opening $50,000 price tag, everyone loosened up a bit. Next we needed a system everybody could use, but wait! There's the Philips N1500, Sony's Betamax, JVC's Video Home System VHS and then Philips again with Video 2000. And just when you were thinking there must be a limit to the number of ways mankind could arrange recording tape in a plastic box, Sanyo offered you V-Cord, and Quasar had a Great Time Machine

(there's also the laserdisc guys to consider, but they were in a cult and quite happy being better than everyone else).

Some older readers are surely now getting ready to fight the bitter videotape format wars all over again. Old allegiances are bubbling to the surface, fierce rivalries are stirring.

'My Video 2000 had an auto-rewind and double the playing time!' PUNCH

'My Betamax had higher horizontal resolution!' KICK

'I've got a VHS. It's cheaper.' VICTORY

So that was all sorted and everyone settled down to watch lots of films. It was hissy, jerky and a bit rubbish, but we didn't know any better so we were happy.

Except for the fact that your TV was *terrible*. Small screen, terrible aspect ratio (though only Dr Kermode complained about this at the time) and *the worst sound you've heard, ever*.

You knew what good audio sounded like – you had one of those new Philips cassette players with its solitary play/rewind/fast forward button, mic on a stand etc – and it was a whole lot worse than that. Your TV loudspeaker was the size of a pea, and in those pre-digital days, this was not a good thing.

Good sound needed big, pulsing, vibrating speakers. And it is a well-known fact that *in TV no one cares about sound*.

Sometimes you could get round this by hauling your proper oak and steel hi-fidelity speakers to a peak audio sweet spot on either side of your TV. Complicated pluggery followed and, assuming your cables could fit, your amp then hummed into action. TV sound was at last coming through decent speakers and, assuming you didn't mind your lounge looking like a vast cat's cradle, you were happy. Sure, you needed to be an Olympic gymnast to contort yourself around the cables, but did you want decent sound or not?

Other than close friends of Stanley Kubrick, no one had heard the words 'home cinema' at this point in time – the very idea was ridiculous. Cinema was what you did in town, in the company of *other people*. Your home was your castle, where entertainment was *private*. Big screen, small screen. Surround sound, barely any sound. You knew where you were.

But as your clunky VHS cassettes were made instantly redundant by groovy DVDs (that sound you can hear is the laserdisc guys partying), this segregated world began to fall apart. You needed a DVD player. This wasn't some vague desire or casual whim, this was a requirement, a necessity, an obligation. It was probably covered in the Human Rights Act too. If you liked movies, you got yourself a DVD player.

This made the Movie Doctors' mission much easier. The films could now do their work with an image that didn't suck and sound that didn't hiss. This is not a small point of minor interest. We have reached a milestone. With the exception of those laserdisc fanatics, whose numbers remained small, no one had experienced *silence* in their home entertainment until DVDs came along. For most of us *there was simply no such thing as silence* before DVD. In the days of video, it was like everyone had tinnitus. If you actually had tinnitus and watched a VHS, you could hardly hear a thing (if you're still suffering, see p.50). The creepily silent house? Couldn't hear the monster for the hiss. The quiet moment of contemplation in the cathedral? Drowned out by fizzing. The awesomeness and sheer emptiness of space? Awash with the sound of eggs frying.

But now as you watch a digital versatile disc, your front room can fill with the sound of digital silence. *Now* you can hear the floorboards, *now* you hear the ecclesiastical stillness, *now* you can hear the soundlessness of infinity.

One TV, one DVD player. Life was simple. But as our ears got used to lovely, pristine digital sound from the pea-sized TV speaker, we naturally wondered what else this new era of marvels could bring us. And the answer wasn't long in coming. Sell your car, remortgage your house and buy a home cinema kit.

It turns out that you don't need all that space in your front room. Why leave a square metre empty when you can fill it with *loudspeakers*. All your life you have had to make do with one tiny, feeble woofer behind a fake wood grill that rattles when anyone plays 'The Theme from Shaft'. Well your days of oppression are over; liberation is at hand. You can now turn your lounge into something better than your local screen 6. No pick 'n' mix, no hooligans, no drug dealers.

Let us count your new bounty. You'll at least need a mid-bass driver, a powerful sub-woofer and a series of satellite speakers arranged in a semicircle. And a Blu-ray disc player (the laserdisc guys giving it one more whoop).

Now, at last, you (and only you, there isn't room for anyone else) can hear the Dolby Surround 7.1 (5.1 is *so* last decade) in all its magnificence. When it rains in a movie, it rains all around you, when a rocket fires it goes right over your head, when a couple are having sex, they're right there in the room with you (it's not all good).

So now when the Movie Doctors come to call, your treatment will be spectacularly efficacious. Please don't adjust your sets.

FERTILITY
CLINIC

To sprog or not to sprog? The Movie Doctors can't make your mind up for you but we can present the cinematic evidence for and against. In our Fertility Clinic you'll find an objective assessment of the **risks and opportunities** as well as a solution to a problem in the 'Mr Happy Department' which is apparently more common than is widely acknowledged.

CHILDREN

An In-Depth Study

t's a tough call. Should you have kids or not? Should you trade your freedom and prosperity for a lifetime of stress and poverty? Imagine only being able to see films once the quite possibly demonically possessed babysitter has been booked? The future could be bleak. Do you really fancy mother and baby screenings at 11 a.m.? Of course you don't. Obviously the Movie Doctors welcome all family set-ups in a non-judgemental we-are-the-world-we-are-the-children kind of way, but here we can offer you the benefit of many years of counselling.

Before you proceed with the rigmarole that goes with bringing more cinemagoers into the world, there is an important question you need to consider: *What if it all goes wrong?*

It's all very well having children and dreaming of them becoming particle physicists, prime ministers or cinema projectionists, but what if they fail? What if they are in fact desperately annoying? What if, instead of turning the world to joy and laughter, they sell weapons to despots? And what if it becomes increasingly apparent that despite all the education, the bedtime stories and the ethically sourced vegetables and holidays, your child has become the spawn of Satan (no offence)? So here we offer a quick cinematic test of your commitment to restock the planet. Consider, if you will, what you might do if you and your other half produced a child like one of these.

DUDLEY DURSLEY
HARRY POTTER AND THE PHILOSOPHER'S STONE *(2001)*

The only child of Vernon and Petunia Dursley from Number 4, Privet Drive, Little Whinging, Surrey. A spoilt, argumentative, cowardly bully. From the very beginning of the Harry Potter story, Dudley is one of Harry's main tormentors. A large blond oaf of a boy, we have all met a Dudley. It isn't that he's been neglected or unloved; in fact, his mum and dad have made sure he has roomfuls of everything. He has the benefit of an expensive education from his father's old school Smeltings and yet he's still as thick as a very thick thing. Draco Malfoy could at least blame his nastiness on his parents. *How do you know you won't produce another Dudley Dursley?* What if your son wears a boater? What would you do if he locked a child under the stairs? Well here's your answer. You'd wish you had never become a parent, that's what.

Spawn of Satan rating ♥ ♥ ♥ ♥

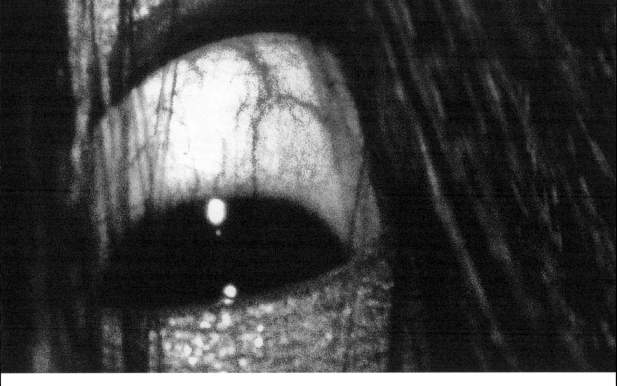

SADAKO
RINGU *(1998)*

Now while it might be true that you won't be drowning your children down a well, you should at least consider the implications of having a child like Sadako. You've begged her to change her clothes but she does seem keen on her blousy white dress. She has such lovely, long black hair but will she tie it up? Of course not. She prefers the dripping-wet, hanging-like-a-curtain-in-front-of-her-face look. But growing up is tricky, isn't it? Always making videos, climbing in and out of televisions, killing people.

So how to parent a future Sadako, or her US cousin Samara? Could you guide and mould her ability to manipulate water for the betterment of humanity? Maybe she could build a reservoir for the needy. Her telepathy could predict the lottery numbers for charity, and just imagine what Simon Cowell would make of her spider walking.

Spawn of Satan rating ♥ ♥ ♥ ♥ ♥ ♥ ♥

ISAAC
CHILDREN OF THE CORN *(1984)*

It may be a Nebraska thing, it may be a let's-dress-like-the-Amish thing, but sometimes a mum and dad end up with an Isaac – a kid who speaks like he's Laurence Olivier for no reason. If this happens, the best advice is to run away. This is because your son and all his weird mates will kill you and everyone over nineteen. It's just what they do. If your child develops a fascination with farm implements, corn husks and barbed wire, it might be time to call social services.

Spawn of Satan rating ♥ ♥ ♥ ♥ ♥ ♥ ♥

THE GRADY TWINS
THE SHINING *(1980)*

Although they're described as being 'about eight and ten', the Grady girls were played by twins and that's how they'll always be remembered. What a blessing! Twice the thrill. Twice the fun. A complete, ready-made family. They'll always have each other for company. Just a few things to watch out for, if we may. If you ever find that, in spite of your usual tastes, you seem to have dressed them in pale blue dresses with a pink trim, whisk them to Topshop as soon as possible. If they start holding hands and asking random boys on bikes to 'come and play with us, for ever and ever', get them to sing 'Let It Go' from *Frozen* like other eight-year-old girls. And avoid Colorado hotels.

Spawn of Satan rating ♥ ♥ ♥ ♥ ♥ ♥ ♥

HENRY MORGAN
THE GOOD SON *(1993)*

A nice, well-mannered child is what all parents hope for. A cute smile, lovely blond hair, and who could be prouder? If you overlook his fascination with death and habit of killing things, this boy is going to grow up to be a well-balanced guy. What to do if you have brought a Henry into the world? Avoid ice skating, cliff tops and bath tubs would be our advice. If the burglars from *Home Alone* had known quite what this boy was capable of, they might have tried next door.

Spawn of Satan rating ♥ ♥ ♥ ♥ ♥ ♥

DAMIEN THORN
THE OMEN *(1976)*

What parent hasn't thought that their child might in reality be the Antichrist? Well, sometimes *he actually is*. Here's the checklist:

- Was his mother a jackal?
- Might his father be Satan?
- Was he born on 6 June at 6 a.m.?
- Do his nannies tend to hang themselves?
- Has he ever crashed his tricycle into his mother, knocking her off a balcony?

If you answered yes to any of the above, ask your local priest if he has any daggers of Megiddo knocking around. You might need one (or maybe seven).

Spawn of Satan rating ♥ ♥ ♥ ♥ ♥ ♥ ♥ ♥ ♥

RHODA PENMARK
THE BAD SEED *(1956)*

The best advice you can give your child is to avoid extreme hairstyles. This is a scientific fact. If you can, stay away from pigtails. Nothing good ever came from a child in pigtails (especially if it's a girl). Also, mothers, avoid being the birth daughter of a notorious serial killer. You never know how that troublesome DNA is going to work its way through your family.

Spawn of Satan rating ❤❤❤❤❤❤

REGINA GEORGE
MEAN GIRLS *(2004)*

That girl you hated at school. The one who was posher, meaner and nastier than all the others put together. The one who ran the most exclusive clique and who told you that you were *way* too unpopular to be allowed to join. What if that is how your sweet little girl ends up? How would you cope? Are you tough enough to take her out of the lacrosse team if that's what's needed?

Spawn of Satan rating ❤❤❤❤❤❤❤❤❤

REGAN MACNEIL
THE EXORCIST *(1973)*

If you're an atheist who allows your daughter to play with a Ouija board, it's all your fault.

Spawn of Satan rating ❤❤❤❤❤❤❤❤❤

DAVID
VILLAGE OF THE DAMNED *(1960)*

Always check your child for glowing eyes, weird hair (again) and unusually narrow fingernails (always the sign of a bad 'un). If he or she tends to have friends who look and dress exactly the same, talks like an adult and can make you crash your car at will, it probably means they are classified now as *gifted and talented*. Grants are available.

If the Movie Doctors ruled the world (and we really feel we could) we would run an inter-village cricket series: *Village of the Damned* versus *Children of the Corn*. Strong umpires would be needed, maybe with guns, but admit it, you'd watch.

Spawn of Satan rating 🔥🔥🔥🔥🔥🔥🔥🔥

THE BROOD
THE BROOD *(1979)*

Nola Carveth (Samantha Eggar) uses psycho-plasmics to lend physical expression to her anger, spawning a crop of murderous 'children of rage' which enact her subconscious bidding. Think *Don't Look Now* with teeth. Cronenberg on top form – again.

Spawn of Satan rating 🔥🔥🔥🔥🔥🔥🔥

So how did you do? If you have made it through the scary kid list and you still wish to procreate, the Movie Doctors endorse your decision. We say go forth and multiply. If you're quaking in your boots, proceed to 'A Cut Below' (see p.126)

A CUT BELOW
To Snip or Not to Snip?

This is, of course, a sensitive matter. A delicate issue. Each family will come to its own conclusion about when the procreation should stop (or if it should ever begin – see p.120). For how long should vas deferens continue to star in your co-authored production? The Movie Doctors would not presume to interfere in this most intimate of matters, but can provide comfort and support (but not that kind of support, obviously) once you have reached your decision. Just be careful not to watch the wrong set of movies.

ANSWER 1 YES PLEASE, SNIP AWAY

Enough of this having a family lark, a new dawn beckons. Movies to watch before, during and after a vasectomy

THE GARBAGE PAIL KIDS MOVIE *(1987)*

Maybe the worst family film ever. A film so appalling, so misguided you'll be urging the surgeon to get on with it. You have *so* moved on from this whole children's entertainment thing. Following on from the Cabbage Patch craze, the Garbage Pail cards were a big fad in the mid eighties, so the movie was all but inevitable. What wasn't inevitable was a monstrosity that featured creepy masks on little people, and a bullied kid who survives an attempt to drown him in sewage. We know how he feels. Oh, and Anthony Newley is the lead. His 1961 hit asked 'What Kind Of Fool Am I?' Well, now we know.

BARNEY'S GREAT ADVENTURE *(1998)*

You've already sat through every TV show that the world's only eight-foot purple dinosaur has recorded. In the middle of the night you have had to bite your pillow as his excruciating 'I love you, you love me, we're a happy family' song runs through your head. You've already imagined telling him that you don't in fact love him and, more to the point, you'd like to punch his lights out. Those shows were only twenty minutes long (though Barney minutes are ten times longer than earth minutes. Scientific fact). This 'adventure' clocks in at seventy-five minutes. Never has time passed so slowly. As you pray for an orc attack, Barney is on the farm with his new best friends Cody, Arabella and a baby called Fig (really?). There are shooting stars, an egg with a creature in it and lots of cowpoke dungaree action. But no orcs, and no dismemberment of any kind. And so you can relax. This is the world you're leaving behind. Thank the surgeon's blade that in a few moments, all that purple T. Rex-induced pain will be gone for ever.

MAC AND ME *(1988)*

So. There's a wrinkly, homesick alien. He has big eyes and long fingers. He's lost and he gets to hang out with a bunch of kids and their single moms. And just when you think that this might be ringing bells, here's the twist. The moment of genius that lets you know you have never seen anything this bad in all your moviegoing days. *This alien can be revived by Coca-Cola.* Who needs to phone home when you can devour gallons of a carbonated, sugary soft drink with natural flavourings? And when everyone gets peckish, where better to spend your time than a McDonald's restaurant? And then, if you need to do a long breakdance sequence, there's always a McDonald's car park nearby. Plus it's really handy for Ronald McDonald, who likes to be all hands on with this kind of thing.

So that Mac of the title? Of course! It stands for Mysterious Alien Creature – hush your cynical thoughts. A film to crush the soul of even the most hardened Republican and free-marketeer. Let go of your rage. Welcome the healing knife. You should by now be comfortably numb.

ANSWER 2 NO THANKS!

Why quit now? Keep those kids coming. Movies to watch while celebrating fertility

TOY STORY *(1995)*, TOY STORY 2 *(1999)* AND TOY STORY 3 *(2010)*

Maybe the best film trilogy of all time. Perfect to enjoy as your children grow. However many times you have seen Woody, Buzz and Mr Potato Head, they never fail to delight. And by the time Stinky Pete, yodelling Jessie the cowgirl and thespian hedgehog Mr Pricklepants join the action, your parent–child viewing couldn't be bettered. There's horrid toy-torturing neighbour Sid to teach us all about respect and not pulling the legs off things. There's Woody's desire for immortality at the toy museum to discuss. And fart jokes.

And who would have thought that grouchy, cynical, caustic songsmith Randy Newman could ever become a children's favourite? The man who brought us 'Rednecks', 'Let's Burn Down the Cornfield' and 'Texas Girl at the Funeral of Her Father' is now the singalong favourite of a generation. 'You've Got a Friend in Me' will keep us at Uncle Randy's piano (sounds fine in America) for years to come. Why limit your options? Keep procreating, keep singing, keep watching.

MARY POPPINS *(1964)*

You might be welling up already. One of the main reasons to have children of your own is to sit them down and make them watch stuff that you liked. And what better place to start than this Oscar-laden classic? A magical nanny, cartoon penguins and the last time bankers (or at least, *a* banker – Mr Banks) were shown sympathetically in a movie. This is still a must-see.

You have so many facts to pass on to the next generation. You know all the words to the Sherman brothers' songs but can still point out the illogicality of saying that supercalifragilisticexpialidocious backwards is docious-ali-exip-ilistic-fragi-cali-repus. Which it clearly isn't. You can explain that Dick Van Dyke's 'cockernee' accent is based on, well, nothing at all really, and that no human being has ever talked like that before or since. And when you're all singing along to 'Feed the Birds', how useful to be able to break off and explain that 'tuppence a bag' refers to old, pre-decimalised money and would be now worth just under one new pence. Your children will love and respect you all the more.

PADDINGTON *(2014)*

The spirit of Mary Poppins lives on in this instant classic. Obviously your children will never *pay* to see a talking-bear movie themselves (will they ever pay for anything?) so this is indisputably *your job*. You do the groundwork ahead of viewing, explaining about the original books and the Michael Hordern-voiced TV series. Then, just when they're switching off and dismissing your lecture as the reminiscences of a madman, the movie starts and the spell is woven. Nicole Kidman is Cruella De Ville from *101 Dalmations*, Hugh Bonneville is Mr Banks from Cherry Tree Lane (not to be confused with *Cherry Tree Lane*, the home invasion/rape/torture/kid-killing horror film, obvs) and Peter Capaldi is the crazy UKIP guy from down the road.

You need children of your own for this movie. Sure, you can borrow other people's kids if you need to (though not in an illegal way) but it's your own flesh and blood that matters here. If they wish to talk further about the issues raised, brief yourself on recent changes to immigration law and just how 'dark' 'darkest Peru' actually is. Hand them sweets, pat them on the head, feel your heart swell. You've done the right thing.

AROUSAL

The Movie Doctors' Casebook	The doctors are IN

INT. MOVIE DOCTORS' SURGERY – DAY

Dr Mayo is wearing casual slacks and a 'Radio 1 FM 1053–1089 My Favourite Radio Station' bomber jacket. Dr Kermode hasn't changed since the last surgery. He is watching a movie on his cracked and useless laptop. He has feeble white headphones in and is paying no attention to anything around him.

> **DR MAYO**
> What are you watching? Is it good? Is there much of it left? We have a patient to see . . . Whatevs.

Dr Mayo presses button.

> **DR MAYO (CONT'D)**
> Mr Russell, do come in.

A middle-aged, casually dressed man enters sheepishly, looks around then dives for the seat as if taking cover. Dr Kermode jumps and removes feeble white headphones.

DR KERMODE

Blimey, Charlie! Where did you come from? Can you get me a coffee?

DR MAYO

It's our next patient. I tried to tell you but you seemed . . . preoccupied. It's Mr Russell.

DR KERMODE

(realising) Oh, Mr Russell! With the . . . problem in the . . . (waves hands) Mr Happy department?

MR RUSSELL

(flushing) A fairly common complaint, I think?

DR KERMODE

Oh yes. I think you're talking about *arousal*. Am I right?

MR RUSSELL

Well . . .

DR KERMODE

Fine. This is easy to sort. Let me tell you what I recommend, though these titles might be tricky to find . . .

MR RUSSELL

Oh well, actually we have one of those stores near us . . . and . . . there are some websites I've been told about . . .

DR MAYO

I don't think he means *that* kind of film, Mr Russell.

DR KERMODE
(ignoring all interruptions) Let's start with *Trotsky*,
the 1993 Russian-language biopic directed by Leonid
Maryagin. Follow that with *Raspberry Festival* from
the Socialist Workers Party Archive of 1944 – classic
collective farm fun.

Dr Mayo is asleep. Mr Russell is aghast.

DR KERMODE (CONT'D)
But my blockbuster, my *banker*, if you know what I
mean, is *Labor's Turning Point: The Minneapolis Truck
Strikes of 1934: A Rank and File Story*. That always
works for me.

DR MAYO
(waking up) Was that two colons in one title?

MR RUSSELL
I was hoping for well, something more . . . you know . . .
(looks at the floor) saucy, maybe?

DR KERMODE
Oh, I see! (looks confounded, briefly). Ah! There's
the Ken Loach back catalogue? *Land and Freedom*,
maybe?

Mr Russell turns to Dr Mayo, pleadingly.

DR MAYO
You could try Meg Ryan in *French Kiss*?

MR RUSSELL
Oh yes, that's perfect, thanks.

Mr Russell rises and makes for the door.

DR KERMODE
(baffled, calling out) There's always *Public Enemy Bukharin*?

The door slams.

DR MAYO
Not sure you got that one quite right, comrade.

DR KERMODE
The lumpenproletariat always surprise me. We should have another *Battleship Potemkin* evening soon . . .

MATERNITY

Ah, the pleasures of motherhood – as **Movie Doctors we love to saunter into our Maternity Clinic to bask in the postnatal glow of our patients**, carefully inserting earplugs to drown out the piercing wails of planet Earth's newest arrivals. As we do so, we mull over those movies that have taken an aeon to reach the big screen, contemplate how the movies make you a better parent and recall some of the more interesting depictions of childbirth captured on celluloid.

BRINGING UP BABY

How the Movies Can Make You a Better Parent

Short-tempered? Shouting too much? Only showing cursory interest in playing mindless, repetitive games? Never despair. All you need to know is this: the movies are here to help! In the movies, *there will always be worse parents than you*. We prescribe the following feel-good parenting films to get you ready for the big push.

HOME ALONE AND HOME ALONE 2 *(1990 & 1992)*

Movies that give and then give some more. Who hasn't warmed to the antics of Macauley Culkin's syrupy-sweet Kevin McCallister? We all cheered as he fought off burglars after being deserted at Christmas. We all whooped as he got the better of New York's evil hotel concierges. But remember the real villains of the piece – his parents. The outrageously bourgeois lifestyle of Peter and Katie McCallister (played by John Heard and Catherine O'Hara) has led them to become symbols of indifference and neglect. You might once forget the name of your child's teacher, the name of his class and maybe even the name of his school, but you would *never* fly to France leaving him in the hands of two burglars. Furthermore, you would never follow up your display of callous disregard by then leaving the little tyke in a crime-ridden city with just your credit card for company. *You can't buy affection, Mr and Mrs McCallister!* And oh, who's that knocking at the door? Is it social services? Can your capitalist lickspittle cronies save you now? Well probably yes, but when you're feeling blue about the extent of your parenting skills, remember the McCallisters. Then make your children watch *Home Alone* and *Home Alone 2*. Don't bother with *Home Alone 3* (1997), *Home Alone 4* (2002), or *Home Alone: The Holiday Heist* (2012). No one else did.

STAR WARS *(1977)*

You'll have bad days. You'll have tricky nights. You'll be irritable. When things go really badly you

might even lash out and kick the budgie. But Darth Vader sets a new standard for bad dad behaviour. Not for him the mere trifles of forgetting the school play or failing to provide child support, he actually, literally totally vaporises his daughter's planet! Not only that, he reveals his parentage to his son, then chops his arm off! You couldn't possibly be this bad, could you?

CARRIE *(1976)*

Well now, mums-to-be. It's time to have a pampering session. Traditionally this may well have involved a spa treatment, a massage and maybe some cheeky aromatic oils rubbed in by Antoine and his magic fingers, but the Movie Doctors are here to suggest something so much better. Get your friends round for a communal viewing of the 1976 Brian De Palma classic *Carrie*.

Meet Margaret White. Carrie's mother is not blessed with the gift of encouragement. Nor is she blessed with the gift of careful, loving insight. It is true she is quite attentive to her daughter's religious education (allow yourself a pang of guilt here, maybe?) and is somewhat concerned about the company her daughter keeps, but all that screaming, Margaret! All that black cape wearing! None of it is helping anyone. Apart from maybe making us feel better. So thanks. As a bonus, once your future offspring have seen this movie, they are guaranteed never to complain about you (though good luck with the whole school prom thing). NB: if your child really does have powers of telekinesis and can move objects like, say, buckets of blood, then the Movie Doctors will see you as an emergency case. Call the number at the back of the book. Stay strong.

MOVIE BIRTHS

Doctors in Discussion

Dr Mayo: Having a child has to be one of the most important moments in any person's life. As doctors, we believe this to be true.

Dr Kermode: Absolutely.

Dr M: It's my contention that Hollywood hasn't dealt with the actual process of childbirth very well. I mean, you get a lot of bog-standard scenes where there's fainting, swearing at the useless father, incompetent doctors, inappropriate blood and so on, but as a rule, Hollywood isn't good at childbirth.

Dr K: Well I guess seeing an actual birth on the big screen might not be everyone's cup of tea. Although now you mention it, there was what appeared to be an actual birth shown in Catherine Breillat's cause célèbre French film *Romance*.

Dr M: An actual birth, producing a real baby?

Dr K: Yep. It made a change from the rest of the film, which had a whole load of photogenic, well-to-do French people having photogenic sex in apartments so large you could land an aeroplane in them. And do you know what they spent all their time doing?

Dr M: Smoking Gauloises and blowing the smoke into a ghostly Charles de Gaulle figure?

Dr K: They complained. Endlessly. No *Romance* whatsoever. Anyway, to get back to the point, movie births are tricky. David Cronenberg's *The Fly* from 1986 originally ended with Geena Davis's character dreaming of giving birth to a 'butterfly child'.

She has been impregnated by Jeff Goldblum who is —

Dr M: Half-man, half-fly?

Dr K: That's right. But when it came to it, this beautiful butterfly child wasn't really all that beautiful – what the designers had come up with was more like a plastic doll with Tinkerbell wings which wasn't going to make anyone swoon in anything other than mirth. So they cut the scene and we never see the Tinkerbell doll.

Dr M: Doesn't sound like we missed much. Of course, the other thing about births is that when a creature does finally emerge it looks nothing like the real thing. I don't know any parents who, when casting adoring eyes on their child for the first time, have seen a sparkling clean tot with side-parted hair.

Dr K: Something that looks like a four-week-old child?

Dr M: Yes, rather than a baby covered in slime.

Dr K: Because it is a four-week-old child.

Dr M: There are some great comedy moments, though – who could forget Franck Eggelhoffer in *Father of the Bride Part II*, when mother and daughter give birth in the same room. What a terrifying thought that is.

Dr K: So, as the Movie Doctors, do we conclude that Hollywood could try harder on the birthing front?

Dr M: Actually now we've discussed it, I'm not sure I'm that bothered, to be honest. I'll be happy in the ante-chamber. Just call me in when it's all over.

PREGNANT PAUSE

Movies That Went Way Past Their Due Date

INDIANA JONES AND THE KINGDOM OF THE CRYSTAL SKULL *(2008)*

Gestation: Three different scripts were produced over a period of fifteen years, none of which lived up to Steven Spielberg's demand for 'double-butter popcorn with extra frosting on top'.

WORTH THE WAIT? Nope – the weakest of the Indy series, with a ropey script, seen-it-before action sequences, and (worst of all) Shia LaBeouf.

THE LEGO MOVIE *(2014)*

Gestation: It took four years, but then animating Lego bricks is more painful than treading on them. Script rewrites were the other reason.

WORTH THE WAIT? Absolutely. Everything is Awesome.

THE THIN RED LINE *(1999)*

Gestation: Twenty years from initial inception to screen, with the screenplay alone taking a decade to complete.

WORTH THE WAIT? Any Terrence Malick film is worth waiting for, although some of the cast may feel differently: Adrien Brody started out as the 'star', but by the time the edit was completed, he was merely a supporting player. Meanwhile Mickey Rourke was excised completely. Neither was amused.

ERASERHEAD *(1977)*

Gestation: Five years, mainly due to funding problems, and the fact that David Lynch had to keep going off to do his paper round. Really.

WORTH THE WAIT? Definitely, unless you're having chicken for dinner . . .

SLEEPING BEAUTY *(1959)*

Gestation: Eight years. An elaborate creative process that included five years of animation, and hand-inking which meant a single frame might take a week to complete.

WORTH THE WAIT? Yes. A Disney classic.

A.I. ARTIFICIAL INTELLIGENCE *(2001)*

Gestation: Stanley Kubrick began developing a film based on Brian Aldiss's 'Super-Toys Last All Summer Long' in the early seventies. By the time the film opened in 2001, Kubrick was dead and Steven Spielberg had taken over as director.

WORTH THE WAIT? On first viewing, no. On second viewing, maybe. On third viewing – Blimey Charlie!

BOYHOOD *(2014)*

Gestation: A whopping twelve years! Now that's what we call a pregnant pause.

WORTH THE WAIT? Yes, you'll watch a boy become a man (literally).

AVATAR *(2009)*

Gestation: James Cameron wrote the original treatment in 1994, but had to wait until the technology he needed to film the script had been developed.

WORTH THE WAIT? Depends on whether you really want to watch *Smurfahontas in Space*. Dr M really enjoyed the 3D. Dr K, blinded by hatred and dark glasses, did not.

APOCALYPSE NOW *(1979)*

Gestation: Ten years. An epic in every sense, it would require a separate clinic to diagnose all the difficulties that beset this Coppola masterpiece.

WORTH THE WAIT? Absolutely, despite the fact that in all that time Marlon Brando never actually read either the source novella (*Heart of Darkness*) or (apparently) the script.

OCCUPATIONAL
THERAPY

Helping people to get through their **daily lives** is a challenge that the Movie Doctors gladly take on. In our Occupational Therapy Clinic we look at the **dangers of 'overpraise'** – and then we tackle those two vexed elements of adult life: **work and holidays.** The movies, we conclude, are always there to help.

HOW PRAISE CAN DAMAGE YOUR HEALTH

A Clinical Examination

From a medical point of view, it's easy to diagnose the symptoms of excessive praise; the history of cinema is littered with examples of directors whose careers have imploded in the wake of reviews declaring them to be the best thing since sliced celluloid. Much has been written about the damaging power of negative reviews, but too little attention is given to the poisonous results of telling a film-maker how great they are. The Movie Doctors are here to help.

An obvious example of this all-too-common ailment is the very talented director John Boorman, who received rapturous acclaim for his Oscar-nominated 1972 thriller *Deliverance*, and became so dazzled by critical plaudits that he promptly made the worst science fiction movie of all time (*Zardoz*, 1974) followed by the worst movie of all time (*Exorcist II: The Heretic*, 1977). Boorman subsequently got his career back on track – after a curative dose of lousy reviews – with such well-loved hits as *Excalibur* (1981) and *Hope and Glory* (1987), and has continued to be a prolific and respected film-maker ever since. Others have not fared so well.

Take the example of Michael Cimino, the American auteur for whom widespread declarations of genius marked an almost immediate end not only to his career, but also to an entire studio. Cimino's background is shrouded in a degree of self-serving mystery. At the time of making *The Deer Hunter*, which won numerous Academy Awards in 1979 including Best Director and Best Picture, journalists reported that he was a 35-year-old film-maker with a background in documentaries who had spent time attached to the Green Berets during the Tet Offensive in 1968. In fact, Cimino was nearly forty, had a background in commercials, and had spent just six months as a reservist in 1962, none of them in Vietnam. As Universal Studios president Thom Mount observed at the time, 'This guy was no more a medic in the Green Berets than I'm a rutabaga.' (A rutabaga is a root vegetable that originated as a cross between a carrot and a turnip – who knew?)

While the director's background was elusive, what *was* certain was that Cimino believed himself to be a genius, and it was only a matter of time until the rest of the world caught up. In his early career (during which time he made his very best films) Cimino had been surrounded by people who thought only that he displayed some talent. It was within this environment that he picked up

co-writing credits on Doug Trumbull's wonderful 1972 sci-fi movie *Silent Running*, and the 1973 Dirty Harry picture *Magnum Force*. All this led to Cimino getting his directorial feature debut gig helming *Thunderbolt and Lightfoot* (1974), which garnered positive reviews and respectable box office. Crucially, Cimino spent the entire production under the thumb of leading man Clint Eastwood, who was the real driving force behind the movie. As first assistant director Charles Okun later observed, 'Clint was the only guy that ever said "no" to Michael.' If the director took too long to prepare a shot, Clint would simply say 'It's good, let's go.' If he did more than four takes, Eastwood would declare 'No, we got enough . . .'

And that was that.

When it came to *The Deer Hunter*, which many consider to be Cimino's masterpiece, plenty of people tried to say 'no' to Cimino. One such was producer Michael Deeley, who originated the movie when he optioned a script entitled *The Man Who Came to Play* by Louis Garfinkle and Quinn K. Redeker (star of the classic *Spider Baby*, 1967). A gripping story about Russian roulette, this script was in need of a rewrite and a director, and Deeley thought he had found both in the shape of Michael Cimino. 'I didn't anticipate [he] would be much bother,' notes Deeley in his terrific book *Blade Runners, Deer Hunters and Blowing the Bloody Doors Off: My Life in Cult Movies*. Indeed, Deeley candidly admits that he picked Cimino partly because 'his CV had a bland look to me' and what he wanted was someone who could do the job efficiently and without fuss. What Deeley actually got was something altogether less predictable.

First, Cimino enlisted his *Silent Running* co-writer Deric Washburn, who delivered a screenplay for *The Deer Hunter* before being told (as Washburn remembers) to 'fuck off'. Next, Cimino began downplaying the input of Garfinkle, Redeker and Washburn, and suggesting that the film was largely autobiographical. The Writers Guild disagreed, crediting Washburn alone with 'screenplay', and naming Cimino as just one of four story writers. But none of this stopped him from continuing to insist that the script was essentially all his own work. Or, as Michael Deeley puts it, 'lying through his teeth'.

By the time principal photography began, relations between Cimino and Deeley were strained. After heated arguments about the American-set opening segment (the director seemed set on making *The Deer Hunter* the same length as *Gone with the Wind* – see Excessive Length p.216), Cimino headed for the River Kwai, where the film's 'autobiographical' scenes of American soldiers being forced by Vietnamese guards to play Russian roulette would be shot. The fact that no such events took place (at least, as far as historical records are concerned) was apparently of minor concern; Deeley subsequently wrote that 'my own view is that it didn't happen' while co-producer Barry Spikings regretted the film's depiction of the war, stating several years later that, 'I didn't realize how badly we'd behaved to the Vietnamese people.'

The director continued to prove troublesome during the shooting, editing and publicising of *The Deer Hunter*, claiming credit where it was perhaps not due, spinning fanciful stories about his own creative roles (both on and off screen), and even earning himself a 'Producer' title, despite Deeley pointing out that he had done nothing which could even vaguely be defined as production duties. That the movie ran over time and over budget was just one of its problems; more worrying was the fact that some of those involved with its production never wanted to work with Cimino ever again. 'The moment couldn't have come too soon,' wrote Deeley of the last time he saw Cimino, having just bagged the Best Picture statuette at the 1979 Academy Awards. 'To this day the only flaw I find in my Oscar is that Cimino's name is also engraved on it. I keep it on a very high shelf, so that I can see the award but not the unpleasantness minutely chiselled there.'

Deeley's bitter misgivings aside, the success of *The Deer Hunter* made Cimino a very respected and bankable director, ranked amongst the world's most celebrated film-makers. Yet his output since then has been disastrous – both financially and artistically. What went wrong? The Movie Doctors' diagnosis is that the growing tidal wave of praise heaped upon the director for his Vietnam epic proved the film-maker's unmaking. Having fought tooth and nail with everyone on *The Deer Hunter* (on which he was, initially at least, a glorified gun for hire), the budding auteur suddenly found himself in a position in which he was able to call the shots, without fear of contradiction. Everyone was telling him that he was a genius, and frankly he believed them. The results were catastrophic.

In his book *Final Cut: Dreams and Disaster in the Making of Heaven's Gate*, United Artists production head Steven Bach remembers the day that he and David Field agreed to let Michael Cimino make a movie for UA – 'the deal that would destroy the company'. Cimino's self-penned script for *The Johnson County War* (a Western based on a controversial period of American history previously addressed in such classic texts as *The Virginian* and *Shane*) had been doing the rounds for some time, and had in fact been rejected by UA back in the early seventies. But now, on the basis of the praise *The Deer Hunter* was garnering, they were ready to let him make the movie – whatever the cost. Originally budgeted at $7.8 million, the film would end up costing UA more than $36 million, thanks to a series of studio capitulations which allowed the budget to spiral without any financial penalty to the director. In short, he could run over time and over budget. Inevitably he did both – on a world-beating scale.

Set in late nineteenth-century Wyoming, *Heaven's Gate* (as the project was renamed) told of the brutal treatment of poor European migrants by rich American cattle barons. With added roller skating. Really. Kris Kristofferson was signed up to play heroic Jim Averill alongside *Deer Hunter* star

Christopher Walken as enforcer-turned-defender Nate Champion. In the role of Johnson County bordello madam Ella Watson, Cimino had his heart set on Isabelle Huppert, a brilliant French actress who had never played the lead in an English-language movie. Despite the producers' insistence that the leading lady must be both comprehensible and saleable to an American audience (this was, after all, a big-budget movie which required big names to ensure success) Cimino stood his ground.

The producers stood theirs.

Cimino threw a hissy fit. ('He accused us of bad faith,' remembers Bach, 'he accused us of cowardice [and] lack of aesthetic judgement . . . finally, he announced it would be impossible for him to make the picture for people as insensitive and talentless as ourselves.')

The producers caved in.

Of course they did. After all, Cimino was a genius. Everybody said so.

As Bach explained to his superiors at UA, 'The star of this picture – it was so clear – was Michael Cimino. We weren't betting that this or that actor or actress would add a million or two to the box office. We were betting that Cimino would deliver a blockbuster with "Art" written all over it, a return to epic filmmaking and epic returns. Yes, Cimino was the star . . .'

Having tested his strength and discovered that he really could do whatever he wanted, the star promptly went off the rails.

Shooting on *Heaven's Gate* began on 16 April 1979, in Montana's Glacier National Park. It would finish nearly a year later, in March 1980, three months after the initially agreed release date of December '79 had come and gone, and with a final cost which missed its original budget by a staggering 500 per cent, of which it would recoup next to nothing. The warning signs were there from the outset. By the end of the first day of shooting, they were a day behind schedule. By the end of the sixth day, they were a week behind. An entire street

was built and then torn down because Cimino thought the road needed to be 6ft wider. When someone suggested that the solution was to simply move one side of the street 6ft back, Cimino threw a strop and insisted that *both* sides be dismantled and moved back 3ft *each*. Otherwise, he insisted, it wouldn't 'look right'.

Other things that didn't 'look right' included the battlefield location on which the climactic confrontation was to be shot, but which wasn't yet green enough to provide contrast for the red blood which Cimino wished to splash cinematically upon it. 'The battlefield is expensive,' explained producer Joann Carelli, 'because we had to clear the land of rocks and stuff and put in that irrigation system.'

'What irrigation system?' asked Bach, dumb-founded.

'For the grass,' Carelli replied.

'What grass?'

'Mike wants grass on the battlefield.'

'Holy Christ, Joann!' screamed Bach, who was desperately attempting to rein in the runaway budget. 'He's talking about hundreds of people and horses and wagons and explosives. Who the hell is going to see *grass*!'

And so on.

Retakes were the order of the day. While Clint Eastwood would simply call cut after the third or fourth take, actors like Brad Dourif grew used to doing forty or fifty readings of the same line as a matter of course. 'How many ways can a guy drop his pants?' asked one witness after thousands of feet of film were wasted taking umpteen shots of a man baring his arse. The crew spent an entire day filming a single shot of Kris Kristofferson waking up drunk in bed and cracking a whip across his bedroom – a shot which would last a matter of seconds on screen (and unremarkable seconds at that). Every morning, the core cast would gather for what became known as 'Camp Cimino' – two hours of horse riding, followed by two hours of roller skating, day in, day out. For one sequence, they would drive four hours to the set in the morning, and four hours back at night. On one particular morning, the entire crew languished, cameras ready, for seven long hours while the director waited for the clouds to do something pretty. When someone suggested that everyone needed a lunch break, he barked, 'This is more important than lunch!'

Apparently determined to outdo Francis Ford Coppola, who had infamously exposed over a million feet of film making *Apocalypse Now* (1979), Cimino ran 1.3 million feet through his cameras – over *200 hours* of exposed film, of which at least 196 would ultimately be thrown away. At one point, *Heaven's Gate* (1980) was said to be costing UA $200,000 a day. The production went on for so long that John Hurt was able to start shooting *Heaven's Gate*, go away and film *The Elephant Man* (1980) in its entirety, and then come back and *finish* shooting *Heaven's Gate*. And all the time, all the UA executives could do was to stand back and watch their studio haemorrhage money.

UA did in fact consider firing Cimino. According to the horrifyingly riveting *Final Cut*, Steven Bach went and talked to a director who may or may not have been David Lean and asked him if he would take over the picture. The unnamed director declined, not least because to do so may well have been in breach of strict Directors Guild guidelines. Worse still, UA would face public outcry if they got in the way of Cimino and his vision. After all, he was a genius.

Everyone said so.

By the time shooting was finally completed, UA were on their knees. Having missed their original projected release date by the best part of a year, the studio was now aiming for a November 1980 premiere. But Cimino still had to pare down his hundreds of hours of footage into a movie of not more than three hours in length. From the moment he changed the locks on the editing room doors, it became clear that he had no intention of observing *any* rules regarding running time. On 26 June,

having been prevented from viewing *any* working assembly of the film on which they had blown every cent they owned, UA executives finally sat down to watch a preview of *Heaven's Gate* from which the director admitted he could probably shave another fifteen minutes.

It was five and a half hours long.

The UA executives went nuts and again considered firing Cimino. But once more, the spectre of his alleged genius prevailed. How could they possibly fire a director whose work everyone loved? Surely they would be branded philistines? And what about all the money they had invested in the film, the budget of which was now fast heading toward the forty million mark, *five times* their original figure. All over Hollywood, film-makers were finding that they couldn't get any movies made at United Artists because Michael Cimino had spent all the studio's money. As Brad Dourif warned him: 'This better be good.'

Sadly, it wasn't. In fact it was very, very bad. When *Heaven's Gate* premiered in New York on 18 November 1980, in a still-sprawling 219-minute incarnation, it was met with gasps of wonder . . . not at its awe-inspiring genius, but at the staggering waste of time, wealth and talent. *New York Times* critic Vincent Canby set the tone for the general critical reaction when he labelled *Heaven's Gate* an 'unqualified disaster', the experience of which was like taking 'a forced four-hour walking tour of one's own living room'. Stunned, Cimino and UA panicked, withdrew the movie, recut it, and re-released it in an abridged 149-minute 'director's cut'. The reaction was no better; reviewing the shortened version, Roger Ebert dubbed it 'the most scandalous cinematic waste I have ever seen,' adding, 'and remember, I've seen *Paint Your Wagon*'. Audiences were no more enthusiastic; by the time the film (in its various versions) finally hobbled out of cinemas, it had earned less than $4 million dollars in total – a tenth of what it had cost. Worse still, it garnered only one Oscar nomination, for Art

Direction and Set Decoration, in which category it lost out to *Raiders of the Lost Ark*, a lively adventure romp made for less than half the price of *Heaven's Gate*. Only at the Razzies did Cimino's movie clean up, picking up nominations for Worst Picture, Actor, and Screenplay, and winning for Worst Director.

So why did the film fare so badly? The simple answer is that it's rubbish; good-looking rubbish, perhaps (the Movie Doctors concur that no one shoots 1.3 million feet of film without some of it being fetching) but boring, mumbling, meandering rubbish nonetheless. Even for those with a fetish for watching men on roller skates play the violin (of which Dr Kermode is one), *Heaven's Gate* is for the most part insufferably dull. In the wake of such a disaster, which effectively sank the studio first set up by Charlie Chaplin, D.W. Griffith, Douglas Fairbanks and Mary Pickford, Cimino's career went into a tailspin from which it has never recovered. Oh, he's made a few movies since then, none of which have been hits: *The Year of the Dragon* (1985), a Mickey Rourke flop best known for promoting racist stereotypes of Chinese Americans; *The Sicilian* (1987), a bomb despite being based on a book by *Godfather* author Mario Puzo; *Desperate Hours* (1990), another box office failure which reminded everybody how much more they liked the Humphrey Bogart original; and *The Sunchaser* (1996), a piece of hippy-dippy nonsense inconsequential enough to be overshadowed by scurrilous rumours of on-set cross-dressing.

The source of all this catastrophe is easy to identify: Too Much Praise. As we noted earlier, all of Cimino's best work was done under circumstances in which he was surrounded by people who thought he was, at best, adequate. In the case of *Silent Running*, he was a struggling screenwriter, one of several who jointly collaborated on a screenplay which director Doug Trumbull then rewrote from scratch (without credit). On *Thunderbolt and Lightfoot*, he was a first-time feature director who got the gig because Clint Eastwood thought he had talent, but who was never more than a second in command to his heavyweight Hollywood star. Even on *The Deer Hunter*, he was considered to be nothing more than a competent re-writer and director of somebody else's material, someone whom Deeley didn't think 'would be much bother' because his CV looked so 'bland'. Only when everyone else started telling Cimino what he wanted to hear – that he was an auteur whose instructions should be followed to the letter – did everything fall apart. And spectacularly so. The failure of *Heaven's Gate* not only resulted in the sale of UA by TransAmerica (who decided to get out of the movie business *fast*), it also led directly to the decline of director-driven films in Hollywood, bringing to a close a so-called golden age of American cinema. In the wake of Cimino's indulgence, studios decided that megalomaniacal directors were financial kryptonite, and started putting their faith instead in producers like Don Simpson and Jerry Bruckheimer, who became the new auteurs of the eighties. In one single stroke, Cimino torpedoed not only his own career, but also that of anyone else who dreamed of dazzling Hollywood with craftsmanship rather than cash accountability. Indeed, one can draw a direct line from the disaster of *Heaven's Gate* to the rise of the kind of franchise film-making which means that today cinemas are stuffed with comic-book movies and smash-'em-up sequels.

In truth, producers at UA had no one but themselves to blame for this unhealthy debacle – something Bach makes abundantly clear in *Final Cut*. All the signs were there with *The Deer Hunter* which, despite its extraordinary success, was a wretched movie. The fact that it beat Hal Ashby's *Coming Home* (1978) to the Best Picture Oscar tells you everything you need to know about its shortcomings – rarely do the American Academy hand their most prestigious gongs to the most deserving films and film-makers. Ashby would go on to direct *Being There* (1979), a film which is loved by audiences and critics alike, and which marked the pinnacle of leading man Peter Sellers' screen career. Cimino, on the other hand, would become a film-maker whose name was forever linked to a famously costly catastrophe.

One good thing did emerge from the making of *Heaven's Gate*, albeit by accident. Early on in the shoot, reports started emerging of the mistreatment of animals on the set by a director who was increasingly behaving like a mini Caligula (incidentally, *Caligula* (1979) is a much better film than *Heaven's Gate*, and crucially has more jokes – see p.205). Stories of live chickens being decapitated for the cock-fighting sequences, of cattle being bled without anaesthetic in order to provide authentic-looking screen blood, and even of a horse being blown up by dynamite charges, were rife. When the American Humane Association complained about these alleged acts of cruelty, Cimino responded by banning them from his set. As a result, the AHA picketed screenings of *Heaven's Gate*, and the subsequent scandal led directly to a change in the rules governing their access to motion picture production. Today, all animal action on mainstream American movies is monitored by the AHA, who strive to ensure that animals are treated with respect by moviemakers – even megalomaniacs.

Meanwhile, the case of *Heaven's Gate* stands as a textbook example of the sickness that ensues when film-makers are told how brilliant they are. Overpraise a director, and their career will wither and die. Give them a hard time, and they will thrive. Look at Michael Bay: critics regularly slate his movies, yet he is currently one of the most successful directors on the planet. Cimino, on the other hand, has all but disappeared from view, despite the recent efforts of the French to 'reassess' his legacy, and to reclaim *Heaven's Gate* as some form of misunderstood masterpiece. *Zut alors!*

From a medical point of view, the remedy is clear: a healthy dose of criticism a day keeps *Heaven's Gate* away.

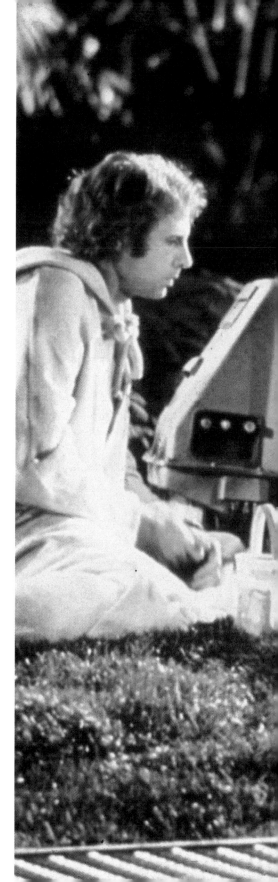

THE MOVIE DOCTORS ON VACATION

How the Movies Can Improve Your Holiday

As part of our ongoing commitment to the general well-being of our patients, the Movie Doctors' work in OT is increasingly being recognised as 'groundbreaking' (also 'ruinously expensive' and 'totally impractical', but hey). Here it is in summary:

- Go on holiday.
- Go to the cinema.

We also know that holidays are not without their unpleasant side-effects – sunburn, mosquito bites, bankruptcy – but rest assured, a trip to the cinema can make it all better. Here are the reasons why.

- The 2kg tub of sugar- and e-number-based snacks you consume at the movies will be the healthiest food you've eaten all holiday.
- At least it's dry.
- You'll be asleep within five minutes.
- Going to the movies will remind you of home. Where your bed is your own, your kids have friends who aren't the wrong sort and your digital radio works.
- Being charged under £25 for four tickets will make you feel you're actually saving money.
- Which will mean you can afford another vat of sweets.
- The cinema has Wi-Fi.
- The ads will remind you about an Indian restaurant just around the corner from this cinema where you haven't been since Tuesday.
- Poor sound, battered seating and the irritating holidaymakers from Sutton Coldfield will make you actually look forward to visiting your local multiplex.
- Wearing flip-flops, shorts and a sou'wester to the movies will make you feel hip.
- You don't need a taxi to get home. You can walk to your tent in under an hour if the moon is out, the locals have drunk themselves into a stupor and witches aren't gathered in the clearing.

GOING HOME AND STAYING POSITIVE

How the Movies Make it Possible

A few thoughts to bear in mind as you prepare for returning home. Mindfulness is all the rage. This is where you accept and focus your attentions on the emotions, thoughts and sensations occurring in the present moment. Which is probably *'I don't want to go home, not now, not ever!'* So let's see if we can do better than that. Focus. Breathe. Smile.

- Your delayed flight will only keep you in the terminal lounge for the duration of a *Transformers* movie. And have better dialogue. And be quieter. And you won't be wearing tiny cut-off shorts (unless you will be, in which case, it's your right to dress as you wish, obvs).

- It's been a while since you've been 'a hard-working family'. Honestly, you've turned into one of the blobby types in *WALL-E*. Go home.

- Your journey back from Cornwall will only be the duration of two *Transformers* movies. And the view will be better. And Marky Mark Wahlberg could do with a visit to a Little Chef. And Gordano services in August isn't far away from a post-apocalyptic nightmare anyway.

- Thank heavens that your local cinema's '9 Tequilas for the Price of 10' offer will keep your life glamorous.

- No need to worry about your fading tan. The next 3D screening and the special glasses will make you – and everything else – 30 per cent darker. Guaranteed!

- Too much exotic cuisine? Fed up with foreign food? A twelve-inch foyer-fresh hot dog will be ideal for your home-loving stomach.

- Your film-free, food-free and politeness-free flight with added scuffling, one-wheel landing and crushed baggage can almost certainly be blamed on Liam Neeson.

OPHTHALMOLOGY

Is sight the most **precious of the senses?** As Movie Doctors we would tentatively suggest it is. And at some point we will all have to wear glasses – either to **boost our fading sight** or to shield us from the blazing sun when we emerge from that midday screening in Cannes. In our Ophthalmology Clinic we look at eyewear options – both practical and cosmetic techniques to surreptitiously 'miss' a gruesome scene in a movie – and we provide a **handy set of sight tests** to see whether you need sight-enhancers in the first place.

THE MOVIE DOCTORS' SIGHT TEST

What Line Can You Read?

That moment when the credits are out of focus *again*. 'What is it with projectionists these days!' you moan, before remembering what Dr Kermode has been telling you for years – *there are no projectionists any more*. 'Well these digital projection cameras are a bit rubbish,' you continue, as you need to be complaining about something. 'How can I be expected to find out how many animals weren't harmed in the making of this movie if I can't even read the cast list?' You throw a glance at the empty projection room just to make the point that that is where the fault lies. Still huffing and puffing as you walk out, you trip over a small child and fall down the stairs. As your partner escorts you squinting and bleeding from the building, it slowly dawns on you that maybe it wasn't the cinema's fault at all. It's you. And it's been you for a while, you just haven't realised. It's time for an eye test.

Y
O   U
S   H   O
U   L   D   H
A V E H I R E
D A P R O J E C
T I O N I S T S T U P I D

E

M   M

A   T   H

O   M   P   S

O   N   C   A   N

D   O   N   O   W   R   O   N   G

Y

O U E

ITHERG

ETBUSYLI

VINORYOUG

ETBUSYDYIN

F

ROMT

HEBIRT

HOFMANK

INDTOTHEDA

WNOFANEWSPECI

ESINTHESPACEOF142MINUTES

FOR EYES

Finest Movie Spectacles

ailed the Movie Doctors' sight test? It's time for glasses. You might have hoped to last a few more years spec-free, squinting at your screens and peering at your food, but no. It's time to join the ranks of the bespectacled. You shouldn't worry that this is the beginning of your slow physical decline (though it probably is – see 'Silver Screenings', p.244). Many movie stars have used glasses to add to their appeal, to sprinkle some intellectual stardust on their image, and you can too. Choosing the right pair can be tricky, but the Movie Doctors, being experts in these matters, can of course point the way. Here we have provided some key cinematic spectacles and, where possible, shopping advice.

HARRY POTTER
HARRY POTTER AND THE PHILOSOPHER'S STONE *(2001)*

The most famous wearer of glasses ever. Those of you who have read the books will know about Harry's lightning scar, his permanently dishevelled hair and that he is lost without his glasses. You will also know they were the classic, round frames, available everywhere for just a few knuts. A boy whose bedroom was the cupboard under the stairs could hardly have emerged sporting a pair of Armani specs.

Looking like The Boy Who Lived doesn't have to be expensive; toy versions can be picked up for only £5.99. (They might also make an innocent Muggle boy look like Stanley Baldwin, but there isn't much call these days for twentieth-century British prime minister lookalikes, so your wizard guise should be obvious.) Those who want the deluxe version, but haven't been able to get their hands on any Polyjuice Potion, could try a pair of Savile Row Warwick frames for around £200. Alternatively find someone else wearing them, use the 'Accio' spell and 'Catch!'

MIKAEL BLOMKVIST
THE GIRL WITH THE DRAGON TATTOO *(2011)*

When Daniel Craig was announced as the new James Bond (to widespread enthusiasm) there was a peculiar group of traditionalists. They believed 007 should never be blond. When Craig was revealed as the male lead in the movie version of Stieg Larsson's bestseller, his hair wasn't the problem – in fact, his fabulous Viking looks were an advantage. What really mattered was making him look intelligent, and for this job they needed glasses.

When we meet Blomkvist we immediately realise he isn't James Bond because of his Mykita acetate glasses. Dark brown, rounded frames set off against his haunted 'I'm a disgraced international journalist' look let you know that Pussy Galore is unlikely to put in an appearance.

WILLIAM FOSTER AKA 'D-FENS'
FALLING DOWN *(1993)*

Joel Schumacher's picture produced one of Michael Douglas's most memorable performances. The frustrated, downtrodden, out-of-work defence worker who goes crazy has some memorable moments: the traffic gridlock meltdown, the baseball-bat demolition of the Korean store and the fast food joint that won't serve him breakfast. Douglas has the buzz cut, the white shirt and tie, but most importantly, the Browline glasses. The heavy plastic upper frame and light metallic lens-surround have been ubiquitous in America since 1947, when they were first manufactured.

If you want to look ordinary, get Browline. If you want to look ordinary but borderline psychotic, crack up one of the lenses and get a shotgun. Cost is around £109.

(Wardrobe NB: Malcolm X also wore Browline. Two unbroken lenses needed.)

GEORGE FALCONER
A SINGLE MAN *(2009)*

Well, what a 'to do' when this movie was released. While some discussed Colin Firth's extraordinary wardrobe of beautiful sixties suits, and others debated his portrayal of a gay lecturer in mourning for his deceased partner, Dr Kermode wanted to talk about his glasses. As directed by Tom Ford, everything about Falconer looked immaculate, but it was his glasses that we had to return to, time and time again. In truth Dr Kermode was not alone. So many people wanted to look like Firth in *A Single Man* that Ford produced replicas. For £230,

the smooth curves of these heavy black frames (model TF 5178) can begin that transition. All you need now is an immaculate designer house and a body like Colin Firth's, and that LA lifestyle is yours.

CLARK KENT
SUPERMAN *(1978)*

Superman is, of course, who we have paid our money to see. We want a man flying, we want a flapping cape and fabulous, Kryptonite-fuelled punch ups with Terence Stamp (or similar). If we're honest, we don't care that much when he is being Clark Kent. Sure, he looks after his mum, is charmed by Lois and, as movie versions of journalists go, he is an abstemious role model. But we are only waiting for the moment when the spandex is back on and Clark gets to kick General Zod's butt.

But let us just pause to praise an inanimate object of extraordinary power. The rocks of Krypton get all the attention, but the real star is Clark's pair of Anglo American Optical Oversize. For frames that cost a mere £70, Clark only has to place them on his face and no one can recognise him. Even Lois Lane doesn't realise that the flying guy who swooped her away from danger and held her inches away from his face is the same guy typing the football results. And all because of the specs (and a touch of hair wax). If it's a cunning and cheap disguise you're after, look no further.

LOOK AWAY NOW

Optical Evasion Techniques for the Squeamish

Not everyone loves horror films, but for some reason everyone goes to see them – at least on occasion (and if this troubles you, see 'Do Sick Movies Make You Sick?', p.194). For teenagers, it can be a rite of passage; for adults, an attempt to 'keep up with what's going on in the cinema' (though Dr K would insist this has never been the case). Whatever, the chances are that at some point you'll find yourself watching a movie which you suddenly realise is more frightening or gory (or both) than you had expected. As 'the fear' starts to wash over you, here are some useful manoeuvres to help you through the movie while maintaining a modicum of self-respect.

- Use the ten-gallon bucket of popcorn, the fizzy-pop container you could train a killer whale in or the bag of sweets the size of a cellophane sleeping bag as a handy shield at moments of extreme tension.

- Borrow a line from pantomime and realise that 'your shoe lace is undone'. Grapple with the wardrobe malfunction until the terror passes.

- Drop a coin down the side of the seat and rummage amongst the detritus accrued during years of cinema-seat abuse until you find it. This worked very effectively for Dr Kermode during one of the most irritating movies of recent years (*Keith Lemon: The Film*, in case anyone's interested).

- Whip out your 3D glasses, muttering, 'I bet this looks great through these.' You'll show how cool you are in the face of horror and how curious and imaginative you are as a cinemagoer. The fact that everything is now dark and out of focus will be a great comfort.

- Try praying. You might not have done this for a while, but maybe now, when you really need a reason to close your eyes, is the perfect time to get religious (suggested words: 'Dear God, please make this stop').

FOR EYES 2

Finest Movie Shades

Prescription sunglasses, of course. All Movie Doctors advice is medically based. This is not a shallow 'style' magazine, full of chiselled young men and gentlemen's-interest articles written by know-nothing boys with beards. This section is exclusively for those who need a tinted version of their regular, day-to-day specs. Shades will also reduce the sun's glare, protect you from dangerous UV rays and make you look ludicrously cool, but that is an added bonus and not our concern here. If you have, on medical advice, decided you need shades, here are the best we can prescribe.

THE MATRIX *(1999)*

Hands down the number one film for sunglasses. Of all time. If ever there was a movie that promoted the highest standards of eyewear and eye care, this is it. Sure, there's lots of nerdy computer, leather fetish and shotgun fanboy stuff, but really this film is about the shades.

Everywhere you look there are styles to choose from. Chances are you won't have cult designer Richard Walker, from Blinde Design, hanging around and making them for you as you limbo under bullets, jump off buildings and fly into helicopters. And if you don't fancy giving your money to one of a hundred firms who jumped on the *Matrix* bandwagon to offer replicas to a desperate market (one company is still offering a gift-boxed set of eight different Matrix sunglasses for $100), you'll have to get inventive. But the question is: who would you like to be? Neo? Morpheus? Random guy with a knife? Choose from these top character styles!

NEO: Our main man. Keanu Reeves sports these lightweight, wire-framed specs with upturned lenses. Try the Ray-Ban 3194 for the closest match. Looks particularly great with a full-length black leather trench coat (underneath which you can hide a small arsenal).

TRINITY: She fights the sentinels, she kisses Neo, they wear the same glasses. As far as we can prescribe, it's the Ray-Ban 3194 again. These square aviators are lightweight, robust and effective against UV (though they let in all references to Descartes First Meditation).

MORPHEUS: Cool dude, preposterous glasses. They defy the laws of gravity, physics and common sense. Small, reflective oval lenses stick to the bridge of his nose for no reason. The classic 'pince-nez' worked if you were a gentleman of the nineteenth century and prone to scholarly exposition, but on the nose of a man fighting cybernetic implants and sentient machines, this is a cyberpunk leap too far. Should cost you around £20.

AGENT SMITH: Agent Smith is the optician's favourite. He's the ruthless enforcer, the owner of the drawled 'Mister Aaannnddeerrsson' line, and he never takes his shades off (we're not counting the very end. Everyone can take them off then). Metal frames, six-sided polycarbonate lenses and hidden powers to make you bend like rubber. You should be able to find them for around £15.

RISKY BUSINESS *(1983)*

If *The Matrix* spawned more sunglasses designs than any other film, Tom Cruise has probably been responsible for more sunglasses sales than any actor in history. The first of his contributions here is as Chicago teenager Joel Goodsen in Paul Brickman's 1983 comedy. The poster has Rebecca De Mornay sprawled over a Porsche, *but we don't even notice her*. This is because, immediately above her, we see a close-up of Cruise and his Wayfarers. These are the classic Ray-Ban Wayfarer RB 2140 and will cover half your head. They say 'crazy', they say 'rock 'n' roll', they say 'we're much too big for your face'. However, if you too would like to drive your father's car into Lake Michigan, these are the shades for you. Expect to pay £80.

TOP GUN *(1986)*

To the strains of Berlin's 'Take My Breath Away', here is Tom's second contribution to the accounts of Ray-Ban owners (at the time) Bausch & Lomb. With the irresistible power of F-14 fighter planes, green boiler suits, sex, death and heroism, we all want to be like Pete 'Maverick' Mitchell. Given that we were unlikely to be accepted into the US navy's elite Fighter Weapons School, the closest we can get is to wear Maverick's shades.

These are, of course, the classic Ray-Ban Aviator 3025s, and for around £95 you can buy the

lustful glances of any passing Iceman, Viper or Cougar. According to *The Times*, post-release sales increased 40 per cent. They'd been around since 1937, but in 1986, men who weren't dressed like Tom were doomed to be shot down by enemy MiGs.

(Scandal NB: your talented, well-qualified – and coincidentally hot – teacher will also find you unbearably desirable. Maybe lose the boiler suit.)

BREAKFAST AT TIFFANY'S *(1961)*

While protecting your eyes is a serious business, sometimes it is necessary to be glamorous too. Glitter and sophistication tends to be unavailable on the NHS these days (those 'cuts', eh?) so that's where the Movie Doctors come in. It's time to step over to the counter selling Oliver Goldsmith's Manhattan sunglasses.

Audrey Hepburn's look in Blake Edwards's classic is one of the greatest ever. These shades will cost you upwards of £300, but for that price you'll get the brown tortoiseshell frames and the light green lenses that proclaim '*I am elegant, sophisticated and only occasionally neurotic!*' Throw in a few pearls, the odd diamond and George Peppard, and you'll have made it.

THE BLUES BROTHERS *(1980)*

Where *Risky Business* sold the RB 2140 Wayfarers (360,000 pairs in one year, apparently), *The Blues Brothers* offered the 5022s. Fast-living John Belushi and Dan Aykroyd needed all the cover the dark lenses and thick acetate frames could provide. It was a good look for those just out of prison and on a mission from God to raise enough money to save their old orphanage from financial ruin. To the soundtrack of Elmore James, Sam Cooke and John Lee Hooker, our heroes put these fabled, trapezoidal glasses through their paces. 'Paces' is a loose term, which here means surviving car chases, flamethrowers, blown-up malls, helicopters, SWAT teams and Nazis. Throughout everything the story throws at them, the boys' beloved Wayfarers do not budge. Originals will cost you around £200, but unless you're a fifties blues legend, where else will you find this amount of cool?

TERMINATOR 2: JUDGMENT DAY *(1991)*

A quick quiz. Where does Arnie get his famous sunglasses from? Or, more precisely, who does he take them from? Back from the future, our Terminator's first stop is a biker bar where pool is cheap and nude men are rare. Dwight Yoakam's 'Guitars, Cadillacs' is playing as the cavemen receive their justice. Once he has helped himself to leathers (and the music has changed to George Thorogood's 'Bad to the Bone'), Termie is followed outside by the barkeeper. In his hands he has his shotgun, in his top pocket he has a pair of Persoli Ratti 58230 sunglasses. Arnie decides that such a rough man shouldn't own such an expensive pair of handmade Italian shades and helps himself. If you want the cyborg look you can either do what Arnie did, or try the more conventional, safer route. It'll cost you $649 (around £400).

THE THOMAS CROWN AFFAIR *(1968)*

Steve McQueen is the star and Faye Dunaway the co-star of this Norman Jewison hit. What if you were to ask Steve to choose between Faye and his sunglasses? The Movie Doctors know he'd pick the shades every time. This is not to show any disrespect to Ms Dunaway, who is McQueen's match throughout – merely to note that he was inseparable from his Persol 0714s. He wore them here, he wore them there, he wore them in *Bullitt* (1968) and *The Getaway* (1972) too. When they came up for auction they fetched £36,762, which makes them our most expensive pair so far. For this you get the rounded teardrop frame, the handmade acetate plastic and their 'meflecto' system, which allows the glasses to fold and make everyone gasp at your cool. They were originally designed for the train drivers of Turin, who were obviously just a little needy.

NORTH BY NORTHWEST *(1959)*

Another vintage film, more vintage shades. In fact these could be the most vintage-y of all. Cary Grant needs to be incognito, he needs to hide, he can't be noticed – what with him being on the run from henchmen and everything. In his desperation he pulls out a pair of what are widely thought to be Vintage Arnells – orange tortoiseshell frames with bottle-green lenses. These sunglasses, made by Tart, have been described by *Slate* magazine as 'the coolest thing anyone has ever owned'. As such they immediately mark our man as the one to chase, capture and interrogate. Maybe he would have drawn less attention to himself with some cheap knock-off shades. You can have the modern equivalent and get that 'I've just been chased by a plane' look for around £100.

THELMA AND LOUISE *(1991)*

Thelma is Geena Davis, Louise is Susan Sarandon, the shades are Ray-Ban W0585 Wayfarer Dekko. They have a '66 Thunderbird, they have a weekend away, but unfortunately they also have a handgun. This belongs to Thelma's idiot husband Darryl, and if they hadn't been heading for a rural cabin (always a disastrous idea) then maybe a map and a compass would have been fine. But while the main plot is working its way through truckers, police and Brad Pitt, Louise's sunglasses have a cameo all of their own. The angular, cat-eyed frames and the thicker ear stems are tricky to come by now, but you might find some for around £285. (Personal health NB: avoid scuzzy men, roadhouse drinks and cliff edges.)

FEAR AND LOATHING IN LAS VEGAS *(1998)*

It's one thing to want to look like a terminator, a sentinel fighter or a New York socialite, but a drug-fuelled journalist? No thanks, even if he is Johnny Depp. Raoul Duke has been sent to cover the Mint 400 motorbike race, but instead gets wasted with his attorney Dr Gonzo. The Movie Doctors would have stepped in now, but sadly chemical stimulants were preferred. Depp has a cigarette in a large holder, a white bucket hat on his head and a pair of Ray-Ban 3138s on his face. These are called 'Shooters', but you'll struggle to find a pair like Johnny's as the yellow tint was specially made for the movie.

PAEDIATRICS

Having children: the **no-win dilemma** of the cinemagoer. (see also 'Maternity', p.133 and 'Fertility Clinic', p.119). You love them unreservedly, you love *some* of the movies they love, *but* they do have a **tendency to inhibit** your moviegoing life. In our Paediatrics Clinic we offer advice on parenting, celebrate the longevity of some of the most enduring child stars and urge our patients to consider the **benefits of the movies** for their precious offspring. We are, after all, here to help.

CHILDREN

What You Need to Know

With the benefit of all our years of experience, we can honestly say that any decision about whether to press on with the procreation task is clarified when there's a cinema nearby. Many families relocate for schools or grandparents but underestimate the importance of the local multiplex. But before doing anything rash, consider these facts.

1 Where else can you legitimately ignore your children for two hours (three if there's a robot hitting a robot)? You don't even have to watch the movie you've paid £30 to see. You can sleep, listen to the football or catch up on your favourite podcast. Afterwards, you can engage the child with a meaningful, post-screening chat.

You: So what did you make of that?
Child in your care: It was fine.
You: Better than *Frozen*?
Child: Don't be stupid.
You: Shall we get some chips?
Child: All right then.

2 With a bag full of cola bottles, sour snakes and gummy bears, your offspring get to experience all of nature's food groups in one convenient paper bag, consumed in a single, convenient, ten-minute session. Hydrogenated syrup, gelatine and glucose make for a powerful cinematic experience. The whole audience will laugh and applaud as your child goes from normal/sullen to hyperactive banshee in seconds. See how many chairs he can kick! See how many pools of vomit she can pirouette in! See how quickly the sugar rush crashes!

3 Surprising nudity. Once you have all, as a family, experienced the exquisite embarrassment of stumbling upon a risqué scene in a hitherto innocent drama, the 'birds and the bees' talk will be so much easier. 'I know! I was surprised, too, when Julie Andrews felt as though she had to take her top off. Maybe she was a little warm . . .' Here are some moments you might have forgotten. You have been warned:

AIRPLANE! *(1980)*

In the unlikely event that you watch this 1980 US comedy on one of its VHS releases, you'll notice the PG certificate. You'll also notice the panicking woman with naked breasts (cult movie star Francesca 'Kitten' Natividad, triv fans), the woman in bed with a horse and the respectable middle-aged woman who snorts cocaine. And maybe the 'shit', 'pisser', 'crap' and 'bastard'. (Thanks IMDb.)

THE RESCUERS *(1977)*

Yes, *The Rescuers*. With or without italics, this is a shocker. It's the 1997 VHS that is the issue here. It is the (surely innocent) story of an international mouse rescue organisation. Two of these mice (Bernard and Miss Bianca) are busy getting down to their rescuing business when the albatross they are getting a lift from (called Orville, should you be wondering) glides past an open window. There, in the evening light stands a lady enjoying the view. There will of course be a good reason why she isn't wearing her top. Maybe she can't afford one, maybe she has forgotten it, or possibly she has a temperature. Either way, the 'Mum, I saw a naughty woman' conversation is a raging certainty.

THE WOMAN IN RED (1984)

The 15 certificate should be a giveaway, but hey it got a mild PG-13 in the States, and all you can remember about this 1984 romcom is that it features Stevie Wonder's lovely 'I Just Called to Say I Love You'. And it has that nice Gene Wilder, who seems like a nice man. And he's trying *so* hard not to get into bed with Kelly LeBrock. Although he seems to have failed. And Ms LeBrock didn't mean to let her bedclothes slip like that . . .

4 Movies help when discussing boundaries with children (as in moral standards, not hitting a six in cricket, as Dr Kermode is insisting on no sports talk in this book. Unless it's about *Field Of Dreams*). For example, let's take *Ghostbusters*, the 1983 movie starring Bill Murray, Dan Aykroyd and Sigourney Weaver. You may remember this with a warm glow of eighties zany, goofball American comedy nostalgia. You may be planning to share this slightly spooky movie with your offspring once they have moved beyond *Frozen* and *The Lego Movie*. I mean, it was only a PG after all (although it's since been reclassified as a 12).

Fine, go ahead. And remember to cough loudly/ pretend to faint/'accidentally' press the mute button when you get to the four 'shits', one 'goddam', one 'dick', four 'asses', one 'bitch', two 'pisses' and two 'hells'.

Once you've exhausted yourself with all the fake hacking and dizzy spells, you will suddenly remember that this 'family comedy' is *full of sex*. It's way, way too late to do anything about it: the family are gathered and places have been taken. You can only grab the arms of your chair in horror. And here it all comes. The masturbation joke with a ghost-tracker machine (you're looking flushed again). Sigourney Weaver saying to Bill Murray, 'I want you inside me' (your family are shifting uneasily now, you're thinking of going for a walk). And there's Murray asking a woman if she's menstruating (OK, that's it, you're off. Your position as the family's moral compass has collapsed forever more).

Never mind the smoking, drinking and cleavages, this is a family feature that could actually put you in therapy. So the Movie Doctors say: avoid unnecessary medical bills and *discuss the movie first*. Ask: what are the acceptable standards of profanity? How much flesh should we tolerate? How much embarrassment can you take before you bail out and take the dog for a walk?

Having kids is a complicated business. If you and your intended disagree on one or more of the above, it may be time to put another bulb in your projector. Refocus. Try a new ratio.

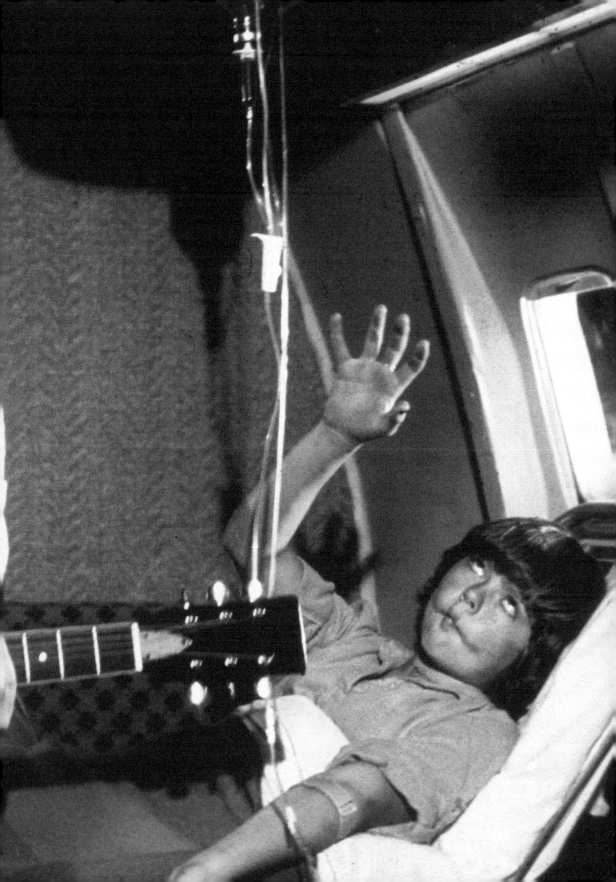

CHALLENGING CHILDREN

The Movie Doctors' Casebook	*The doctors are IN*

INT. MOVIE DOCTORS' SURGERY – DAY

Dr Kermode is wearing a black suit and tie matched with inappropriately scruffy shoes. Dr Mayo is sporting a T-shirt that was in its prime circa 1989 and skinny jeans. He thinks he's twenty-three. A black coffee and a green tea are on the desk. They are ready to go.

> **DR KERMODE**
> Hey.

> **DR MAYO**
> Hey.

This *Friends*-style banter continues for a few minutes.

> **DR KERMODE**
> First patient?

> **DR MAYO**
> Reckon so.

Dr Kermode fumbles with the technology then realises he doesn't know what he's doing.

> **DR KERMODE**
> How does this work?

Dr Mayo presses the button marked 'To call in patient press here and speak'.

> **DR MAYO**
> Miss Templeman, please.

> **DR KERMODE**
> (muttering) I've been here years and no one shows me anything . . .

A tall, middle-aged woman walks in and sits down in front of the Movie Doctors. She looks tired and somewhat pale.

> **DR MAYO**
> Hello, and what seems to be your problem, madam?

> **MISS TEMPLEMAN**
> Help me, Movie Doctors, you're my only hope.

> **DR MAYO**
> (smiling his DJ smile of condescension) Perhaps try coming in again, Miss Templeman?

> **MISS TEMPLEMAN**
> Of course. (She leaves and re-enters) Hello, I wonder if you can help me?

> **DR KERMODE**
> Much better! Yes, of course! What seems to be the problem?

MISS TEMPLEMAN

Well, it's my kids, really. They argue all the time and show me no respect whatsoever. It's really getting me down and I wondered if you might have the right medicine for me?

DR MAYO

Have you tried shouting and then becoming distressed?

MISS TEMPLEMAN

They can yell and scream louder than me.

DR MAYO

How about bribing them? Have you tried paying?

MISS TEMPLEMAN

They have more money than me.

DR KERMODE

Don't worry, Miss T., we have the answer. Have you tried *Parenthood*?

MISS TEMPLEMAN

Well, really. I didn't come in here to be insulted. I'm doing my best . . .

DR MAYO

No, no, no you misunderstand, we mean the movie *Parenthood* starring Steve Martin. Have you seen it?

MISS TEMPLEMAN

A long time ago, maybe. How will it help?

DR MAYO

Ah well, first of all it'll put a song in your heart. Try this. It's sung by two kids in the back of Steve Martin's car after a ball game.

Both Doctors sing, Dr Mayo conducts.

DR MAYO and DR KERMODE

When you're sliding into first
And you're feeling something burst
. . . diarrhoea diarrhoea

When you're sliding into third
And you lay a juicy turd
. . . diarrhoea diarrhoea

DR MAYO

When the brats are getting you down, a song that has unexpected poo references will always surprise and confound. It'll give you the upper hand.

DR KERMODE

Then later you'll watch the travails of Jason Robards as he deals with all his family. Tom Hulce has money problems, Keanu Reeves has attitude problems . . .

MISS TEMPLEMAN

Keanu Reeves? Are you kidding?

DR MAYO

Don't worry, Miss T., it's not like *Little Buddha*. He's actually acting in this one.

MISS TEMPLEMAN

If you say so. But this is making me stressed.

DR MAYO

Oh yes, I forgot, there's actually quite a good, er, stress-relieving scene too.

MISS TEMPLEMAN

What happens?

DR MAYO

(flushing slightly) Ah. Well, you'll find out.

MISS TEMPLEMAN

What's the ending like? What's the conclusion?

DR MAYO

That there's no end in sight. The troubles with your children go on for ever, you just swap one set for another. There's no finishing line.

MISS TEMPLEMAN

(looking downcast) I see. And how does that help?

DR MAYO

We're all in this together, Miss T. The problems you have are the same as in families the world over. Doesn't it help to know that?

MISS TEMPLEMAN

I guess so. Can I watch it with my kids?

DR MAYO

Er, most of it. Apart from the stress-relief section, obviously. That helped earn it a 15 rating . . .

DR KERMODE

. . . and there's a joke about an electrical appliance which Dianne Wiest makes. You might want to miss that bit too.

MISS TEMPLEMAN

How many times should I be watching this film?

DR MAYO

As many times as you need, until you've learned the diarrhoea song.

MISS TEMPLEMAN

I think I may have the gist of it already . . .

DR KERMODE

Excellent! You'll be feeling better in a matter of days.

MISS TEMPLEMAN

Thank you, Movie Doctors, you've saved the day again!

CHILD STARS

How Young?

STAR	BORN	FIRST FEATURE FILM	AGE
RIVER PHOENIX	1970	EXPLORERS *1985*	15
MARK LESTER	1958	THE COUNTERFEIT CONSTABLE *1964*	6
EMMA WATSON	1990	HARRY POTTER AND THE PHILOSOPHER'S STONE *2001*	11
DAKOTA FANNING	1994	TOMCATS *2001*	7
DANIEL RADCLIFFE	1989	THE TAILOR OF PANAMA *2001*	11
SHIRLEY TEMPLE	1928	RED-HAIRED ALIBI *1932*	4
HALEY JOEL OSMENT	1988	FORREST GUMP *1994*	6
KIRSTEN DUNST	1982	NEW YORK STORIES *1989*	7
ELIJAH WOOD	1981	BACK TO THE FUTURE PART II *1989*	8
MACAULAY CULKIN	1980	ROCKET GIBRALTAR *1988*	8
JUDY GARLAND	1922	PIGSKIN PARADE *1936*	14
NATALIE WOOD	1938	HAPPY LAND *1943*	4
RICKY SCHRODER	1970	THE CHAMP *1979*	9
DREW BARRYMORE	1975	ALTERED STATES *1980*	5
BROOKE SHIELDS	1965	COMMUNION (AKA ALICE, SWEET ALICE) *1976*	11
JODIE FOSTER	1962	NAPOLEON AND SAMANTHA *1972*	10
TATUM O'NEAL	1963	PAPER MOON *1973*	10
KURT RUSSELL	1951	IT HAPPENED AT THE WORLD'S FAIR *1963*	12
HAYLEY MILLS	1946	TIGER BAY *1959*	13
ELIZABETH TAYLOR	1932	THERE'S ONE BORN EVERY MINUTE *1942*	10
MARGARET O'BRIEN	1937	BABES ON BROADWAY *1941*	4
MICKEY ROONEY	1920	ORCHIDS AND ERMINE *1927*	7

ISOLATION
CLINIC

In our **Isolation Clinic**, we host movies that you really don't want to watch when you're feeling in the least bit peaky – those films that are guaranteed to induce a feeling that you've got *it*, no matter what *it* is. We also offer some original research on the subject, **'Do Sick Movies Make You Sick?'** – it's controversial, but life in the Movie Doctors' Isolation Clinic isn't all *On Golden Pond*, you know.

HIGHLY CONTAGIOUS

Movies to Avoid When Sick

hen you are ailing and weak, the Movie Doctors are armed and ready to alleviate your suffering with just the right movie (see 'Prescription Medication', p.304). But for extreme cases, we administer a few words of caution – there are some films that must not be viewed unless in tip-top condition. Over the years you will have learned that in movies no one 'just gets a cold'. If a character sneezes or coughs unexpectedly, they'll be dead before tea. This is probably not the type of thing you need to see if you're under the weather. So here's our tried and tested list of what *not* to watch. Spoilers abound, but as you're not going to be watching these films anyway, who cares?

OUTBREAK *(1995)*

This movie tells the story of an outbreak (oh, I see) of the fictional Motaba virus in Zaire. The huge advantage of this illness is that because it doesn't exist, director Wolfgang Petersen can make up its characteristics to suit his story. Here's a virus that you can catch from pretty much anything, including monkeys and Dustin Hoffman. But – good news – a cure is at hand. The bad news is that it was developed by the US army, who didn't feel the need to share it with anyone. Avoid at all costs.

THE STAND *(TV, 1994)*

Stephen King's 1978 novel was first filmed as a TV miniseries back in the mid-nineties (with Molly Ringwald and Gary Sinise, no less), and at the time of writing a much talked-of feature movie is finally on the way. Possibly. If it does ever make it to your local plaza, stay away if you have a temperature. Ignore. Do not touch with a disinfected barge pole. It's another apocalyptic tale that starts with a strand of the flu which is weaponised by our friends in the military (who knew they were such a health risk? Apart from all the guns and so on). This strain is known as Project Blue and is accidentally released from an army base, wiping out 99.4 per cent of the earth's population. Awkward. Though Las Vegas gets destroyed too, so it's not all gloom.

CONTAGION *(2011)*

It's not monkeys this time and not even the American army. It's pigs, bats and bananas. A super swine flu with bells and whistles named Meningoencephalitis Virus 1, or MEV-1. Symptoms you should check for if worried: fever, foaming at the mouth and general scenes of death. If even Matt Damon can't prevent the resulting social breakdown, what hope is there for the rest of us? The moral of the film appears to be: 'Don't have extra-marital sex with Gwyneth Paltrow if she's just returned from Hong Kong'. Even if this temptation is unlikely to present itself, this is an uncomfortable watch for the healthy, never mind the sick. You might be tempted to watch *Contagion* just to see the crazy homeopath–conspiracy theorist played by Jude Law get his comeuppance Resist. Just because you're sick, doesn't make you feeble.

I DRINK YOUR BLOOD *(1970)*

In the 1970s, Satanist hippies who ate pies infected with the blood of rabid dogs were a real problem. It often led to unpleasantness and dismemberment on a wide scale. In contemporary culture we rarely encounter Satanists, hippies or rabies, but they are out there, waiting for us to drop our guard. Stay vigilant. Avoid listening to any Jefferson Airplane until you feel better.

28 DAYS LATER . . . *(2002)*

Never go to hospital. Stay at home and be tended to by your nearest and dearest. If you succumb and visit your nearest A & E (see p.11), you might suffer the same fate as Cillian Murphy. He wakes up from a coma to find that the whole of London is deserted. Some animal liberation types have released a diseased (wait for it) chimpanzee, and its Rage virus has infected everyone. You may feel a little zombie-like already, slowly shuffling from room to room, so it won't help you to see scenes of energetic zombies running around in this film. And just for balance, this time it's the turn of the British army (or what's left of them) to be thoroughly unhelpful and terrifyingly dangerous.

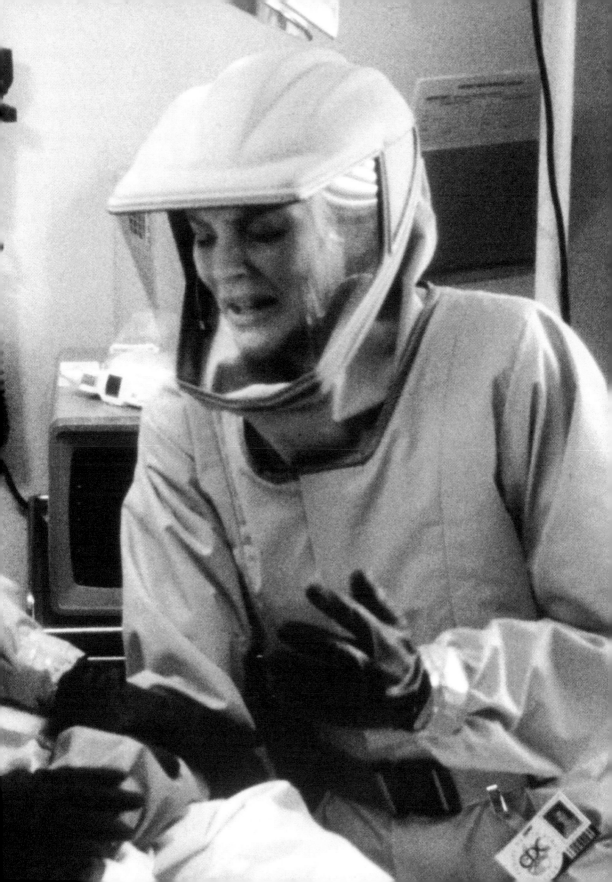

DO SICK MOVIES MAKE YOU SICK?

A Clinical Examination

One of the questions the Movie Doctors get asked on a regular basis is, 'Why on Earth would someone want to watch something scary?', usually in conjunction with the inevitable follow-up question: 'Are these people sick or something?'

Explaining the appeal of horror films to those who don't like them is as impossible a task as attempting to explain the offside rule to someone with no interest in football. Like haiku poetry, coarse fishing and traditional Morris dancing, the lure of horror cinema is baffling and mysterious, even to those who love it. The short answer is that you either get it or you don't; it's not something that can be rationalised, and it's not in the least bit bad for you. Horror films work on both a cerebral and (more importantly) gut level, and for those who appreciate their dark charms they are thrilling, challenging, intriguing, life-affirming and (most importantly) healthy!

The problem is that many people who *don't* like – or understand – horror movies imagine that they must be corrupting, dangerous and diseased. From the earliest days of Robert Wiene's *The Cabinet of Dr Caligari* (1920), F.W. Murnau's *Nosferatu* (1922), Tod Browning's *Dracula* (1931) and James Whale's *Frankenstein* (1931), scary movies have been putting the fear of God into those who imagine the power of horror cinema to be fearsome and perverse. Battles with censors, fights with moral guardians, and all-too regular run-ins with the media made horror films the real bogeyman of the first century of cinema. Even in the enlightened twenty-first century, there remains a thinly veiled suspicion of any and all movies that

set out to terrify, unsettle and even repulse an audience. Surely such movies are sick – and the audiences who watch them even *sicker*?

The question of whether twisted movies make twisted people (or vice versa) has long plagued the movie business and its regulators. When *The Texas Chain Saw Massacre* was first submitted to the British Board of Film Censors (now 'Film Classification') back in the early seventies, it was banned outright by then-chief censor James Ferman on the grounds that the film represented 'the pornography of terror'. Ferman had attempted to trim the movie to rid it of some of its appalling power, but the cuts had made no difference whatsoever. So stifling was the atmosphere of anxiety which director Tobe Hooper had conjured on a shoestring budget that the film remained effectively immune to the censor's scissors. But was Ferman attempting to protect an audience from being terrorised and tortured beyond their own capacity for pain? Or was he more concerned that the film might somehow *infect* them with its fetid air, turning formerly decent citizens into potential marauding maniacs?

This complex question lies at the very heart of film classification. Since 1977, films and videos in the UK have been subject to the Obscene Publications Act (OPA), under which a work of art may be deemed legally obscene if it demonstrates

a tendency to deprave and corrupt a significant proportion of its likely/intended audience. This is a very specific test, thrashed out over a number of years by lawyers, and centring on the notion that good people can be turned into bad people through contact with sick (or 'obscene') material. When it comes to films, that means the BBFC can't rubber stamp anything which is likely to have a depraving effect on the kind of people who would probably see it. Which, in medical terms, is the equivalent of ensuring that the viruses and bacteria are safely quarantined away from the kind of healthy people who would be likely to come into contact with them. If you see what we mean.

In theory, this is a prescription for a healthy society, a world in which moviemakers are free to express themselves in whatever manner they like as long as their films don't turn their audience into homicidal maniacs. That sounds eminently sensible, but in practice the diagnosis is notoriously hard to get right.

Take the case of *The Evil Dead*, Sam Raimi's epochal horror classic from 1981, which found itself at the centre of Britain's so-called 'video nasties' scare during which its distributors were prosecuted under the Obscene Publications Act. A savagely comedic shocker described by its creator as 'the Three Stooges with blood and guts for custard pies', *The Evil Dead* became something of a cause célèbre when video dealers were hauled through the courts for supplying the title in the early days of VHS. (See 'In-Home Care', p.114, for more format fun!) At a time when legislation hadn't yet caught up with the rise of home viewing, tapes of uncut horror movies which would previously have been cut or banned in UK cinemas (*Cannibal Holocaust* (1980), *Zombie Flesh Eaters* (1979), *I Spit On Your Grave* (1978) etc) were being widely circulated with little or no regulation. For some, this meant the end of civilisation as we know it.

Hailed by Stephen King as 'the most ferociously original horror film in years', *The Evil Dead* had already suffered minor amputations at the hands of the BBFC, who performed plastic surgery on several of its more gory scenes before giving it a clean bill of health for cinema audiences aged eighteen and over. But even in this pre-cut form, the film was deemed infectiously offensive on video by a number of magistrates' courts who were asked to pass judgement on scenes of zombie (or, more accurately, 'possessee') dismemberment which were now playing not in cinemas, but in people's front rooms. Despite a high-profile victory at Snaresbrook Crown Court, where *The Evil Dead* was officially cleared of obscenity charges, the title's involvement in several successful OPA prosecutions of video dealers left it labelled as unclean. When the rushed-through Video Recordings Act was introduced in 1984, Sam Raimi's lively shocker was one of several titles deemed unfit for video classification, quarantined from a potentially corruptible audience to prevent its alleged sickness spreading through the population at large.

A couple of decades later, the cutting and banning of *The Evil Dead* looks quaintly ridiculous, on a par with such archaic medical treatments as the application of leeches and the brutal procedure of 'bloodletting'. In today's more media savvy world, the BBFC no longer apply their scalpels to movies willy-nilly and bring out the scissors only as a last resort, particularly in the case of movies clearly designed for adult audiences. Yet censorship is not dead. Consider the recent case of *The Human Centipede* (2009) and its uneagerly awaited sequel *The Human Centipede 2* (2011). Directed by outré Dutch auteur Tom Six, *The Human Centipede* follows the misadventures of a cracked scientist who kidnaps unsuspecting victims, drugs them, and performs mouth-to-anus surgery with unsurprisingly sick-making results. The film is essentially a vulgar satire, with heavy doses of the kind of scatological fetishism which has long made Dutch/German 'special interest' material a no-go zone for the faint-hearted. Approaching the movie with admirable even-handedness, the BBFC reported that while it was 'undeniably grotesque and revolting' their legal team had advised that 'The Human Centipede is not in breach of the Obscene Publications Act 1959 [because] the scenario is so far-fetched and bizarre that there is no plausible risk of emulation.' In short, they concluded that the chances of someone becoming infected by the movie's unabashed sickness and deciding to go out and make a human centipede of their own was next to nil.

The movie was, in effect, uncontagious, and thus remained unbanned.

The same could not be said of the sequel, which, with peculiar perversity, depicted a scenario in which the very thing the BBFC had argued simply could not happen with the first film (a viewer becomes contaminated enough to reproduce its on-screen atrocities) happened! Shot in the unremittingly ugly hues of art house black and white, The Human Centipede 2 starred Laurence R. Harvey as a lonely car park attendant who becomes obsessed with Tom Six's original schlocksterpiece, kidnapping his victims and stapling them together to create his very own poo-eating chain of human degradation. Jovial highlights include Mr Harvey watching The Human Centipede while rubbing sandpaper onto his Mr Happy; scenes of victims having their teeth smashed in with a hammer; extensive depictions of rape, torture and 'explosive defecation'; and – to cap it all – the sight of a newborn baby being killed. The film is horrible in every sense of the word, and the BBFC were initially minded to refuse certification outright. But in an age in which the Human Rights Act has enshrined into UK law the principle of free speech and freedom of artistic expression, movies are generally no longer banned simply for being revolting, or rubbish, or even (as in this case) both. In order to be quarantined from contact with the outside world, they also have to be dangerous – representing a threat to the mental health and well-being of the public, or infringing the existing laws of the land.

Thus, having given the matter some lengthy consideration, the BBFC took the surgical approach, deciding which particular areas of cancerous nastiness would need to be excised in order to turn the movie from a malignant horror into merely a benign cinematic tumour. As always, their report on the operation is as detailed and forensic as a set of medical notes, distinguished by a doctorly sense of detachment.

'In line with the consistent findings of the BBFC's public consultations and The Human Rights Act 1998,' they explain in sober fashion, 'at "18" the BBFC's guideline concerns will not normally override the principle that adults should be free to choose their own entertainment. Exceptions are most likely in the following areas [. . .] where material or treatment appears to the BBFC to risk harm to individuals or, through their behaviour, to society – for example, any detailed portrayal of violent or dangerous acts, or of illegal drug use, which may cause harm to public health or morals.'

Having ruled that 'the original version of the film was potentially harmful in its portrayal of violent acts and sexual and sexualised violence', the BBFC classified a heavily cut version of The Human Centipede 2 which 'omits the most explicit moments of sadistic violence [and] does not pose a credible harm risk, although some viewers may find it very distressing.'

And indeed very rubbish.

But now harmless rubbish (or, as Douglas Adams would have it, 'mostly harmless').

While censorship and classification in the modern age is perhaps more of an art than a science, a brief look back to the earliest days of the BBFC shows us how much more humane our regulatory surgeons have become. Back in the 1920s, the Board refused to classify F.W. Murnau's now-canonised gem Nosferatu (1922), possibly influenced by reports that Bram Stoker's widow was pursuing a copyright claim against the film-makers, whom she insisted (with some

justification) had plagiarised her husband's novel *Dracula* without permission or payment. In the thirties, the Board banned Tod Browning's now widely acclaimed *Freaks* (1932) because 'it was felt that the film exploited for commercial reasons the deformed people that it claimed to dignify'. *Freaks* was rejected again in the fifties on much the same grounds ('an unbroken succession of scenes of which the only point was the display of deformity and abnormality which no amount of cutting could tone down') and wasn't finally deemed fit for UK audiences until the sixties, when it earned an X certificate, with the caveat that 'people should be warned of the nature of the film so that those to whom such sights are displeasing will not see it'.

In the meantime, the BBFC had banned *The Wild One* in 1955 because they were alarmed by the sight of a tightly-leathered Marlon Brando on a motorcycle, and had taken the scissors both to the James Dean teen classic *Rebel Without a Cause* (1955) and Richard Brooks' *Blackboard Jungle* (1955), the latter of which arrived in the UK amidst claims that Bill Haley and his Comets were about to destroy civilised society with their balding and slightly portly brand of rock 'n' roll. Cannily using 'Rock Around the Clock' over its opening credits, *Blackboard Jungle* became the source of endless tabloid scare stories about beat-crazed rockers going wild in the aisles and slashing their local cinema seats – although the BBFC report that the film's eventual UK release passed largely without incident.

In the sixties, sex and drugs became a prime target of the censors' wrath, with exploitation maestro Roger Corman's psychedelic *The Trip* (1967) being banned outright over the course of four separate submissions (it wasn't certificated until the twenty-first century) on the grounds that it amounted to 'an advert for LSD'.

The seventies saw the BBFC wrestling with such scandalous cause célèbres as *Straw Dogs* (1971), *The Devils* (1971), *The Exorcist* and, of course, Stanley Kubrick's *A Clockwork Orange* (1971), the last of which remains one of the very few instances

WE'RE GOING TO NEED A BIGGER PLASTER

Unexpected and Unwanted Medical Attention in the Movies

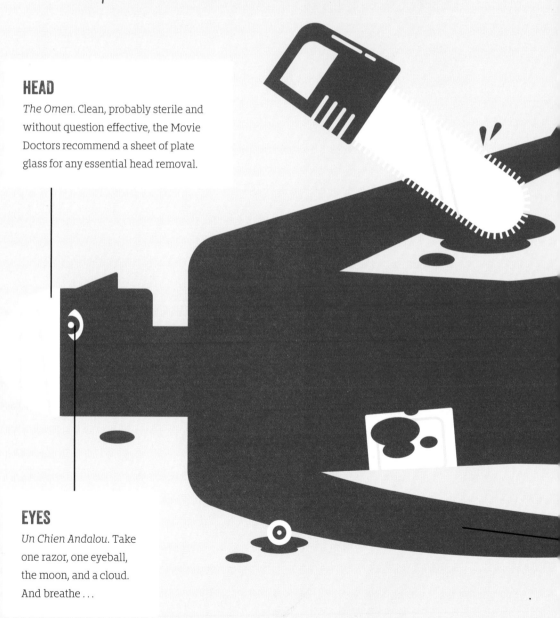

HEAD

The Omen. Clean, probably sterile and without question effective, the Movie Doctors recommend a sheet of plate glass for any essential head removal.

EYES

Un Chien Andalou. Take one razor, one eyeball, the moon, and a cloud. And breathe . . .

HANDS

Evil Dead 2. When your hands become possessed by evil spirits, it's time to reach for the chainsaw. Twice.

FEET

Misery. If your ankles are troubling you, you could do worse than to call for Kathy Bates, who can work wonders with a block of wood, a piece of string and a sledgehammer.

PRIVATE BITS/UNMENTIONABLES

Caligula. A man who has proven troublesome to Malcolm McDowell's Emperor has his testicles roughly removed and thrown to the dogs. Luckily, two young women are on hand to pee on him – presumably for disinfectant purposes. Sadly he is already dead . . .

ARMS AND LEGS

Boxing Helena. Sherilyn Fenn has her arms and legs amputated by Julian Sands – for love! Kim Basinger was signed on to play the role, but strangely bailed out at the last moment.

of a film that was banned by its own director. Based on the novel by Anthony Burgess, *A Clockwork Orange* had been passed uncut by the BBFC, who had previously deemed a 1967 screenplay 'unlikely to be acceptable'. Yet despite the fact that the first half of the movie presents a weirdly intoxicating cocktail of 'rape and ultraviolence', chief censor Stephen Murphy concluded that 'by the end of the film it could not be accused of exploitation; quite the contrary, it is a valuable contribution to the whole debate about violence'. The media took a rather different view, with stories of copycat teenage violence (the film had an over-18s-only X rating) becoming a tabloid staple in the wake of the film's release. Such stories disturbed the American-born but now UK-based Kubrick, as did the threats to himself and his family which reportedly ensued. Thus, in 1973, after *A Clockwork Orange* had completed its first-run tour of UK cinemas, Kubrick struck a deal with Warner Brothers to remove the film from British distribution, although it remained available in other territories around the world.

So adamant was Kubrick that *A Clockwork Orange* should never again darken the inside of a UK cinema that when the much-loved Scala cinema in London's King's Cross secretly screened the movie in 1992, Warners sued (at the director's insistence), and soon after losing an expensive legal battle the once-proud haven of alternative and cult cinema closed. It wasn't until Kubrick's death in 1999 that Warners finally plucked up the courage to allow *A Clockwork Orange* back into UK cinemas, with VHS, DVD and television releases following in double-quick fashion, and nary a raised eyebrow.

Fast-forward to the present, and despite the widespread impression that today anything goes, the BBFC continue to fight the good fight against movies which they believe have the power to do harm to viewers. In 2009, they rejected Kôji Shiraishi's Japanese sexual torture shocker *Grotesque*, which was publicised with the claim that it 'could make even the most extreme splatter horror fan vomit'.

UNWATCHABLE

*A Brief Guide to Movies
Banned by the BBFC*

BATTLESHIP POTEMKIN *(1925)*

Banned because of its 'inflammatory
subtitles and Bolshevist propaganda'
First passed 1954, rated X
Current status PG uncut

FREAKS *(1932)*

Banned because of 'an unbroken
succession of scenes of which the only
point was the display of deformity'
First passed 1963, rated X
Current status 12 uncut

THE WILD ONE *(1953)*

Banned because 'burgeoning juvenile
delinquency . . . could only be aggravated
by young people seeing this film'
First passed 1967, rated X
Current status PG uncut

GLEN OR GLENDA *(1953)*

Banned because of themes of
transvestism and transsexuality
First passed 1995, rated 15
Current status 15 uncut

SHOCK CORRIDOR *(1963)*

Banned because it 'could well cause grave
concern to people who have friends and
relatives with mental illness'
First passed 1990, rated 15
Current status 15 uncut

'Cuts were not considered viable,' reported the BBFC with customary understatement. In 2011, they banned *The Bunny Game* for its 'unremitting sexual and physical abuse of a helpless woman', noting that 'aspects of the work such as the lack of explanation of the events depicted, and the stylistic treatment, may encourage some viewers to enjoy and share in the man's callousness and the pleasure he takes in the woman's pain and humiliation'. In their press statement, the BBFC took issue with 'media reports [which] have repeated the mistaken claim that the BBFC has only ever refused classification to 11 works. Over the Board's entire 99-year history, the true figure is approaching 1,000 such decisions,' the press release announces proudly. 'Many of these decisions date from the early years of the Board. In more recent years, the Board has typically refused classification to 1–2 works a year.'

As recently as March 2015, the Board banned the home-invasion torture fest *Hate Crime*, which depicts 'the terrorisation, mutilation, physical and sexual abuse and murder of the members of a Jewish family by Neo Nazi thugs'. Noting that 'little context is provided for the violence beyond an on-screen statement at the end of the film that the two attackers who escaped were subsequently apprehended' (a neatly deflating plot spoiler) the BBFC declared with a splendidly straight face that: 'We have considered the attempt at the end to position the film as against hate-crime, but find it so unconvincing that it only makes matters worse.'

In all of these cases, the underlying principle remains the same – that a movie runs the risk of being cut or banned not because it is 'bad' (the BBFC admit that *Grotesque* is 'well made') but because it has the potential to make its *viewers* bad; to infect them with its bad ideas and images, and make them morally (rather than physically) sick. Clearly, this is a tricky thing to judge; like the medical diagnoses which use the term 'syndrome' in the absence of definitive physical or biochemical proof, there is no absolute positive or negative test for moral turpitude. Bound by the somewhat convoluted rubric of the Video Recordings Act, the BBFC interpret the vague legal concept of 'harm' as referring not merely to 'behavioural harm' (the possibility of a viewer acting out that which they have seen on screen) but also 'more insidious risks . . . for instance, moral harm and possible desensitisation'. On 24 January 2008, the 'the harm test' was 'clarified' by Mr Justice Mitting in a High Court ruling which simply instructed the Board 'to have special regard to any harm that may in future be caused to potential viewers' – a ruling which must be balanced with the demands of the Human Rights Act's equally vague definition of freedom of expression.

And you thought being a censor was easy.

The Movie Doctors would like to leave this particular minefield with a little light relief, with the story of the infamous seventies porno-epic *Caligula*. Originally based on a screenplay by Gore Vidal (itself inspired by Suetonius's *Lives of the Twelve Caesars*), *Caligula* had been disowned by its writer, director (Italian schlockmeister Tinto Brass) and many of its A-list cast (which included Malcolm McDowell, Helen Mirren, Peter O'Toole and John Gielgud) long before it ever ran into trouble with British authorities. Accurately described by Mirren as 'an irresistible mix of art and genitals', what had begun life as a quasi-philosophical film about 'the orgy of power' turned into a lurid romp about 'the power of the orgy' after producer and *Penthouse* magazine proprietor Bob Guccione inserted a bunch of hardcore scenes against the wishes of Brass. Removed from the editing room, Brass demanded (like Vidal) that his name be taken off the film. Several years of litigation ensued before *Caligula* finally premiered at Cannes in 1979, garnering reviews littered with such colourful phrases as 'sickening, utterly worthless, shameful trash' (Roger Ebert) and 'a trough of rotten swill' (Rex Reed).

When a print of *Caligula* arrived in the UK in April 1980, it was promptly seized by HM Customs and Excise, and was only allowed to remain on British soil on the proviso that it was escorted directly to the Soho offices of the BBFC, who would set about removing any potential obscenities, of which there were apparently many. With its orgiastic scenes of unsimulated sex and genital-mangling violence, *Caligula* ticked a number of problematic boxes, and it took more than *fifty* separate cuts (totalling around eleven minutes of screen time) to turn it into something which could be passed with an X rating. Yet even with these hefty edits and a clean bill of health from Customs and Excise, *Caligula* was deemed a threat to the moral health of areas such as Cardiff, Blackpool and Portsmouth, where local councils exercised their legal right to ban the movie from their boroughs, thus safeguarding the well-being of their respective populations.

Fast-forward to 2008, and the complete uncut *Caligula* which had caused such public health anxieties back in the early eighties found its way back to the BBFC. 'The passage of nearly 30 years had significantly diminished the film's impact,' the BBFC reported, 'and after careful consideration it was decided that it could now be classified 18 uncut.'

But what about those scenes of sex and violence which Her Majesty's own Customs and Excise officers had found likely to deprave and corrupt back in 1980? Was the film really no longer a danger to innocent UK viewers? Apparently not. As the BBFC pointed out, 'Although there are scenes in *Caligula* that some people will find shocking, offensive or disgusting, the film does not contain . . . any material that is likely to give rise to harm for adult audiences, most of whom will be well aware of its controversial reputation.'

And with that, the once terrifying threat of an uncontrolled outbreak of moral ill-health spurred on by the sight of famous actors in togas doing unspeakable things to each other's private parts was contained and neutralised.

In the world of cinematic obscenity, the Movie Doctors must conclude that time really does cure all ills.

PHYSIOTHERAPY

How and where you seat yourself in the theatre becomes an increasingly important matter as age **takes its toll** on your physique, your hearing and your eyesight – to name but three common **health issues** for the older generation. The Movie Doctors are here to help on that front. In our Physiotherapy Clinic we also provide the necessary tools for keeping film stars and directors **in check.**

POSTURE CLINIC

Are You Sitting Comfortably?

The Movie Doctors diagnose some of the common ailments relating to cinemagoers' posture.

FEET ON SEAT IN FRONT

Puts undesirable pressure on the lower back muscles. Causes tension in the neck of the person sitting in front.

UPRIGHT, DOMINATING ARMRESTS

Try to relax and share space with neighbours. Observe the drinks rule – container in holder reserves armrest. Better still, win the lottery and buy the seats around you to avoid any unnecessary contact.

HUNCHED OVER PLATE OF FOOD AND GLASS OF WINE

Some theatres serve dinner and drinks at screenings now. Indigestion is a potential problem, as is not seeing much of the movie (you can't pause the film when you drop half a burger on the floor). Consider watching the film, then going to a restaurant.

SLUMPED IN SEAT

Either a gradual response to disheartening movie experience, or habitual teenage posture. Causes stress in the row behind if slumpee is particularly tall, as sudden periodic resurfacings, in response to movie shocks, can obstruct view of screen at vital moments.

BEAN-BAGGED

A recent 'innovation' commonly found before the front row at multiplex screenings. Guaranteed to induce discomfort and shuffling, and also a headache due to proximity to vertiginous screen. Best avoided if over fifteen.

V.I.P.ARANOIA

Panic caused by sitting in the 'premium' seats in the middle of the theatre without paying the extortionate supplement. Occupants commonly spend duration of movie worrying that they will be the first people in the history of cinema to be ejected for sitting in the wrong seat.

PHYSIOTHERAPY AT THE MOVIES

Doctors in Discussion

Dr Mayo: Well the first point is this: you have to sit strategically depending on the cinema, don't you?

Dr Kermode: You do. The bigger the screen the further back you want to be. If you're at an IMAX screen, for example, you should be in the back row. If you're close to the screen for 3D the eye strain is worse. Ideally, in 3D screenings, you should be far enough back that you're actually in a different screen altogether, watching something else.

Dr M: Not that you have a medical objection to 3D, Dr Kermode?

Dr K: Don't get me started . . .

Dr M: (interrupts) Moving on. Let's get back to getting the right positioning in a cinema for maximum comfort.

Dr K: OK. So when you sit in the cinema your head needs to be at a natural angle, or the Movie Doctors' Tilt/Length Rule comes into play.

Dr M: And what does that mean?

Dr K: Well take us . . . We both wear glasses – when we sit down to watch a movie the top rim of the glasses should be aligned with the top of the screen. If you have to tilt your head back to see the screen, it means that the movie will need to be shorter, otherwise pain will result. *Interstellar* may be a terrific movie, but if you're having to tilt your head to watch it, imagine the crick in your neck. It's very bad for you.

Dr M: That's very helpful. And then of course there's the issue of who you have sitting in front of you.

Dr K: Yes. There's a medical syndrome . . .

Dr M: . . . called 'Why Does the Man with the Top Hat Always Sit in Front of Me in the Cinema?' It's a well-known condition, for which we have a suggestion – adapted from *The Goodies* all those years ago.

Dr K: I remember it well.

Dr M: Cinemas should impose a system called 'Apart-height' whereby the shortest people sit at the front because otherwise the tallest people will automatically sit in front of the shortest, and that makes for neck ache and misery.

Dr K: There is also the slightly less heightist solution of simply choosing a cinema that has an adequate rake.

Dr M: And I take it by that you don't mean a half-decent eighteenth-century philanderer?

Dr K: I mean the angle at which the seating rows are placed one behind the other.

Dr M: But cinemas don't advertise this, do they? They don't say, 'Come inside, we've got a great rake.'

Dr K: Some of them do, actually, but they should make more of it.

Dr M: OK, so what's the ideal rake?

Dr K: The perfect rake is when the head of the person in front of you is at your knee level.

Dr M: Given that such a scenario might not always be available, isn't there a third solution to this problem? If you have the money, just buy the seat in front of you.

Dr K: Well, yes, but if you have the means, I'd suggest you actually buy five seats. Your seat, the seat in front of you, the seat behind you and the seat either side.

Dr M: I suspect, Dr K, if you are being totally honest, you'd suggest buying *all* the seats in the cinema.

Dr K: You're absolutely spot on as usual, Dr M.

Dr M: This is the Misanthrope's Guide to Minimising Physical Discomfort at the Movies.

Dr K: And then there is the issue of so-called 'Premium Seating'.

Dr M: Isn't that elitist and wrong?

Dr K: In essence, yes, unless one agrees that in a proper cinema, *all* seats should be 'premium'. Seat 'grades' are like being asked when you buy your ticket: 'Would you like a seat from which you can see the screen in comfort? Or one from which you can't see the screen without dislocating your spine?' Every seat should be premium.

Dr M: And there you have it – top physio tips to minimise physical discomfort during your visit to the cinema.

DOCTOR'S BAG

The Essential Movie Doctors' Kit for Interviewing Film Stars and Directors

STETHOSCOPE

To check if actor is still alive after five hours of press junket.

TONGUE SUPPRESSOR

For when well-rehearsed film promo spiel becomes too much to bear.

REFLEX HAMMER

For keeping red-eye shuttle victims awake long enough to provide necessary sound bites. Plus, with careful self-application, the only chance you'll get to kick a movie star.

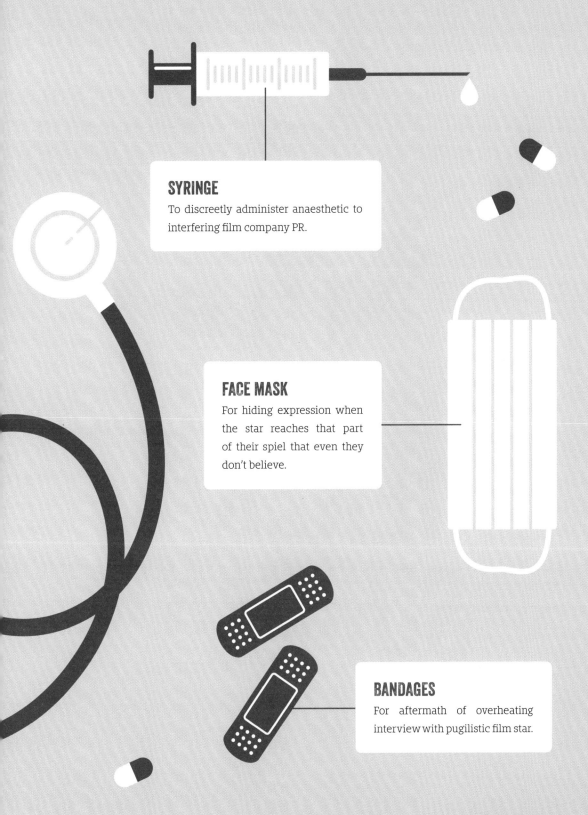

SYRINGE

To discreetly administer anaesthetic to interfering film company PR.

FACE MASK

For hiding expression when the star reaches that part of their spiel that even they don't believe.

BANDAGES

For aftermath of overheating interview with pugilistic film star.

GENERAL
SURGERY

There's no question that surgery of whatever kind is a **painful and distressing experience** for the patient, and has the potential to induce anxiety either during or after the procedure (or in extreme cases, before). Taking a knife to a movie (aka 'editing') can have the same effect. But exactly like real surgery on real people, editing is **necessary and beneficial** to the health of the patient. The Movie Doctors' General Surgery Clinic explains the necessity of making **appropriate and timely cuts** – something that directors often seem reluctant to tackle.

EXCESSIVE LENGTH

A Clinical Examination

The satirist P.J. O'Rourke once observed (in only mildly sarcastic fashion) that conclusive proof civilisation was improving rather than declining could be found in the fact that bad works of art were getting shorter rather than longer. Writing in the mid nineties, O'Rourke pointed out that 'Wagner's *Ring Cycle* takes four days to perform while "Mmm Mmm Mmm Mmm" by the Crash Test Dummies lasts little more than three minutes.' As far as he was concerned, this was an indication that things were getting better. Musically speaking, less is more.

The Movie Doctors believe that the same prognosis may be applied to cinema, a medium in which size really does matter – although not in the way that most people think. While an apparently endless stream of young men continue to be enticed into quack clinics on the promise that various parts of their anatomy may be artificially elongated (just look at how much internet spam promises to make Mr Happy even happier (see 'Arousal: The Movie Doctors' Casebook', p.130)) movies requiring medical attention are usually more in need of length reduction. Think about it: when was the last time you came out of a movie and said 'Well, that was really great, but you know what – I thought it was a bit short'? Even as devout cinemagoers who hold the medium dear to their hearts, the Movie Doctors struggle to recall an occasion on which they left a cinema feeling short-changed in terms of running time. While many movies have proved sorely lacking in wit, invention and visual delight, very few have managed the frankly unimaginable feat of under-staying their welcome. Even the films we love the most rarely leave us wanting more, although several have left us longing for less.

In terms of cinematic ailments, a superfluity of length is the movie equivalent of the common cold: a condition with which everyone is painfully familiar, but for which there appears to be no known cure. Or to put it another way: how come we can put a man on the moon, but we can't stop Quentin Tarantino from making bum-numbingly long films? For Quentin, it's clearly a case of 'never mind the quality, feel the width', and there is a suspicion that his much vaunted preference for celluloid over digital is primarily driven by the fact that film reels take up more space than Digital Cinema Packages (DCPs). Tarantino makes films by the yard, and if you ask him what any of his movies are about, he'd probably tell you that they are 'about three hours – give or take'.

Film critics have always been suspicious of directors who don't know when to stop. At the beginning of every press screening, as the critical glitterati assemble in the foyer, one question can be heard above all others: 'What's the running time?' If the answer is a nippy eighty-nine minutes, you can almost feel the atmosphere in the room change from one of barely veiled hostility to merriment, jubilation and delight. Indeed, the phrase 'four-star running time' has long been part of the habitual film critic's private vocabulary, describing in glowing

terms any film lasting less than an hour and a half. The reason for such sight-unseen approval is simple: people who spend most of their working days in screening rooms tend to look more kindly upon anything which doesn't involve large amounts of bladder-management ('Yes, I would love a third cup of coffee, thank you kindly!'). Conversely, the announcement that the film you're about to view is 'just under three hours' (an increasingly common occurrence nowadays) leads to a palpable sense of doom and gloom, with critics nodding sagely and silently at each other in the manner of troops in the trenches of France during the Great War preparing to go over the top. Some will even wish you a fond farewell before heading to the back of the screening room, hoping to drift into the abyss of sleep, waking just in time to catch the end credits on which their entire review will then be based.

And it's not just critics who get sniffy about movies being excessively lengthy. Audiences, too, are keenly aware of the multiple problems caused by bloated running times. Bearing in mind that no cinema programme is now complete without forty-five minutes of trailers and commercials before the main feature begins, any movie clocking in at over two hours presents nightmarish logistical problems for anyone with less than infinite amounts of leisure time.

Let's say, for example, that you have decided to go and watch the fourth *Transformers* movie, tellingly subtitled *Age of Extinction* (2014). Skipping over the fact that anyone who willingly pays to watch a Michael Bay movie is clearly in need of medical attention, try doing the sums on the amount of time it will take you to accomplish this seemingly simple task. We'll start with the journey to the cinema which, here in the UK, averages out at somewhere between twenty and forty minutes door-to-door (although for many, it'll be more like an hour). You arrive at said movie emporium and queue for ten to fifteen minutes to purchase your ticket from the popcorn counter which, for reasons best known to the multiplex chains, is doubling as an admissions centre. (You could, of course, purchase your ticket online, but chances are you'll wind up spending fifteen minutes standing in the popcorn-and-tickets line anyway when the automated machine in the foyer eats your credit card.) Then it's off to your chosen screen, where you sit through three quarters of an hour of pre-feature gubbins and annoying anti-piracy waffle before Mark Wahlberg finally arrives on screen to thrill you with his quick wit, firm abs, and inappropriate jokes about statutory rape (we're not making this up – *Transformers: Age of Extinction* really does feature an extended 'comic' interlude on the subject of the legality of underage sex. Classy! For a handy list of other movies that should never have been made, see 'Doctor, No!', p.270).

By the time the movie ends and Mr Bay has grown tired of looking up young women's skirts while enormous robots hit each other, you are 166 minutes older than you were when the opening credits rolled – nearly three hours of your precious life that you will never get back. Battered, bruised and somewhat soiled, you crawl out of the cinema and head back to the safety of your home, another twenty to forty minutes melting away like snow. Add it all together, and the entire adventure has taken you somewhere between four and a half and five hours, and that's assuming you don't stop for a stiff drink on the way home to steady your nerves after peering deep into Michael Bay's foul soul.

Now let's say you have kids and had to arrange a babysitter: that's five hours at anywhere between five and ten pounds an hour – an average cost of £37.50 just to buy yourself the time necessary to go to the movies where the accumulated price of a ticket, a soft drink and (most annoyingly) 3D glasses made you think that Mr Wahlberg was going to appear and perform the movie for you, personally. Honestly, when you've invested this amount of time and money, the least the film-makers could do would be to say 'thank you'.

And therein lies the rub. Because invariably the curse of the overlong movie has more to do with a film-maker's desire to please themselves than an urge to satisfy their audiences. Back in the late eighties, Dr Kermode was one of a gaggle of overeager cineastes who proclaimed that the very best thing about video (a new-fangled invention in those heady days – see 'In-Home Care', p.114 if you need a reminder) was the fact that it would allow film-makers to issue extended cuts of movies which had been unfairly truncated for cinema. A key case was that of James Cameron's 1986 movie *Aliens* (tag line: 'This time it's war!'), which had been trimmed for its cinema release from an original 'director's cut' and was now to be reissued on video in its full uncut glory under the punning banner 'This time it's MORE!' (geddit?). This, Dr K declared at the time, was a great leap forward – no longer would directors be constrained by the brevity enforced upon them by cinema chains eager to pack in five performances a day with enough time in between for the sale of overpriced sweets and obnoxious-smelling fizzy drinks. Home viewing had offered directors the chance to throw off the shackles of shortness and to express themselves at whatever unwieldy lengths they wished. If only cinemas could follow suit.

Twenty years later that dream has come to pass, and those who argued for a film-maker's right to go on and on and on as long as they please are wishing we had kept our big stupid mouths shut. Contrary to expectations, very few films turned out to be improved by being allowed to straggle beyond the 120-minute mark which was once a timely limit. On the contrary, allowing directors to use elongated running times as a form of cinematic status symbol had precisely the reverse effect upon their work. As exploitation maestro Roger Corman famously observed, it is hard to think of any movie which would not benefit from shedding a third of its original running time (he found 82 minutes to be the ideal length). Yet somehow we were all hoodwinked into believing otherwise, and the interminable legacy of that sorry misapprehension has turned much modern cinema into an endurance test.

Which is not to say that all long movies are *ipso facto* 'bad'. By a perverse coincidence, at the exact same time that Michael Bay was demanding nearly three hours of your time for his bloody awful *Transformers* movie, director Richard Linklater was making the same request for his really rather brilliant drama *Boyhood*. Shot in thirty-nine days over a period of twelve years, *Boyhood* was one of the outstanding cinematic treats of 2014, a film which seemed to treasure every one of its 166 minutes, and which rewarded its audience richly for each second of their viewing. Despite its lengthy running time, it's hard to find a single scene in *Boyhood* which could be dropped without detriment to the overall movie. The film may be long, but it is exactly the length it needs to be, and the time simply flies by. Crucially, you never get the feeling that Linklater is keeping you there to satisfy himself; rather, he is taking whatever time is needed to ensure that you get the most out of the movie.

The same is not true of many (most?) other directors, for whom lengthiness may be more a symptom of either pride or vanity. Indeed, sometimes it can actually become competitive. When Spike Lee was putting together his sprawling 1992 epic *Malcolm X*, he was told by both the completion bond company (who guarantee that a film gets finished as agreed) and the studio that the picture must be no longer than two hours and fifteen minutes. Noting that Oliver Stone's 1991 Kennedy biopic *JFK* had gone on for over three hours, Lee turned to donors like Oprah Winfrey, Bill Cosby and Michael Jordan, who stumped up the money to allow him to finish the film to his own satisfaction – and length. As he told the press at the time: 'I will do the film the way it ought to be, and it will be over three hours . . .'

Which is exactly what he did, handing in a movie which was twelve and a half minutes longer than Stone's. You have to admire the logic, if not the outcome: *Malcolm X* is a very fine film, with a barnstorming central performance by Denzel Washington, but there are several occasions on which it is fully possible to pop to the loo and then return with no discernible dramatic lacunae whatsoever. As for *JFK*, having laid down the overlong template which Lee would claim as his own, Oliver Stone decided that his movie needed to be even longer, and set about assembling an extended version which exceeded Lee's film by another four minutes. Ha! There's a brilliant *Simpsons* episode in which we see a brief clip of *JFK: The Director's Cut* which simply goes: 'back and to the left, back and to the left, back and to the left, back and to the left . . .' ad infinitum. (Not to be beaten, Francis Ford Coppola cooked up *Apocalypse Now Redux* – longer than *Malcolm X* but shorter than *JFK: Director's Cut* – in which he re-edited *his* movie to include a heated discussion of the First Indochina War on a French rubber plantation which had presumably been cut the first time round because it was boring as sin.)

In general, when it comes to movie lengths, the Movie Doctors apply what we like to call the '2001 rule', which states that 'If Stanley Kubrick can go from the birth of mankind to the dawn of a new species in the space of 142 minutes (the premiere version was longer, and an interval still bumps up the overall running time) then anyone who needs any more time than that to tell their story better have a damned good reason.' Generally speaking, they don't. Key offenders include the aforementioned Quentin Tarantino, whose movies have been getting longer and longer without crucially getting any better for pretty much the entire duration of his career. While 1992's *Reservoir Dogs* (still one of Tarantino's finest works) clocks in at around an hour and a half, *Django Unchained* is closer to three hours – nearly twice as long. (Was it nearly twice as good? Er, nope.) As for *Kill Bill*, rather than cutting to the chase and reining in his nerdy, fanboy excesses, Tarantino managed to persuade Miramax to allow him to release it as two movies with a combined running time which ventures

THE SNIPS

Movies That Should Have Been Trimmed

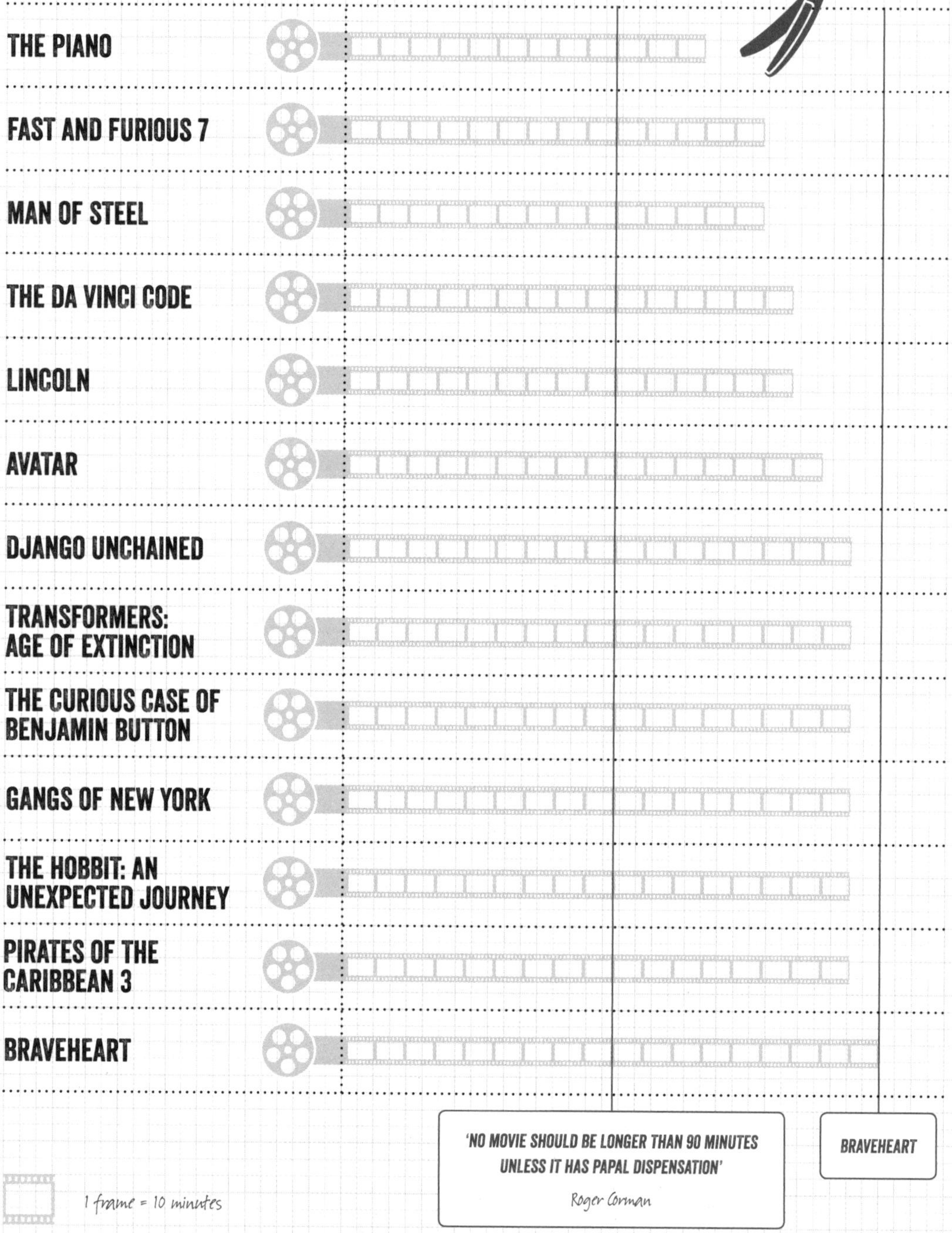

THE PIANO

FAST AND FURIOUS 7

MAN OF STEEL

THE DA VINCI CODE

LINCOLN

AVATAR

DJANGO UNCHAINED

TRANSFORMERS:
AGE OF EXTINCTION

THE CURIOUS CASE OF
BENJAMIN BUTTON

GANGS OF NEW YORK

THE HOBBIT: AN
UNEXPECTED JOURNEY

PIRATES OF THE
CARIBBEAN 3

BRAVEHEART

1 frame = 10 minutes

'NO MOVIE SHOULD BE LONGER THAN 90 MINUTES
UNLESS IT HAS PAPAL DISPENSATION'

Roger Corman

BRAVEHEART

north of four hours and somehow manages to feel even longer. Honestly, in the time it takes to watch *Kill Bill Vol. 1* and *2* (2003 and 2004), you could grow an entire new set of teeth. More and more, you don't come out of a Tarantino movie asking what time it is; you want to know what day it is.

So why doesn't anyone stop him? How come Quentin is allowed to make movies that test the audience's patience (not to mention their bottoms) for so little return? The answer, of course, is a lack of editorial control. Ever since movie mogul Harvey Weinstein described Miramax as 'the house that Quentin built' and the Weinstein Company as 'the house that Quentin saved' it was clear that no one in either of those organisations was ever going to argue with Tarantino about the extent of his brilliance. Rather than standing over him in the cutting room with a stopwatch and a very big stick (as he had done with countless other directors), Harvey chose to give Tarantino perpetual final cut as a reward for the studio-building box office bonanza of his first two features. Clearly, Weinstein felt that he owed Tarantino, and running time was the currency of his repayment.

Thus, while other film-makers (including such legends as Martin Scorsese) would have to fight for every frame with the so-called 'Harvey Scissorhands', Quentin would be allowed to let his ego run rampant – to make movies with running times which screamed 'LOOK HOW IMPORTANT I AM!', simply because he could.

The result? His movies got worse.

So what's the solution? Is there a cure for this most prevalent film-maker's ailment – temporal incontinence? Or are movies destined to just carry on getting longer – and worse?

The answer lies in the hands of producers and editors, the latter of whom are the most important – and often least visible – people in the moviemaking process. A good editor can make or break a movie. For proof, look no further than film editor Ralph Rosenblum's page-turning *When the Shooting Stops*

... The Cutting Begins, an account of his days working with the likes of William Friedkin, Mel Brooks and Woody Allen, all of whom required a strong guiding hand in the cutting room. In the case of Allen, Rosenblum recounts how the director had set out to make a film called *Anhedonia* ('the inability to experience pleasure') which dealt with a number of unmarketable philosophical and religious issues, and which reportedly languished under a succession of spoof working titles including *It Had to Be Jew* and *Me and My Goy*. The first cut came in at an unwieldy two hours and twenty minutes, a version with which no one was satisfied. 'Far from being the story of a love affair,' wrote Rosemblum, 'it was the surrealistic and abstract adventures of a neurotic Jewish comedian who was reliving his highly flawed life and in the process satirizing much of our culture.' Yet while sifting through the thousands of feet of raw film which he had shot, Allen and editor Rosenblum stumbled upon the heart of something which would (with a couple of weeks of reshoots) emerge as *Annie Hall*, a film which American critic Roger Ebert would correctly describe as 'just about everybody's favourite Woody Allen movie'. Not only was the newly reconfigured movie (which had now been transformed into a love story) far better than anything Allen or co-writer Marshall Brickman had originally imagined, it was also far shorter – a mere ninety-three minutes. To this day, the Doctors have never met anyone who really wanted to see an extended cut of *Annie Hall* which put back in all that stuff that the editor took out. After all, as Allen has said many times, they took those scenes out because they just didn't work. Perhaps more than any other movie, *Annie Hall* stands as proof that less really is more.

Other directors who have benefitted from 'cutting their luvvies' include Paul Thomas Anderson, whose best movie, *Punch-Drunk Love* (2002), is a taut ninety-five minutes of pure bonkers beauty. Most of Anderson's films (*Boogie Nights* (1997), *Magnolia* (1999), *The Master* (2012)) clock

QUENTIN UNCHAINED

The Tarantino Snorometer

The point in Quentin's oeuvre when he should have shouted *'That's a wrap!'* and put his camera away.

RESERVOIR DOGS *(1992)*

PULP FICTION *(1994)*

JACKIE BROWN *(1997)*

KILL BILL VOL 1 & 2 *(2003/2004)*

DEATH PROOF *(2007)*

INGLOURIOUS BASTERDS *(2009)*

DJANGO UNCHAINED *(2012)*

 = 10 minutes

in at somewhere around the two-and-a-half-hour mark, and several of them manage to justify their length – just about. But *Punch-Drunk Love* is an hour and a half of pure perfection; a movie from which you could not remove a single scene without the whole piece falling apart.

This, of course, is the key to the surgical procedure which has proved most efficacious in the treatment of over-running: forcing a director to go through their movie scene by scene (starting with their favourite sequence) and then cutting it out and seeing whether the movie lives or dies without it. It's a cruel-to-be-kind process, based upon the principle that that which does not kill me strengthens me. Unsurprisingly, most film-makers baulk at the very thought of it. Yet, like a patient with a tumour who needs an unblinking surgeon to take a knife to their body, most films don't need mollycoddling – they need cutting. If you applied this process to Tarantino's back catalogue, most

of his films would run no longer than 100 minutes, and would be all the better for it. There would be exceptions – *Jackie Brown* may drift way beyond the two-hour mark, but for once it's worth it. In general, however, Tarantino's body of work could be vastly improved by the celluloid equivalent of liposuction – if only the patient would consent to surgery.

In the meantime, audiences must decide for themselves just how much of their time they are willing to commit to any film or film-maker. While directors may be unable to cure themselves of long-windedness, audiences can vote with their feet and demand that the movies they pay for don't end up simply wasting their time. Box office remains the blunt instrument with which cinemagoers can influence film-making, and if enough of us simply refuse to accept the flatulent bloating which has become an epidemic in Hollywood of late, then maybe there's still time to save modern cinema.

Hand us that scalpel.

LET'S PLAY DOCTORS

A Medical Movie Game

See how many of the following well-worn medical movie tropes you can spot in your next movie...

'He/she won't remember anything.'	Operating theatre lights	■
Flat-lining heart monitor	'Rosebud.'	Assassination attempt in helicopter
Curtains drawn around bed	■	'His/her new face will look completely different ...'
'Is Kenneth Williams in this one?'	'Take these.'	Assassination attempt in ambulance
■	James Robertson Justice	'A suicide pill, with a mild laxative side-effect ...'

'You'd better sit down.'	Stethoscope	View from inside anaesthetic mask
■	Defibrillator spasm	Helicopter
Doctor in white coat	Bed chart	'But will he/she also be taller?'
Operating table	Bernard Bresslaw in a hospital gown	Surgical gown
■	Hospital gurney	'What seems to be the problem?'

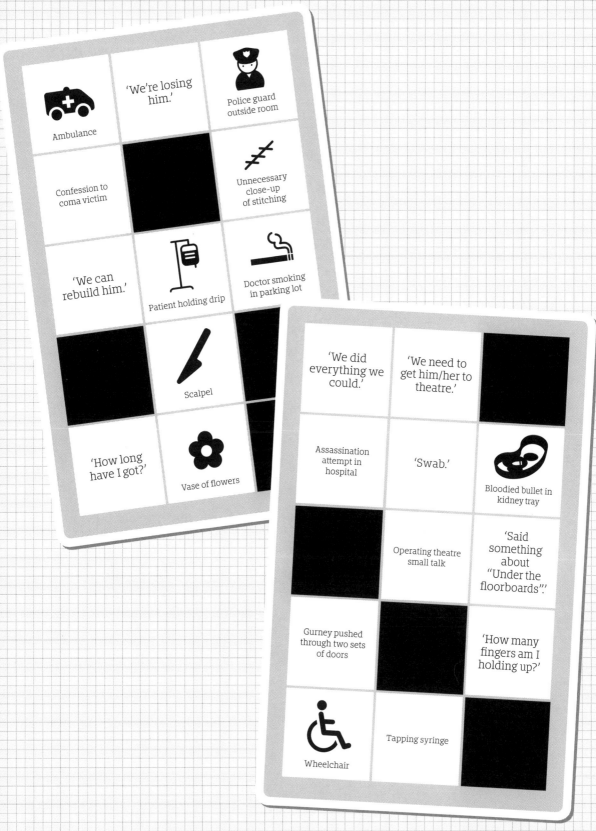

Card 1

Ambulance	'We're losing him.'	Police guard outside room
Confession to coma victim		Unnecessary close-up of stitching
'We can rebuild him.'	Patient holding drip	Doctor smoking in parking lot
	Scalpel	
'How long have I got?'	Vase of flowers	

Card 2

'We did everything we could.'	'We need to get him/her to theatre.'	
Assassination attempt in hospital	'Swab.'	Bloodied bullet in kidney tray
	Operating theatre small talk	'Said something about "Under the floorboards".'
Gurney pushed through two sets of doors		'How many fingers am I holding up?'
Wheelchair	Tapping syringe	

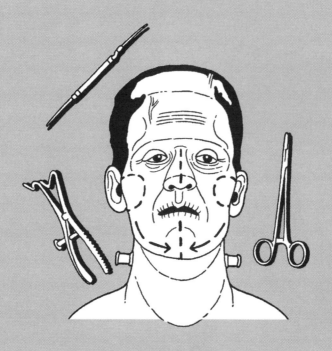

COSMETIC
SURGERY

Celluloid? Humanoid? We all want to look our best. In Hollywood, this is simpler than in real life. The Movie Doctors' Cosmetic Surgery 'salon' helps you understand the pitfalls of **appearance-enhancing surgery**. Think Rob Lowe as the cosmetic surgeon in *Behind the Candelabra* who can't close his eyes because he's had so much work done. When challenged that this might not be a good thing, Lowe reassures Michael Douglas's newly stretched Liberace: *'You'll always be able to see people's reactions when they see how wonderful you look!'* In Hollywood, anything is possible and it's all good.

MOVIES CHANGED BEYOND RECOGNITION

A Clinical Examination

'Real nice party, Hapsburg,' says Leslie Nielsen in *The Naked Gun 2½: The Smell of Fear* (1991). 'I see a lot of familiar facelifts . . .' It's a line which has been bandied around in Hollywood circles for decades, an open acknowledgement that Tinseltown has long been a feeding ground for some of the world's most highly paid plastic surgeons. Indeed, the Movie Doctors have often been told that they should abandon their current practice and take up the knife – after all, that's where the money is. Yet rare are those performers who will admit to having had 'work'.

Despite the fact that most moviegoers can spot an injection of Botox or a discreet nip and tuck a mile away (when someone's face is blown up to the size of a house, you tend to notice these things), we have all got used to hearing publicists explain that the radical transformation of a star's appearance has been brought about by nothing more than a fitness regime and an alternative diet. How come Renée Zellweger is suddenly unrecognisable as the former star of the Bridget Jones movies? Must be all those healthy vegetables she's consuming. Why did Mickey Rourke look like he'd been in a fire in the early nineties? Endless hours spent punching away in the gym. As for Cher, the Movie Doctors remember vividly watching a screening of *Burlesque* in a very small preview theatre in Soho and worrying that if she smiled too broadly her entire face would snap off and give the front row whiplash.

The reason for Hollywood's infatuation with 'cosmetic assistance' is easy to understand: in a town in which youth is prized above all other commodities and actors are actively punished for the crime of growing old (unless you're Judi Dench – see 'Ageing in Hollywood', p.252), anyone who wants to keep working beyond the age of thirty had better find themselves a friendly surgeon pronto. The pressure is worse for women than men, with leading ladies being forced to succumb to lip implants and skin stretches the minute they exit their teenage years, while stalwarts like Robert Redford are still able to play romantic leads despite having faces like saddlebags. But in general, there's a revulsion for the natural process of ageing which means that Hollywood movies are increasingly populated by people who look like Barbie dolls (both male and female), and anyone over the age of twenty-nine starts to think they're living in a real-life remake of *Logan's Run*.

But it's not just people who are the recipients of all-too-pervasive cosmetic surgery. Movies themselves are regularly submitted to a process of cosmetic realignment to disguise not their age but their entire *raison d'être*. Outspoken columnist Molly Ivins may have described Michael Jackson as 'a poor black boy who grew up to be a rich white woman', but such radical transformations are not unusual in the wonderful world of films.

Take the case of the recent British movie *Pride*, one of the very best films of 2014, and a movie which would melt the heart of all but the most cynical and mean-spirited of viewers. Based on a stranger-than-fiction true story, the film (brilliantly scripted by Stephen Beresford) recounts an unlikely alliance between striking Welsh miners and out-and-proud gay Londoners in the darkest era of the Thatcher years. Charting the rise of the inelegantly but accurately named fundraising group 'Lesbians and Gays Support the Miners', this feel-good treat had UK audiences punching the air with joy as its disparate anti-heroes discovered common cause in the battle for equality and justice for all. Having been a Manchester Trot at the time of the Miners' Strike, Dr Kermode remembers well the bonds forged by LGSM, but even those too young to have witnessed those struggles first-hand found that the film hit a nerve. Despite its apparent cultural specificity, it really is a universal story – a tale of ordinary people engaged in a David and Goliath battle against the unthinking machinery of a capitalist state. You don't have to be a badge-wearing leftie to love the movie, you just have to have a beating heart (and if *Pride* doesn't get you going, we refer you to our Cardiology Clinic for a prescription of movies that really will get your heart racing – see p.96).

When *Pride* opened in the UK in September 2014, it was met with almost universally positive reviews. But when it came to the United States, the film's home-viewing distributors decided that

Pride was in need of a fairly radical makeover. They weren't trying to change the film itself, merely to 'reposition' its appearance in a fiercely competitive market place. The way they did this was to erase from their promotion and advertising words which might inform potential viewers that the film had anything at all to do with the potentially thorny issue of homosexuality. In short, they tried to sell a film about 'Lesbians and Gays Support the Miners' by taking out the lesbians and gays, and pretending that it was really just about the miners.

Thus it was that potential DVD viewers in the USA were greeted with a cover image of our heroes on London Bridge, their fists raised in joyous defiance, but their LGSM banner neatly Photoshopped out of the picture, replaced instead by an azure sky and a handsomely erect Big Ben. Turn the DVD over and the blurb on the back described the film as being about 'a group of London-based activists' (rather than lesbian and gay activists) who decide to help out 'a tiny Welsh village'. Apparently, any mention of homosexuality ran the risk of persuading punters to drop the DVD and run screaming from the store in a fit of rampant, homophobic panic.

That such attitudes still exist in the twenty-first century is depressing enough, but the idea that a distributor should attempt to *hide* the gay theme of a film which overtly celebrates a key chapter in gay history is frankly unfathomable. What did they think was going to happen? That bigots who really like miners but have no time for gay people could be conned into taking home a movie which brought images of Imelda Staunton playing with a large pink rubber dildo into their God-fearingly straight homes?

Picture the scene:

'Martha, you going down to that there video store?'

'Sure am, Hank, honey. Want me to pick something up?'

'Absolutely. Something good and wholesome

SEPARATED BY A COMMON LANGUAGE

Different Movie Titles Across the Pond

RELEASED	UK TITLE ➡	US TITLE	JUSTIFICATION
1946	A MATTER OF LIFE AND DEATH	STAIRWAY TO HEAVEN	The studio were advised that you couldn't use the word 'death' in a title in the US. It was released just after the Second World War.
2005	A COCK AND BULL STORY	TRISTRAM SHANDY: A COCK AND BULL STORY	To ensure audiences understood it was a literary adaptation, and not something else altogether!
2009	THE BOAT THAT ROCKED	PIRATE RADIO	The film didn't work well in the UK so was retitled for the US.

RELEASED	US TITLE ➡	UK TITLE	JUSTIFICATION
2007	LIVE FREE OR DIE HARD	DIE HARD 4.0	'Live Free or Die' is the official state motto of New Hampshire. Not well known outside the US. Dr K dubbed the UK release 'Die Hard Four Point-Less'.
2001	JOY RIDE	ROAD KILL	Joy Ride has a different meaning in the UK – stealing cars and a hit for Roxette in 1991.
1950	YOUNG MAN WITH A HORN	YOUNG MAN OF MUSIC	Allegedly because of the rude connotations of 'horn'.
2012	THE AVENGERS	MARVEL AVENGERS ASSEMBLE	In case UK viewers complained about the absence of Patrick Macnee …

that you and I can watch and enjoy together under the shelter of our nice safe heterosexual roof.'

'OK, Hank. You got any suggestions?'

'Your choice, honey. Whatever catches your eye. Just so long as it doesn't feature any of them queer fellas. Maybe something uplifting about decent honest working folk.'

Thirty minutes later:

• 'Hi Hank, I'm home! I got some great gritty grits and the new edition of *Christian Science Monitor – and* I picked up a new British movie about a group of Welsh miners being helped out by some very clean-cut-looking "London-based" activists.'

'Well, that sounds terrific, Martha. As long as it doesn't deal with any of those light-footed types I keep hearing about on Fox News then I'm sure it'll be wonderful. Slip it into the machine.'

Five minutes later:

'Aaaaargh! Martha! You have a committed a terrible crime. You have invited the sodomites into our, until now, entirely heterosexual home!'

'Oh Hank, I'm so sorry! I didn't realise that's what "London-based" meant!'

'Jeez, Martha, have you never heard the word "metrosexual"?'

'Is that what they are, Hank?'

'It sure looks that way, Martha. Fetch me my gun so I can shoot the TV set . . .'

Commenting on the rebranding of *Pride* in the US, director Matthew Warchus agreed that the heterosexual make-over was both 'clumsy' and 'foolish', adding that 'considering that it's called *Pride* I don't know how you'd persuade a potential audience that it's got nothing to do with gays or lesbians'. But he also expressed sympathy for the US marketing department's attempts to 'try to remove any barrier to the widest possible audience and to avoid it being misunderstood as exclusively a gay film'. Emphasising that he didn't want his movie to be merely preaching to the converted, Warchus stressed the importance of attracting a non-liberal audience, whom he was sure the film would win over. The problem, of course, is that in doing so the distributors fell foul of accusations of homophobia – the very thing against which the film itself argues so powerfully.

This idea that you can trick an audience into watching a movie which they'd usually cross the road to avoid is at the root of much modern cinematic cosmetic surgery. Take the example of the bloated sci-fi epic *John Carter* (2012), adapted from the writings of genre king Edgar Rice Burroughs. Largely based on the book *A Princess of Mars*, Andrew Stanton's film was originally entitled *John Carter of Mars*, making clear that most of the action takes place . . . on Mars! However, as the production progressed and the budget spiralled, wonks at Disney started to worry about having so much money invested in a science fiction movie, a genre which (their number crunchers insisted) was no longer popular with audiences. Noticing that the 2011 animated feature *Mars Needs Moms* had been a total bomb, the studio's head of marketing, M.T. Carney, decided that it would be much better to leave any references to sci-fi in general and Mars in particular out of the movie's publicity. This despite the fact that the studio had just spent $263 million making what was (*whichever* way you looked at it) a science fiction film set on Mars.

According to Andrew Stanton, the marketing department were certain that by retitling the movie *John Carter* (arguably the most boring film title in the history of cinema), they would capture the attention of moviegoers eager to find out who this John Carter guy was without scaring them off with talk of Mars. In effect, they could con punters who don't like science fiction, or Mars, into seeing a film about both, simply by shortening their original title. Imagine the howls of derision when, about twenty minutes into the film, Mr Carter hides in a cave in Arizona only to be suddenly and mysteriously transported . . . to Mars, where he spends the rest of the movie!

Perhaps unsurprisingly, this ruse failed. In May 2012, Disney announced that its dismal quarterly figures in which 'operating income decreased $161 million to a loss of $84 million' were due largely to 'the performance of *John Carter*', a performance which seemed to demonstrate that no amount of cosmetic surgery could have made the movie appealing to audiences.

Such jiggery-pokery is nothing new. Early trailers for Tim Burton's *Sweeney Todd* worked very hard to sell the movie as a stylish gothic revenge drama full of deranged passion, and featuring Johnny Depp wielding a bloody cut-throat razor. What those trailers were notably lacking was any singing, a key element of *Sweeney Todd* which is, of course, a musical. Adapted from Stephen Sondheim and Hugh Wheeler's Tony Award-winning stage hit, *Sweeney Todd* tells its tale of murder and malice through the medium of song. But once again, some marketing whizz-kid decided that it would be better to withhold that salient detail from the audience, convinced that once punters had paid to see the movie they'd just get used to the fact that everyone kept bursting into song. In fact, they did no such thing; reports of enraged responses to the all-singing *Sweeney Todd* made national headlines in the UK. A number of complaints were lodged by punters who resented being lured into the cinema under 'false pretences', and who argued that the distributors had deliberately misrepresented their product by producing a trailer which pretended that this was anything but a musical.

Official complaints about misleading trailers are becoming increasingly common. In 2011, Michigan resident Sarah Deming attempted to sue both the distributors and exhibitors of Nicolas Winding Refn's bleakly stylish existential thriller *Drive* for selling the movie in a manner which suggested that it was very much in the vein of the inexplicably successful *Fast and Furious* series.

It wasn't. Rather than endless shots of glamorous muscle cars tearing up the highways to testosterone-pumping effect, *Drive* spent much of its moody, melancholic running time with low-key, character-building scenes which establish a growing relationship between Ryan Gosling's secretive stunt driver and Carey Mulligan's lonely mother. Yes, there *are* some action sequences (the heist scenes are tense and expertly choreographed) but the film's most notorious scene finds Gosling stomping an adversary's head to a bloody pulp in an elevator – not quite the kind of explosive action for which Ms Deming was hoping.

The main problem for Ms Deming was insufficient car activity. In her suit, filed at the Sixth Judicial Court in Oakland, she complained that *Drive* 'bore very little similarity to a chase, or race action film . . . having very little driving in the motion picture'. Clearly she should have been referred to the Movie Doctors' A & E, where there's enough car chases to satisfy any petrolhead – see p.11. Her grievances didn't end there, however. Having failed to fulfil her automotive desires, *Drive* further invoked Ms Deming's ire because it was (she claimed) jam-packed with 'extreme, gratuitous, dehumanising racism directed at members of the Jewish faith, and thereby promoted criminal violence against members of the Jewish faith'. Ms Deming hoped to turn her complaint into a class action suit which would enable other stateside punters to join in should they find themselves unexpectedly watching a movie which did not adequately fulfil the remit of its publicity.

In response, the cinema in question pointed out that it would have been happy to refund the cost of the ticket had Ms Deming taken her complaint directly to them, something which is apparently becoming more and more commonplace in the modern movie marketplace.

Early in 2014, a US cinema showing *The Wolf of Wall Street* went to the extraordinary lengths of placing a large placard in the foyer which read:

SO SUE ME

Hollywood Legal Peculiarities

BEN HUR *(1907)*

Copyright infringement. The first case of a movie being sued for adapting a story without buying the rights. Lawsuit upheld, which established the precedent that all film companies had to secure the film rights to a story before commissioning a screenplay.

THE COOGAN ACT *(1939)*

Aka 'The California Child Actors Bill'. Named after child actor Jackie Coogan who starred in films such as Chaplin's 1921 classic *The Kid*, but who discovered upon reaching adulthood that his parents had spent all the money he earned.

LUXO JNR *(1986)*

Lamp copyright infringement. A Norwegian lamp manufacturer claimed that the Pixar lamp (first featured in *Luxo Jnr*) violated their trademarks. Pixar settled out of court.

SUPERSTAR: THE KAREN CARPENTER STORY *(1987)*

Richard Carpenter sued the young director Todd Haynes claiming that the rights to use the Carpenters' songs were never acquired (he wasn't crazy about him and his sister being portrayed by Barbie and Ken dolls either). The case was upheld, and all prints of the movie were removed from circulation – although last time we looked the whole thing was on YouTube. Ha!

BORAT *(2006)*

Multiple lawsuits. A Romanian village sued because it portrayed them as 'stupid and incestuous'; frat boys sued for defamation; an etiquette coach from Alabama and a driving instructor from Maryland all complained about their portrayal in the film. All suits unsuccessful.

AVATAR *(2009)*

Fantasy plant design. The graphic artist Roger Dean claimed that fourteen of his paintings had been copied by director James Cameron in his design of the planet Pandora. Case dismissed.

THE HANGOVER PART II *(2011)*

Tattoo copyright infringement brought by Missouri tattoo artist S. Victor Whitmill, claiming that one of his designs was used without permission. And it was Mike Tyson's tattoo at that. Settled out of court.

TED *(2012)*

A company called Bengal Mangle Productions claimed that the character 'Ted' was an unlawful copy of their own creation ('Charlie') who appeared in the internet series *Charlie the Abusive Teddy*. Dismissed.

CAPTAIN PHILLIPS *(2013)*

The real ship's crew claimed that the captain deliberately took the ship into known pirate waters to save time and money. Lawsuit still under discussion.

THERE ARE NO REFUNDS FOR THE WOLF OF WALL STREET

Some are offended by language and explicit scenes in the film but Mr Scorsese is an auteur and his work is rated brilliant by academic bastions of thought

Which is basically a polite way of saying, 'Hey, people who are *way* smarter than you think this film is really clever, so don't come pissing and moaning to us just because you had to watch Jonah Hill waving a rubber willy around on screen. OK?'

Frankly, how anybody could go to see *The Wolf of Wall Street* without expecting to be drenched from head to foot in salacious sleaze is beyond me. The film is based on the real-life memoir of loathsome scoundrel Jordan Belfort, a man who achieved notoriety (and a prison sentence) by ripping off hard-working Americans so that he could bury himself in hookers and cocaine, and whose entire life seems to have been dedicated to masturbatory self-aggrandisement on a scale which would make a Roman emperor blush. This was made abundantly clear both in the publicity for the film and also in the reviews which attended its release; indeed, for many it was a major selling point. As for Scorsese, he may have won a Best Director Oscar for the relatively tame 2006 thriller *The Departed*, but anyone familiar with the violent climax of *Taxi Driver* (1976), the religious controversy of *The Last Temptation of Christ* (1988) or the staggering drug consumption of *Goodfellas* (1990) would have been hard pressed to argue that they weren't prepared for *The Wolf of Wall Street.* Yet still the complaints rolled in.

In the end, the Movie Doctors are forced to conclude that anyone who manages to be 'tricked' into seeing a film under false pretences is guilty of failing to do their homework. In an age in

THERE ARE NO REFUNDS FOR THE WOLF OF WALL STREET

Some are offended by language and explicit scenes in the film but Mr Scorsese is an auteur and his work is rated brilliant by academic bastions of thought

which the internet allows everyone at the touch of a button not only to discover all the salient facts about what's *in* a movie, but also to read the entire script before a single scene has been shot (and probably to download a pirated copy of the finished movie before it ever makes it into cinemas), the 'I didn't know what I was getting' line really doesn't wash.

More importantly, the fine art of misrepresenting movies is a grand tradition which is as old as cinema itself, and anyone getting suckered in has no one but themselves to blame. Roger Corman once told budding director Joe Dante (who cut his teeth editing promos for Corman flicks) to 'jazz up' a particularly boring trailer. Dante responded by simply splicing in a shot of an exploding helicopter, which Corman found improved the trailer hugely. On the subject of whether this addition was ethical, Corman simply observed, 'There is no law that says that everything in the trailer has to be in the film!' In the wake of which, people really should be a little more savvy about how movies are marketed to maximise their audiences. Is it really possible to feel sympathy for those European audiences who were allegedly lured into watching Steve

McQueen's brilliant *12 Years a Slave* (2013) on the basis of a massive portrait of Brad Pitt, one of the film's producers, whose on-screen appearance can best be described as fleeting? How hard can it be to do a Google search which will inform you that the star of the film is actually Chiwetel Ejiofor, and the movie is based (very faithfully) on the memoir of Solomon Northup, who is unlikely to be played by the blond-haired, blue-eyed Mr Pitt?

Back in the eighties, video viewers were duped into renting *Savage Island* (1985) on the strength of cover artwork which featured *Exorcist* star Linda Blair in a revealing outfit, brandishing a machine gun in a tropical hell – despite the fact that Ms Blair is hardly in the movie, remains thoroughly clothed throughout and never goes anywhere near an island, savage or otherwise. Turns out Blair had simply been hired for ten minutes of wraparound footage to repackage some misbegotten Italian exploitation fare, and her star billing was nothing but a cheap trick. Did anyone sue? Did they heck as like. When it comes to marketing movies, the Movie Doctors conclude that anyone who takes marketing literally deserves everything they get.

GERIATRICS

Unlike in Hollywood, in our Geriatric Clinic actors of more **advanced years** are treated with the deference and respect they deserve. So here you'll find some movies to ease the transition into the more serene phase of your life, a nudge-nudge look at those actors who may have been trying to **hang on to youth** a bit too long and an examination of 'old age' as portrayed in the movies. We said, 'AN EXAMINATION OF "OLD AGE!" AS PORTRAYED IN THE MOVIES!'

SILVER SCREENINGS
How the Movies Can Help the Ageing

You might feel that this area of our clinic is not for you. But you'd be wrong. Science tells us that, I'm afraid, you may well have peaked already. By the time you've reached your late twenties you are already in decline. You may well still be developing qualities you have been noticeably lacking in so far – wisdom, grace and sobriety, for example – but physically? It's all heading south and you know it.

THE MOVIE DOCTORS' GERIATRIC CHECKLIST

* Do you walk down the stairs and feel all of you moving?
* Do you watch a movie and the thing you take in first from a kitchen scene is how much nicer the appliances are than yours?
* Do you notice you are beginning to look like your dad? Or mum? Or, more terrifyingly, a strange amalgam of them both?

If you answered yes to any of the above, you are getting old. From now on the movies are a whole different ball game.

Those 'anarchic' frat-boy comedies will now start to really annoy you. The crazy young things hanging out after school and looking for adventure seem like irresponsible subversives who need stricter parental controls. The 'dancing' scenes at parties seem unbelievably exhausting. This is the ageing process in action, and you may find the cinema a cruel mistress.

If you are an actor, the future holds a combination of roles which have eluded you until now: tramps, witches, matriarchs, patriarchs, bishops, God, dead people on slabs, Father Christmases, old hags, wicked stepmothers etc. For the cinemagoer, whole new worlds are also opening up and surprising emotions will take hold. 'What's that you say? Another "gritty" drama where the kid gets kidnapped and the bleak landscape is a parable for the alienation forced on us by globalisation? With Liam Neeson? No, thanks.' You get the picture.

But all is not lost. Fortunately a common side effect of getting older is finding yourself less poor (if this isn't you, see 'Movies for Wastrels' below). This means your money gives you power. And if the film industry want you to spend your cash on their popcorn – and they really, really do – they will want to make movies that appeal to you, the ageing film fan. Here comes the Movie Doctors' selection of encouraging, supportive movies for the silver screeners.

DRIVING MISS DAISY *(1989)*

Not just a film for the anxious and stressed (see p.80). Here we take inspiration from Miss Daisy herself – Jessica Tandy. Although she had been winning theatrical plaudits since 1932, it wasn't until she was eighty that she delivered what was widely considered to be her greatest performance. Roger Ebert called it 'one of the most complete portraits of the stages of old age I have ever seen in a film'.

This is encouragement on a grand scale. Imagine being eighty and at the top of your game. You might not be able to quaff a gallon of vodka like you used to – and nowadays actually prefer a small sweet sherry, if you're asking – but you can still win your equivalent of Best Actress at the Academy Awards. It is the Movie Doctors' belief that your best is yet to come (also, you haven't exactly done much of note so far).

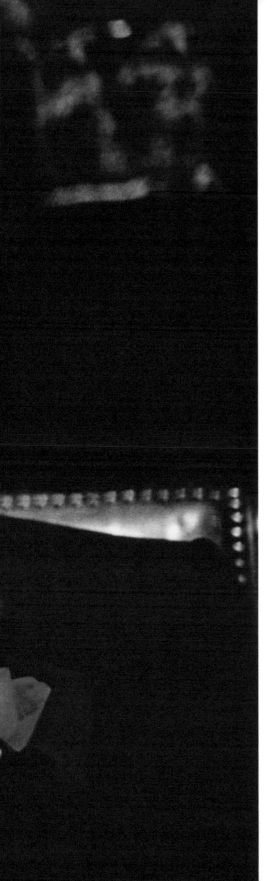

THE GODFATHER *(1972)*

Growing old can be stressful. You worry. You're not looking your best any more – a little bit puffy around the face and maybe your jaw barely moves when you speak. In fact you tend to whisper not talk these days, it seems easier. And more menacing. You look at your children and you wonder whether they're up to anything much. You've done your best, set them a good example. You got involved in community projects, encouraged loyalty (you're *especially* good at that) and made generous payments to worthy causes. You've made sacrifices but still you worry.

Who can take over the family business and run it properly? You've always had standards but they are looked down on now, derided as 'old fashioned'. Your eldest is a bit of a hothead – he might go shooting his mouth off and upset customers and competitors (and the police). Your favourite son is young and fresh-faced (for now, the scars come later) but he shows little interest in the old ways. And then there are the drugs. You've told them all you won't be dealing. You've been OK with the prostitution, revenge, greed, treachery, random violence and murder, but you know where to draw the line. You have standards. Here is a movie that cares for your family as much as you do. It is the cinematic equivalent of that Michael Parkinson insurance ad but without the free pen. (Travel and lifestyle advice NB: avoid small Italian restaurants, massages, revolving doors, steps, hospitals, bridges, prostitutes, churches, elevators and Sicily.)

COCOON *(1985)*

Ron Howard's double Oscar winner might seem a shoo-in – any film that lists the Sunny Shores Rest Home and St Petersburg Shuffleboard club as two of its key shooting locations has to be a prime candidate for the silver-screener list. Well, maybe. Here we have a bunch of old folk (Don Ameche, Wilford Brimley, Jessica Tandy again) in an old folk's home doing old folk things. One of these is breaking into the house next door because it has an indoor pool. It's free, it's warm and there are no irritating children bombing, petting or smoking. But the house – wouldn't you know it? – has been rented by some friendly aliens in human form. They want the pool to house their cocoons – each one contains another powdered alien waiting for release – and while they are stewing, these pods emit a life force. This proves to be quite helpful to the trespassing veterans, as they become rejuvenated – they climb trees, get healed of cancer and have sex in the water.

These aliens turn out to be amongst the most genial in the universe (we're guessing here) as they offer to take thirty residents back with them to their home planet of Antarea. This is an attractive offer, as apparently there they will not get ill, die or get beaten up by the staff.

This is a controversial choice, we admit, as it really is a film about cheating old age rather than running with it and seeing what happens. But we include it here so that the next time you're swimming and the pool feels a little over-warm, you could convince yourself it's Antarean life force cocoon juice, not someone else's urine.

A CHRISTMAS CAROL *(1951)*

It was, of course, the estimable Alan Parsons Project who sang of the joys of being 'Old and Wise' in 1982. It told of a time in the future when your sadness will be gone and bitter words will mean little. And then let's recall Uriah Heep's 'Wise Man' which, through hilariously clunky, preposterous, fourth-form-style poetry, associates wisdom with advanced years. Grey hairs = Solomon. Normal hair = Prince Andrew.

We may well think that we too show better judgement now than we did in our youth; we make better choices, have better taste, eat fewer crisps. But sadly some of us have gone astray: made bad choices, taken the wrong path, eaten too much Monster Munch. Similarly, Ebenezer Scrooge is not in a good place (obviously most of Dickensian London is 'not a good place', but bear with us).

Salvation can always be at hand. You could turn to *The Muppet Christmas Carol* (1992) and watch Michael Caine take up the role of the most famous miser in history. Or maybe *Scrooged* (1988), where we can all boo and hiss at Bill Murray. Even Disney's Scrooge McDuck has his supporters. But really this story of geriatric redemption is best viewed with Alastair Sim in the title role.

This is the version that feels like 'the original', even if that title actually goes to the 1901 *Scrooge or Marley's Ghost* from director W.R. Booth, who tells the whole story in five minutes. Audiences in the 1950s might have felt slightly short-changed if that was all they got here, so director Brian Desmond Hurst's film clocks in at a still brief eighty-five minutes.

There are many reasons that we have prescribed this adaptation. You get Michael Hordern, later to become the voice of Paddington, as Jacob Marley. There's Patrick Macnee, destined for *The Avengers* (unassembled) as the younger Marley, and even George 'Arthur Daley' Cole as the younger Scrooge. But primarily it is for Alastair Sim. He shows us, better than all his illustrious rivals, that we can still find giddy excitement in realising that we have actually been wrong about everything.

ARSENIC AND OLD LACE *(1944)*

Pensions are a complicated area and, for many, extremely off-putting. How to negotiate the ridiculous piles of booklets that promise you a relaxed, carefree retirement? You may well navigate their pages, sign their forms (ageing visibly in the process) and end up with an annual income of £36.50. How much easier to spend your latter years murdering people, then. It's quick, easy and terrific fun. All you need to take part is a graveyard that provides you with elderberries, some arsenic from your dad's old chemistry set and the ability to look like a sweet, innocent old maid.

The Scrooge path of finding childish joy in repentance is not for everyone, so turning to serious crime late in life is a valid alternative lifestyle choice. Frank Capra filmed this with Josephine Hull and

Jean Adair as the cheery killers Aunt Abby and Aunt Martha. They are in cahoots with a crazed nephew who takes the bodies to the cellar, and it is up to another nephew, Cary Grant, to piece together what is happening. Hanging over anyone who messes up (apart from the electric chair) is the threat of finishing your days at the Happydale Sanatorium. We never quite see what life is like there, but we guess it won't have an indoor pool with life-giving aliens hiding in pods.

The hidden subtext here is beware home brewers. Anyone who has enough time to make alcohol which everyone knows will be inferior to and more expensive than the shop-bought alternative is up to no good.

HOW OLD?!

Discrepancies Between Age of Actor and Age of Character

ACTOR	CHARACTER	FILM
Leslie Caron	GIGI	GIGI 1958
Audrey Hepburn	HOLLY GOLIGHTLY	BREAKFAST AT TIFFANY'S 1961
Gary Burghoff	CORPORAL WALTER EUGUENCE O'REILLY	MASH 1970
Susannah York	JANE EYRE	JANE EYRE 1970
Malcolm McDowell	ALEX	A CLOCKWORK ORANGE 1971
Sissy Spacek	CARRIE	CARRIE 1976
Stockard Channing	BETTY RIZZO	GREASE 1978
Olivia Newton-John	SANDY	GREASE 1978
Barbra Streisand	YENTL	YENTL 1983
Michael J. Fox	MARTY MCFLY	BACK TO THE FUTURE PART III 19
Stacey Dash	DIONNE	CLUELESS 1995
Emma Thompson	ELINOR DASHWOOD	SENSE AND SENSIBILITY 1995

CHAR. AGE	ACTUAL AGE	DIFFERENCE
15	26	11
18	32	14
18	26	8
18	31	13
17	28	11
17	26	9
17	34	17
18	29	11
26	41	15
17	29	12
17	28	11
27	35	8

AGEING IN HOLLYWOOD

Doctors in Discussion

Dr Kermode: You know Dame Judi didn't get her first Oscar nomination until she was sixty-four – in *Mrs Brown* – and she is now one of the most nominated actors of all time?

Dr Mayo: What's your point?

Dr K: I think that perhaps, just perhaps, Hollywood is starting to push beyond that terrible ceiling that has restricted actors with a more 'mature' profile. It used to be the case, as they say in *The First Wives Club*, that there were only three roles for women in Hollywood – babe, district attorney and *Driving Miss Daisy*.

Dr M: And do you think the success of movies like *The Best Exotic Marigold Hotel* and *The King's Speech* are proving that the silver-pound audience is worth catering for?

Dr K: You know they put screenings on specifically for the older crowd?

Dr M: What used to be called the blue-rinse brigade.

Dr K: Yes, you get free tea and biscuits and a cut-price movie screening – and believe me, there are riots if the tea and biscuits run out. I know – I've started a few.

Dr M: I presume by riots you mean 'mild protestations and harrumphing in the aisles'.

Dr K: Well yes, obviously they're not ripping up the seats and throwing them at the screen like they did[n't] when they saw *Blackboard Jungle* for the first time in 1955. But my point is that both the more mature audience and the stars are getting a better deal these days.

Dr M: That's handy as we, the Movie Doctors, are approaching Peak Maturity with as much speed as our reluctant knees can muster.

Dr K: But it's a relatively modern idea that the cinema is for the 'young'. It didn't used to be the case – movies used to cater for audiences of all ages. The first *Pink Panther* movie in 1963 had all the elements of an old-fashioned variety show. There was a cartoon at the beginning for the kids, a bit of action and adventure for the grown-ups, and even a musical number for those who would rather have been at the theatre. It was only with television that the cinema audience got broken up by Hollywood into these depressing age demographics: 2–8; 8–12; 12–15; 15–21; 21–30 and then everyone else. After 30, you're all just old!

Dr M: And the movies have only recently started to cater again for the silver-pound market. To be fair though, I think your tastes change as you get older. It's like the fairground. I remember when I was a teenager I'd go for the biggest dipper, the whirliest waltzer and go again and again. Now if I so much as look at one, I think, 'No, that's just going to make me feel sick,' and move along to show off my prowess at hooking a plastic duck.

Dr K: You're right. I'd still defend the right of horror fans to watch *The Last House on the Left* uncut, but my desire to see it again is less now than it was when I was sixteen or seventeen. You definitely change in terms of what you want from a movie.

Dr M: And given that the world is often a savage place, my desire to see a savage movie is certainly diminished.

Dr K: I do remember watching *The Human Centipede 2* thinking I'm just too old to have to do this.

Dr M: I think you are, too. In fact no one is the right age to go through that ordeal.

TRANSPLANTS

On occasions **drastic movie surgery** is required to **save face** and **make money**. An actor and a role might seem like a **match made in heaven** – until you start filming. Sometimes it's an **honest mistake**, not in the least motivated by recent big box office success. Other times you just have to say, *'What were they thinking?'*

FULL FACE (AND BODY) TRANSPLANTS

A Clinical Examination

'I don't know what I hate wearing worse; your face or your body . . .' In John Woo's rip-roaring 1997 thriller *Face/Off*, a bizarre surgical procedure is employed to swap the faces of 'freelance terrorist' Castor Troy and FBI agent Sean Archer, played respectively by Nic Cage and John Travolta. The procedure is described as 'experimental' but apparently produces results so seamless that no one can tell the difference between the real and the 'face-swapped' patients.

Despite recent advances in the real-world practice of facial transplants, the Movie Doctors can report that 'the *Face/Off* machine' of which Jason Statham speaks so hilariously in *Spy* (2015) is still a work of fiction. Thus, when making his rip-roaring identity-swap movie, it wasn't actually possible for John Woo to rip the faces off his leading men and then have them neatly transplanted onto each other's bodies (Hitchcock may have famously said that 'all actors should be treated like cattle' but even he drew the line at surgical intervention). Instead, it's left to the performers to reproduce the necessary medical illusion through thespian skills alone, cavorting around the screen pretending to be each other . . . pretending to be each other. So, John Travolta pretends to be Nic Cage pretending to be John Travolta, while Nic Cage pretends to be John Travolta pretending to be Nic Cage. And they do it rather well.

It's dizzying, head-spinning stuff which left critics breathless, and not a little confused. Writing about the quirky spin which Cage (who had recently starred in such action vehicles as 1996's *The Rock* and 1997's *Con Air*) brings to his role, American critic Roger Ebert wrote that 'when he first sees Travolta's daughter, he [Cage] quips "The plot thickens". But of course it is Travolta who sees Travolta's teenage daughter, because it is Travolta playing the Cage character . . . All through the movie, you find yourself reinterpreting every scene as you realize the "other" character is "really" playing it.'

Face/Off screenwriters Mike Werb and Michael Colleary cited both the classic 1949 Jimmy Cagney gangster flick *White Heat* and the 1966 face-swap weirdie *Seconds* as inspirations for their modern-day thriller which went on to become both a critical and box office hit. It's easy to see a genetic link with *Seconds*, in which a disconsolate character originally played by John Randolph consents to extensive facial surgery in order to start a new life, and emerges from the operating table in the reborn form of handsome Rock Hudson. But there's also a strong hint of Georges Franju's French shocker *Les Yeux Sans Visage/Eyes Without a Face*, a stunning black and white nightmare from 1960 in which an increasingly deranged doctor attempts to find a new face for the daughter whose own features have been horribly disfigured. Wracked with guilt, Pierre Brasseur's Dr Génessier kidnaps and performs surgery upon young women whose flawless faces he steals. Meanwhile his daughter, played with unforgettably haunted eyes by Edith Scob, walks the lonely corridors of their house, her features obscured by an eerie white mask which would itself provide inspiration for John Carpenter's epochal *Halloween* (1978). (It also prompted Billy Idol to co-write the soft rock ballad 'Eyes Without a Face', although the less said about that the better . . .)

If you've never seen *Les Yeux Sans Visage*, then the Movie Doctors prescribe a screening (it's recently been re-released on Blu-ray and DVD by the BFI) as soon as possible. This really is one of the ten greatest movies of all time, not least because its facial-transplant sequences are some of the most genuinely disturbing scenes ever filmed. When the movie played at the Edinburgh Film Festival in 1960, seven audience members were reported to have fainted, prompting Franju to remark sarcastically, 'Now I know why Scotsmen wear skirts.' Yet more importantly, from the Movie Doctors' point of view, the film perfectly illustrates our long-standing fascination with the strange process of replacing one person's face with another – a process which is utterly commonplace when it comes to making movies.

The script for *Face/Off* had been doing the rounds for several years before John Woo finally took it into production, and during those years a number of actors were mooted as possible contenders for the lead roles. Having recently scored a hit in 1993 with *Hard Target*, Woo toyed with the notion of working again with 'the muscles from Brussels', Jean-Claude Van Damme. Michael Douglas (who wound up with an executive producer credit) also looked like a possible candidate. By the time Cage and Travolta signed on, their famous faces were merely the latest in a long line of casting mug shots – the faces that finally fit.

This process of disparate actors dropping in and out of the frame for any particular movie is business as usual in Hollywood, as *Face/Off* star John Travolta knows all too well. Indeed, for years Travolta and Richard Gere appeared to be engaged in some peculiar real-life face-swap soap, with Travolta turning down a string of roles upon which Gere would effectively build his career. Bill in Terrence Malick's *Days of Heaven* (1978); Julian Kaye in Paul Schrader's *American Gigolo* (1980); Zack Mayo in Taylor Hackford's *An Officer and a Gentleman* (1982); Billy Flynn in Rob Marshall's 2002 Best Picture winner *Chicago* – all these parts were at one time earmarked for Travolta, but eventually wound up putting a blinky smile on Gere's face. It has been suggested that if Travolta had made better career choices, Gere would never have become a movie star, and looking at the list of hand-me-down hits which Gere inherited from Mr Saturday Night Fever himself, it's hard to disagree.

Travolta also offered an inadvertent helping hand to Tom Hanks by passing on projects like *Splash* (1984) and *Forrest Gump* (1994), the latter of which earned Hanks his first Oscar statuette, causing Travolta to admit that turning the film down had been a mistake. As for Hanks, the list of projects for which *his* face was originally in the frame includes *Field of Dreams* (1989), *The Shawshank Redemption* (1994) and *Jerry Maguire* (1996), on the last of which he commented: 'I think you look at it now and it couldn't have been anybody other than Tom Cruise.' (In a peculiar twist of fate, a copy of the *Jerry Maguire* script was at one stage accidentally sent to Hugh Grant. 'I rang up my agent,' Grant recalled, 'and said, "There must be some mistake because you sent me a good script . . ."')

Other famous pre-production face transplants include Harrison Ford being parachuted into

1981's *Raiders of the Lost Ark* after original choice Tom Selleck proved unavailable because of his commitment to the ongoing TV series *Magnum P.I.*, and Sean Connery saying no to Gandalf in Peter Jackson's *Lord of the Rings* movies because he hadn't read the Tolkien books and didn't understand 'Bobbits'. In the late eighties Bob Hoskins was reportedly paid £20,000 *not* to play Al Capone in Brian De Palma's crime thriller *The Untouchables* (1987) after the director managed to persuade Robert De Niro to take the role instead. 'I phoned him up,' Hoskins remembered after receiving the cheque in the post, 'and said, "Brian, if you've ever got any films you don't want me in, son, you just give me a call!"'

More peculiar, however, are the stories of actors being replaced once the cameras have started rolling – a procedure which inevitably comes with a good deal of trauma, after which it can take several years for the scars to heal. Take the case of *The Wizard of Oz* (1939), a timeless classic which has continued to be embraced by new generations of viewers thanks to cinema revivals and emergent home-viewing formats. Many (if not most) viewers know *The Wizard of Oz* (1939) off by heart, every frame of its weird phantasmagorical magic burned deep into their hearts. Yet, as with so many classic movies, the face of that film could easily have been very different. For a while, Shirley Temple was being lined up for the key role of Dorothy, cheekily telling news reporters 'There's no place like home!' before leaving Judy Garland to don the red slippers. Both Ed Wynn and W.C. Fields were tentatively cast as the Wizard, but reported disputes over money and prominence ultimately left the way clear for contract player Frank Morgan to pull the levers behind the curtain. Meanwhile Gale Sondergaard pulled out of a commitment to play the Wicked Witch of the West and was replaced by Margaret Hamilton just days before the cameras turned.

Most alarmingly, the role of the Tin Man was originally essayed by Buddy Ebsen, who had to

THE ONES THAT GOT AWAY

Directors and the Movies They Didn't Direct

SERGIO LEONE found directing *The Godfather* to be an offer he *could* refuse; he wanted to work on *Once Upon a Time in America*.

DAVID LYNCH was asked by George Lucas if he would helm *Star Wars Episode VI: Return of the Jedi* but instead he made *Dune*.

QUENTIN TARANTINO was offered both *Speed* and *Men in Black*. Apparently.

JAMES CAMERON terminated any involvement in *Terminator 3: Rise of the Machines*.

TERRY GILLIAM was brave enough to decline Mel Gibson's request to direct *Braveheart*.

DANNY BOYLE nixed *Alien: Resurrection* but made the bizarre short *Alien Love Triangle*.

GUILLERMO DEL TORO was 'too busy' to consider helming *Star Wars Episode VII: The Force Awakens*. He also walked away from the *Hobbit* movies.

DAVID CRONENBERG turned down *Basic Instinct 2* (although he toyed with the script).

STANLEY KUBRICK turned down *The Exorcist*, but went on to make *The Shining*.

JOHN BOORMAN turned down *The Exorcist* but went on to make *Exorcist II: The Heretic*

be dropped ten days into shooting following a near-critical reaction to his character's aluminium powder make-up. Ebsen had first been signed up to play the Scarecrow, but switched with Ray Bolger, who had been longing to have his head stuffed with straw ever since he saw Fred Stone play the part on stage in 1902. Desperate for the role, Bolger persuaded producer Mervyn LeRoy to recast him, leaving Ebsen to go to town on the equally prestigious Tin Man part. But during the second week of filming, Ebsen's lungs became coated in aluminium-powder and the actor had to be hospitalised. When Jack Haley was brought in to fill Ebsen's shoes, he fondly imagined that his predecessor had simply been fired, since no one told him that the original Tin Man had in fact been poisoned by the role! As for Margaret Hamilton, she spent several weeks in hospital after being burned during the Wicked Witch's explosive exit from Munchkinland, although unlike Ebsen, her on-set injuries didn't cost her the role.

Elsewhere, actors have been removed and replaced for altogether less fiery reasons. Woody Allen shot the Chekhov-inspired 1987 drama *September* with a cast which originally included Sam Shepard, Maureen O'Sullivan and Charles Durning, then decided he didn't like it and went back to reshoot the whole thing with Sam Waterston, Elaine Stritch and Denholm Elliott. (When asked what he thought of the finished film, Allen stated that he'd like to go back again and have one more crack at it.) Harvey Keitel famously began work on Francis Ford Coppola's *Apocalypse Now* back in 1976 having landed the starring role of Willard, the narrator who leads us into a cinematic heart of darkness in search of Marlon Brando's deranged Colonel Kurtz. Coppola had first tried to persuade Steve McQueen to take the part, but the star didn't want to work on any project which would involve him being away from America for a substantial period (he turned down the lead role in William Friedkin's *Sorcerer* (1977) for the same reason). Al Pacino, with whom Coppola had worked on *The Godfather 1 & 2*, was similarly unhappy about the prospect of decamping to the Philippines, particularly since Coppola seemed set on making the kind of epic which could easily overrun its schedule (principal photography ended up sprawling from March 1976 to May 1977). In the end, Coppola settled for Keitel because he'd liked his work in *Mean Streets* (1973), although it was widely known that he really wanted Martin Sheen for the role and was settling for a second (or perhaps third) choice. Out in the jungle, Keitel tried to give Coppola what he wanted, but it soon became clear that things just weren't working out. So, having viewed the rushes and been thoroughly disappointed with the outcome, Coppola dropped Keitel and headed back to Hollywood, determined to get Martin Sheen in the picture.

'The nature of Willard in *Apocalypse Now* is that he is the eyes through which you watch the events,' editor Walter Murch would later explain. 'And on a simple biological level, Martin Sheen has very big eyes that look at the world, and Harvey Keitel has very narrow eyes.' Thus, according to Murch, this wasn't so much a case of a face transplant as an eye transplant, Keitel losing out to Sheen simply because his peepers were the wrong shape. (Murch also claims that Keitel can in fact be glimpsed in the finished *Apocalypse Now*, in a helicopter shot as the boat leaves the dock near the beginning of the film: 'It's such a long shot you can't tell, but he is in the film!')

Years later (and probably as a direct result of what happened on *Apocalypse Now*) Keitel would find himself the subject of an utterly apocryphal story about getting fired from Stanley Kubrick's naff 1999 erotic thriller *Eyes Wide Shut*, the director's final film. Having been cast in the role of Victor Ziegler, Keitel left mid-shoot, provoking rumours that he had been removed for over-exerting himself during a sex scene with Nicole Kidman. The rumour was nothing but mischief (no such sequence ever existed in the script, let alone the film) but such was its persistence that Keitel found himself having to publicly deny it. When asked about the stories by writer Jason Matloff, the actor replied, 'Nonsense, utter nonsense. When Kubrick stopped the movie, they wanted me to wait for months without getting paid, which I couldn't do.' As a result Keitel quit, meaning that all his scenes had to be reshot, with film-maker Sydney Pollack stepping in to take over the role of Ziegler. 'What an insult,' Keitel joked, 'not only was I replaced, I was replaced by a director!'

Considering how things worked out on both *Apocalypse Now* and *Eyes Wide Shut*, Keitel would probably have welcomed the opportunity to jump into a souped-up DeLorean and travel back in time to the period before he signed on to make either movie. The same would probably be true of poor old Eric Stoltz, who had been shooting *Back to the Future* for a full five weeks before director Robert Zemeckis decided that Marty McFly really needed a whole new face. Having initially set their sights on Michael J. Fox, the film-makers reluctantly sought an alternative because their first choice couldn't get time off from shooting the *Family Ties* TV series.

With Fox out of the picture, and a start date looming, the producers opted for Stoltz, who had recently completed work on Peter Bogdanovich's Oscar-winning *Mask*. Although *Mask* wouldn't open in theatres until March 1985, Zemeckis knew that Stoltz's portrayal of a young man with craniodiaphyseal dysplasia (or 'lionitis') was something very special. Despite having large sections of his face and head obscured with complex prosthetics, Stoltz had brought warmth, wit and charm to the role of Roy 'Rocky' Dennis, for which he would receive a well-deserved Golden Globe nomination. Clearly a rising star, Stoltz seemed more than able to handle Zemeckis's Freudian fantasy about a school kid who travels back in time and finds himself bizarrely embroiled in his mum and dad's faltering first dates.

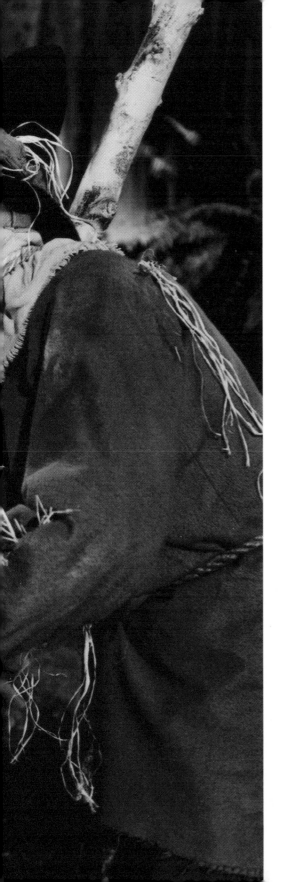

With a projected budget of $14 million, *Back to the Future* was by no means an extravagant affair; indeed, an original ending involving an atomic explosion in the Nevada desert had been ditched because it was deemed too costly. But by the end of the first month of filming, Zemeckis was becoming so alarmed by the lack of laughs in the material he had shot that money became the least of his worries. In a state of growing despair, Zemeckis showed the footage to executive producer Steven Spielberg, who agreed that it wasn't anything like as funny as it needed to be. Drastic action was required. And so, despite the fact that it would add another $3 million to the already overstretched budget, the film-makers decided to ditch their leading man and start again from scratch with their original first choice, Michael J. Fox.

Watching interview footage of Spielberg, Zemeckis and co-writer Bob Gale recalling the moment they decided to cut their losses and amputate Stoltz from the production, it's clear that this operation was as painful for them as it was for the young actor. In fact Stoltz himself had been having doubts about his suitability for the role, and had apparently confided in Bogdanovich that he didn't think he was right for the picture. Nevertheless, being fired from a movie that far into production is a big deal which can cause irreparable damage to a performer's reputational health. 'It was the hardest thing I ever had to do,' Zemeckis said, confessing that he was 'sick about it for days. [Eric] is a magnificent actor, but his comic sensibilities were very different from what I had written with Bob, and he and I were just never able to make that work.' According to Spielberg, Zemeckis felt that Stoltz was simply too 'dramatic' for what was essentially a comedic role, while Gale worried that he just never looked at home on a skateboard. Not so Michael J. Fox, who merrily admitted that 'All I did in high school was skateboard, chase girls and play in bands.' And so, a complex shooting schedule was constructed which allowed Zemeckis to reshoot *Back to the Future* around the

ORGAN TRANSPLANT

Mismatched Actors and Roles

Sometimes transplants go wrong – the body rejects the organ. This applies to films as well.

COURAGE UNDER FIRE Meg Ryan is a helicopter pilot

THE UNTOUCHABLES Sean Connery is 'Irish' (1)

JACK REACHER Tom Cruise is the very tall Jack Reacher

ALEXANDER Colin Farrell is Alexander the Great (as one critic noted, the film is 'full of brilliant highlights, and they're all in Colin Farrell's hair')

TOUCH OF EVIL Charlton Heston is Mexican

THE LAKE HOUSE Keanu Reeves is an architect

THE BACK-UP PLAN Jennifer Lopez can't find a man (yeah, right)

RUN FOR YOUR WIFE Danny Dyer is a lovable bigamist

DOGMA Alanis Morissette is God (Emma Thompson could have pulled it off . . .)

MARY REILLY Julia Roberts is 'Irish' (2)

edges of Fox's *Family Ties* commitments, and Stoltz simply vanished – just as Marty himself disappears from the talismanic time-travelling photograph which he carries throughout the movie.

Stoltz was stoical about his experiences on *Back to the Future*, and has frequently stated that he has no regrets about getting dumped from the movie. Indeed, his career seems to have done just fine without Marty McFly. (As for original co-star Melora Hardin, she had to weather the indignity of being dropped along with Stoltz simply because she was deemed too tall to play the famously diminutive Michael J. Fox's love interest.)

Stranger still, however, is the story of what happened to Crispin Glover on *Back to the Future Part II*, during the course of which the film-makers were charged with attempting to steal his face. Having proved to be something of a wild card on *Back to the Future*, in which he played Marty's gawky dad George McFly, Glover was notably absent from the cast of the sequel, even though his character appears in the film. Exactly what happened remains the source of much heated speculation, with producer Bob Gale insisting that Glover was dropped for demanding salary parity with Fox, something the actor denies. According to Glover, the real problem was that he had argued with Zemeckis about the ending of *Back to the Future*, claiming that it gave its audience a negative message about wealth by equating Marty's moral victory with his family's financial success. 'I had a conversation with Robert Zemeckis about it,' Glover recalled in 2012, 'and said, "If the characters have money, if our characters are rich, it's a bad message. That reward should not be in there."' Instead of finding a shiny new truck parked in his garage, Glover argued that Marty's reward should be realising that his mother and father are happily married and 'in love with each other'. This was something Glover felt quite passionate about, and apparently that made his director 'pissed'.

When it came to the sequels (Parts II and III were shot back to back) the actor felt that the film-makers were actively attempting to sabotage his involvement, making a derisory financial offer ($125,000, considerably less than the amount Lea Thomson had reportedly been offered) and making it 'very clear they didn't want me in the film'. What they did want, however, was Glover's face – just not with Glover attached to it. 'They already had this concept that they were going to put another actor in prosthetics,' Glover explained. 'They thought that was funny. They knew that they could basically torment me, either financially or by this mean-spirited [replacement], what ultimately was an illegal thing to do. I'm sure they laughed and joked about it.'

Unsurprisingly, Glover refused to sign on the line, so the film-makers simply proceeded without him, actor Jeffrey Weisman playing George McFly with an assortment of facial prosthetics (nose, chin, cheekbones) designed to make him look like Crispin Glover. Techniques such as placing George in the background of a scene or hanging him upside down (he's meant to have a bad back) were also employed to obfuscate the fact that the original actor hadn't returned, and combined with some out-take footage from the original film the result was oddly convincing. To this day, many viewers watching *Back to the Future Part II* are convinced that Glover has a small but significant role in the film. In effect, the moviemakers had stolen his face. And now, he wanted it back.

Claiming that the film-makers had effectively hijacked his likeness without his permission, Glover filed a lawsuit which resulted in a landmark ruling by the Screen Actors Guild. 'My lawsuit was about copyright infringement,' Glover told Doctors Mayo and Kermode on their Radio 5 Live Film Review show in 2011. 'They put another actor into prosthetics they made from a mould of my face they had from the original film, and they inter-spliced that actor's performance with small portions of myself which I had done for the first film, to fool audiences into believing that I was in the film. They owned the character that they wrote but they didn't own me, they didn't own my face.' Glover protested, and as a result, SAG now has 'rules that make it so that actors and directors are not allowed to do that. So I'm proud that I stood up for that – it was an important thing to make sure it doesn't happen, because it's not right.'

Of course, Glover's lawsuit didn't mean that an actor's face can never be used without their permission – particularly if the actor is no longer around to raise a fuss. Brandon Lee's face was digitally imposed onto a body double after the star died during the filming of *The Crow* (1994) in the early nineties; Oliver Reed's digitally transplanted face made a fleeting posthumous appearance in Ridley Scott's 2000 Oscar winner *Gladiator*; and Paul Walker's starring role in *Fast & Furious 7* (2015) was completed by his brothers Caleb ('primarily for body size and mannerisms') and Cody ('for the eyes') alongside 'a three-camera crew from New Zealand's Weta Workshop' performing a process now known simply as 'face replacement'. Apparently this is a growth industry. In April 2015, the *Guardian* reported that Bruce Lee's estate was seeking legal redress to prevent his computerised likeness appearing in the forthcoming action movie *Ip Man 3*. Meanwhile, it was revealed that Robin Williams had gone to some lengths to 'prevent his image, or any likeness of him, being used for at least 25 years after his death'. These restrictions prevent 'any posthumous exploitation of the actor, be it through the use of CG to resurrect him in *Mrs Doubtfire 2* or as a live hologram performing comedy on stage – something that the advancement of technology has made an increasingly likely occurrence.'

In an age in which 'face replacement' is making the fantasy of *Face/Off* an everyday reality (maybe The Stath was right after all), it seems that the face of cinema has never been more open to change . .

THE TALKIES
Voice-over Transplants

It's not just actors' faces which are interchangeable. Back in 2014, Colin Firth made a surprisingly moving announcement about his voice being removed from the digitally enhanced *Paddington* reboot, declaring that he and the bear were undergoing a 'conscious uncoupling'. 'It's been bittersweet to see this delightful creature take shape, and come to the sad realisation that he simply doesn't have my voice,' Firth announced in splendidly straight-faced fashion. And he was right, his departure making way for Ben Whishaw to carry out one of the screen's most successful vocal transplants. Samantha Morton was equally gracious about her departure from Spike Jonze's *Her* (2013), a movie in which Joaquin Phoenix falls in love with a computer operating system, Throughout the production, Morton performed the role of 'Samantha', reading her lines off-screen (sometimes from the confines of a soundproofed box), interacting with Phoenix, aiding and guiding his performance. But when Jonze got the film into the editing room, he decided that Sam needed a new voice, and enlisted Scarlett Johansson to re-record all her lines in typically alluring fashion. The resulting film was a critical hit, but there are some (the Movie Doctors included) who would still love to hear what Morton made of the role she first created.

MORGUE

When it's all over, you've shuffled off and are en route to whatever place you believe in (see 'A Chapter Too Far', p.286 if you're still undecided), you'll spend a little time in the staging post known as the **Morgue**. Here you'll find movies that should never have seen the light of day and some **characters who have left the movies in spectacular style.**

DOCTOR, NO!

Movies That Should Never Have Been Made

PAINT YOUR WAGON *(1969)*

Hear Lee Marvin sing, 'I was born under a wand'rin' star'! Or, on second thoughts, don't.

EXORCIST II: THE HERETIC *(1977)*

Richard Burton flies to Africa on the back of a locust. After which a man dressed as a leopard spits out a cherry and a house in America falls down. The End.

1941 *(1979)*

Because when you think of all the things that Steven Spielberg does really well (action, drama, thrills, spills, historical intrigue etc) the word 'comedy' doesn't leap to mind . . .

THE VANISHING *(1993)*

Dutch director George Sluizer's US remake of his own Euro-chiller *Spoorloos* turned a film about the banality of evil into one about the evil of banality.

AN ALAN SMITHEE FILM: BURN HOLLYWOOD BURN *(1997)*

Director Arthur Hiller attempted to take his name off *Showgirls* screenwriter Joe Eszterhas's terrible movie about a director who attempts to take his name off a terrible movie. Meta or what?

PARTING SHOTS *(1998)*

Portly, bearded MOR popster Chris Rea stars in Michael Winner's serial killer 'comedy' about a man diagnosed with cancer who decides to go on a humorous *Death Wish* murder spree. Japes ensue.

PSYCHO *(1998)*

What better way to honour Alfred Hitchcock's timeless classic than to allow Gus Van Sant to do a shot-for-shot remake – in colour!

ALI G INDAHOUSE *(2002)*

It's a popular short-form TV series in which brevity is its strength. Let's turn it into an hour and a half movie. What could possibly go wrong?

THE RING *(2002)*

Do you know what's wrong with Hideo Nakata's 1998 Japanese chiller *Ringu*? Nothing! So let's have Gore Verbinski make it again – in American!

SEX LIVES OF THE POTATO MEN *(2004)*

The UK Film Council handed its opponents all the ammunition they needed to bring about its demise with this tale of chips and intercourse. If you never want to see a man masturbating over a squid and jam sandwich, look away now.

SEX AND THE CITY 2 *(2010)*

AKA 'Consumerist Pornography Goes to Abu Dhabi'.

FILM SOCIALISME *(2010)*

Nouvelle vague funster Jean-Luc Godard wonders how far he can push it before fawning critics realise he's taking the piss. The answer turns out to be: Very Far Indeed.

THAT'S MY BOY *(2012)*

Adam Sandler ups the downmarket ante with this jaw-dropping comedy about statutory rape. Apparently, child molesting is really funny. Apparently.

ENTOURAGE *(2015)*

A bunch of hateful wealthy misogynist assholes roam around Los Angeles while we are expected to smile and cheer at their soulless antics. How bad is it? A smug, self-aggrandising cameo appearance by Piers Morgan is the least of its problems. Yes, it's *that* bad …

WAY TO GO
Movies for the Grand Finale

Well there's no way around it. People die in movies all the time and it would be wrong if your Movie Doctors avoided the subject of death here. There is a place for sensitive grief counselling and, you will be relieved to hear, this is not it. But *talking* and *sharing* can help. And in that spirit we thought we'd share some classic departures in the hope that we can find a common story, a way to move forward together in these difficult times and face the challenges of tomorrow (unless you're dead, in which case there isn't one – see 'A Chapter Too Far', p.286).

STAR WARS: EPISODE IV A NEW HOPE *(1977)*
OBI WAN

David Prowse is fighting Alec Guinness. David is forty-two and dressed in the bad clothes of a bad man – black swirly cape and evil helmet. Alec is sixty-one and wearing the good clothes of a good man – cream robes and a rust-brown, coarsely-knitted overgarment. 'I've been waiting for you Obi Wan, we meet at last,' says Dave (in the voice of James Earl Jones). Alec isn't too keen to hear this, but at least his lightsaber is a righteous blue, contrasting pleasingly with David's wicked red.

Neither are the most nimble swordsman we have seen but they both have their moves. They cut, thrust and parry. There's a twirl from Alec, a menacing advance from David, but that's about it. After one of the least energetic sword fights ever, they both seem rather tired. Alec sees young Mark Hamill arrive and decides he's had enough of this Jedi nonsense. He does his beatific smile, holds his saber to his chest and is struck down, his body disappearing and his robes folding in on themselves.

LESSON LEARNED If you're a Jedi master, you come back stronger, so dying is no big deal anyway. Enjoy life a little. Lose the hood.

HARRY POTTER AND THE GOBLET OF FIRE (2005)
CEDRIC DIGGORY

Oh the pain! Oh the heartache! Let it not be so! Alas poor Cedric (Robert Pattinson) – our noble Hufflepuff champion – meets his end at the hand of the Dark Lord (it's Tim Spall's really, but he was only obeying Ralph Fiennes's orders). Moments before it had all seemed so different; the Triwizard Tournament had been won, Cedric and Harry had grabbed the cup together, and teamwork had triumphed over nasty neo-Thatcherite individualism.

But the cup was a port key (of course!) and our heroes have landed in a graveyard. Harry has dreamt about this place before, and when he sees Tom Riddle's gravestone he knows they are in trouble. Right on cue, enter Peter Pettigrew (Tim Spall) with a ventriloquist dummy-like Voldemort under his arm. Even though his voice is squeaky and hoarse (so would yours be if you were only a head), the Dark Lord's 'Kill the spare!' are still chilling words of execution.

With an 'S'-shaped wand movement and the 'Avada Kedavra' incantation, Pettigrew performs the killing curse. A flash of green light envelops Diggory, who is thrown backwards, then drops instantly to the ground. Hufflepuff has lost its champion and Robert Pattinson can move on to another money-spinning franchise.

LESSON LEARNED The killing curse is not a bad way to go. A bit sudden, admittedly, but wildly glamorous and heroic.

THE DARK KNIGHT (2008)
UNKNOWN HOODLUM

The gangsters of Gotham have turned weedy. Where once they could spread their menace unhindered, now they cower under the Bat symbol, a pale shadow of their former selves. They gather to discuss matters at a ruffians' away day but are interrupted by the chortling, face-painted Joker (Heath Ledger). Because he isn't on the agenda, one hoodlum wonders why he shouldn't get 'my boy here to pull your head off'.

Caked in make-up that is clearly past its best-before date, the Joker offers to perform a magic trick. He takes a pencil and rams it into the table top. Scientists have proved that this always ends in a ruined pencil but here the Joker, presumably using a 9H, succeeds in embedding it into the table. The pencil is now rubber-end up and the Joker is waving his hands around it like some kind of ridiculous magician.

'I'm gonna make this pencil disappear,' he says, and as he is approached by the hoodlum's henchman, the Joker smacks his head right onto the upturned pencil, which duly disappears inside his skull.

'Ta-dah!'

This makes the victim the first eraserhead since 1977 and he falls from our view.

LESSON LEARNED A simple but memorable way to go. The murder weapon only cost 65p, so economical too.

ALIEN *(1979)*
OFFICER KANE

Executive Officer Kane (played by John Hurt) is hungry. Possibly the hungriest he's ever been. He's had a stressful time recently, what with the trip to that strange planet and its even stranger aggressive eggs. Then there was the unfortunate business with the eight-fingered facehugger with acid for blood and a tube down his throat. Anyway that's all behind him now and he wants one huge meal before he and all the crew of the *Nostromo* head back to cryosleep.

There's pasta, noodles and cigarettes to be enjoyed before Kane starts his coughing fit. As we have established elsewhere, no one coughs in the movies without reason; it usually means you'll be dead before the reel is out. In Kane's case he doesn't even make it to coffee. He chokes his way onto the table, where he writhes and contorts before his chest bursts, throwing litres of blood onto the horrified crew. As Kane's hands spasm and twitch, the titular alien appears where his guts should be. The xenomorph (as it is lovingly referred to) then gets his only laugh of the entire franchise. Using the animal impersonation skills of the late Percy Edwards, it squawks rather weekly, like an asthmatic badger. Then, with all the mannerisms and style of Kermit or Gonzo the Great, it exits the frame. Thinking they are hunting a Muppet, the crew set off in pursuit. The Muppet wins (kind of).

LESSON LEARNED Endoparasitic species have to live somehow. Your death is a noble one – you have sacrificed your body for science and extraterrestrial cooperation between species.

BAMBI *(1942)*
BAMBI'S MOTHER

For one generation of children, it was *Pingu* episode four, 'Pingu Helps to Deliver Mail' (Pingu and his father deliver a black-edged telegram to a tearful pensioner penguin). For another it was *Transformers* (Frenzy decapitating Jazz. Or was it Bonecrusher ripping up Blackout? Who knows? Who cares?). But for many others it was the slaying of Bambi's mother that was their introduction to death.

We know she's in trouble from the moment the music changes. One minute Bambi and his mother are enjoying the new spring grass (orchestra plays 'pastoral'), the next she is sniffing the wind (orchestra plays 'smelly hunters on the way'). They run for the thicket, Bambi in the lead, his mother exhorting him to 'keep running and don't look back!' Two shots ring out. The fawn thinks they have escaped but then realises he is on his own. Snow falls, the forest darkens and an old stag appears (as they tend to in moments like these). The Giant Prince of the Forest, no less, says 'Your mother can't be with you any more.' This is all too much and we dissolve into hysterical sobbing. Our world has darkened, maybe for ever.

LESSON LEARNED Die off camera. Don't make a big thing about it, no one likes a moaner. Taking this option is *graceful* and *classy*.

BONNIE AND CLYDE *(1967)*
BONNIE AND CLYDE

They're young. They're in love. They kill people. Faye Dunaway and Warren Beatty star in this Oscar-winning film (Best Supporting Actress and Cinematography), robbing anything that moves, humiliating cops and shooting bank managers in the face. This is only going to end badly.

Their final scene, however, is one of the longest executions in movie history. An ambush has been planned and Bonnie and Clyde drive straight into it. Thinking they are helping an associate's father fix a tyre, they pull over and Clyde gets out to help. When the old-timer dives for cover and birds clatter from a bush, we, and they, know the end is nigh. They just have time to exchange swift 'I know we're about to be riddled with bullets but I love you anyway' looks, and then all hell breaks loose. The five hidden cops fire and keep firing their Thompson sub-machine guns for twenty-two seconds, Bonnie and Clyde bouncing like puppets as the bullets hit. Clyde falls and rolls toward the car; Bonnie collapses sideways, dangling from the passenger seat. The lawmen emerge to inspect their handiwork, joined by the old-timer and two passing farm workers. A small part of us hopes for a Pythonesque 'I'm not dead yet' from Clyde, or a Bond-style firing off a final round from Bonnie that takes out the sheriff, but instead the screen fades to black. Just so everyone knows this is 'The End'.

LESSON LEARNED This is a memorably flashy and flamboyant death, the stuff of legend and a number one hit song for Georgie Fame. Get this right and we'll gloss over the fact you were nasty, brutal killers whose lawlessness set its own death warrant.

JURASSIC PARK *(1993)*
LAWYER ON THE TOILET

If you're a lawyer, the movies can sometimes be a tough watch. Unless it's another John Grisham adaptation you're seeing (do tell us, John, about your latest heroic lawyer who saves the day against the evil corporations), chances are the screenwriters, producers and directors have surrendered enough of their hard-earned cash to the legal profession. This means that sometimes justice for your sort can be fearfully brutal.

On John Hammond's (Richard Attenborough) Isla Nubla, the prehistoric beasts are on the rampage, and a Tyrannosaurus Rex is munching on a jeep containing our John's grandchildren Lex and Tim. Before it reaches the terrified kids, the T. Rex gets distracted by flares (not the seventies trousers) and it sets off after chaos theorist Dr Ian Malcolm (Jeff Goldblum). On the way it demolishes a toilet block where we find Hammond's lawyer sitting with his trousers around his ankles. This is Donald Gennaro, who is on the island to represent Hammond's investors, but right now is staring straight into the eyes (and nose and, very soon, throat) of a seven-ton beast. Earlier we have heard him look in awe at the revitalised dinos and exclaim, 'We're gonna make a fortune from this place!' We, however, understand instantly that 1) he won't make a cent and 2) he will be chopped in two by dino-teeth at the next available moment. Recalling Woody Guthrie's line 'Some rob you with a six gun / Some with a fountain pen', we nod sagely and know justice has been done.
LESSON LEARNED Outdoor poos can be fatal. Be careful out there, people.

BUTCH CASSIDY AND THE SUNDANCE KID *(1969)*
BUTCH AND SUNDANCE

The only scene in this list where, maybe, no one dies. I mean they *could* have got away, couldn't they? Those hundred or so Bolivian troops shooting their guns . . . they could all miss, maybe? The many cries of 'Fuego!' which close the film might mean the troops *are fighting each other*, not slaying Butch and Sundance. We all know what undisciplined troops those South Americans are! (See p.43)

These final moments in a deserted house also feature some sparkling dialogue (written by William Goldman) in which our badly wounded cowboys discuss the attractions of moving to Australia. Butch says the horses, banks and women all look good and that everyone speaks English. Sundance hopes they won't get there only to find it stinks. Putting all thoughts of Darwin behind them, they make a break for it, firing into the day's last sunlight. The camera freezes on Butch and Sundance and, as the sound of the volley from soldiers' guns rings out, the image fades to sepia then black and white. Not a bad exit. They may well have been blown apart by scores of army rifles, but we'll never know.
LESSON LEARNED Have some witty exchanges lined up for your exit. It's your final bow so make it count.

BLADE RUNNER *(1982)*
ROY BATTY

While we are on the subject of words, here's one of the noblest of passings. If gruff man-banter isn't appropriate (see above) then try a Shakespearean-style soliloquy. You could have one planned or, like Rutger Hauer, here playing the replicant Roy Batty, you could improvise. He'd been a given a script by screenwriters Hampton Fancher and David Peoples, he had a first-rate director in Ridley Scott but Rutger had a few ideas of his own (see also p.34).

The dying replicant has just saved Deckard (Harrison Ford) from falling off a building. They have been fighting a while. Realising he is needed in the next Spear of Destiny video, Roy has reached the end. With Vangelis noodling away in the background, he kneels in the neon-lit torrential rain, and begins.

'I have . . . seen things you people wouldn't believe . . . Attack ships on fire off the shoulder of Orion. I watched c-beams glitter in the dark near the Tannhäuser Gate. All those . . . moments . . . will be lost in time, like [small cough] tears . . . in . . . rain. Time . . . to die . . .'

Cue applause and tears on set, man-hugs and a few 'Tannhäuser Gate?' queries.

LESSON LEARNED If possible, deliver your final lines sitting stripped to the waist. Release a dove as you pass, letting everyone know you've finished.

WHITE HEAT *(1949)*
CODY JARRETT

No one died like James Cagney. Faye and Warren (above) may have gone out with panache, but next to James, they appear almost demure. Here he is Cody Jarrett, a thoroughly nasty, messed-up gang leader with a bit of a 'mother complex'. He is married to Verna (Virginia 'Granny!' Mayo) but it is his ma who he confides in, as he sits on her lap.

Jarrett and his gang have botched up a payroll raid at a chemical plant. Jarrett himself has fled to the top of an ominously large gas tank where he takes a few hits from the lawman's rifle. Lesser actors would now tumble to their deaths or, realising the game is up, take the whisky and revolver option. Not Jimmy. Appreciating that a gas tank is only ever in a movie for one reason, he starts to shoot it up. As flames leap from the ruptured metal, the lawmen run for cover. Engulfed by smoke and fire, Cagney, arms wide, his face in raptures, yells: 'Made it, Ma! Top of the world!' The gas tank duly obliges.

LESSON LEARNED Don't go on your own. If you can take your gang and half of California with you, so much the better.

POSSESSION

| The Movie Doctors' Casebook | *The doctors are IN* |

INT. MOVIE DOCTORS' SURGERY – DAY

Dr Kermode is wearing a Harrington jacket (light grey), Levis with turn-ups and muddy DMs (it's a 'not-on-TV' day). Dr Mayo has a cardigan (blue, same as ever), Radio 2-appropriate jeans and ankle boots (every day is a 'not-on-TV' day).

> **DR KERMODE**
> Hey.

> **DR MAYO**
> Wassup.

Dr Kermode has a 'Please stop it, you're not fifteen or from the Bronx' look on his face again.

> **DR MAYO**
> (shrugs) You happy?

> **DR KERMODE**
> I haven't been really happy since the days of the old X certificate.

A dishevelled middle-aged woman walks in. She looks concerned and slightly spooked.

> **DR MAYO**
> (scanning his patient list) Hello, Mrs Travers. Do sit down.

> **DR KERMODE**
> What seems to be the trouble?

> **MRS TRAVERS**
> Well it seems my daughter is possessed by the demon Pazuzu.

> **DR MAYO**
> Oh, here we go . . .

> **DR KERMODE**
> (leaning forward, animated) Have you been abroad recently?

> **MRS TRAVERS**
> Not really. Just a brief archaeological dig in Iraq.

> **DR KERMODE**
> (turning pale) Did you find anything?

> **MRS TRAVERS**
> Well, there was this weird figurine, but I don't think . . .

Dr Mayo goes to throw himself out of the window but is hauled back by Dr Kermode.

> **MRS TRAVERS**
> (nodding at Dr Mayo) Is he possessed too?

DR MAYO
No, I just can't stand to hear about *The Exorcist* again!

MRS TRAVERS
Are you sure I need an exorcist? I thought Paul McKenna maybe had an app I could download or something . . .

DR KERMODE
Why do you think your daughter is possessed?

MRS TRAVERS
Well, she swears a lot.

DR KERMODE
Hmmm.

MRS TRAVERS
That's an annoying sound to make, Dr Kermode. Your tone implied scepticism, while on the surface expressing agreement.

DR MAYO
That happens quite a lot . . .

DR KERMODE
(moving on) Anything else that your daughter does to suggest demonic possession?

MRS TRAVERS
She spends a lot of time in bed.

DR KERMODE
Is the bed on the ground?

MRS TRAVERS
Mostly.

DR MAYO
Mostly?

MRS TRAVERS
The rest of the time it's floating in the air. Sometimes her head spins around a bit. Oh, and she talks backwards...

DR MAYO
Well, I think we get the picture. Dr Kermode, any thoughts?

DR KERMODE
(smiling) Absolutely. I think we should let BUPA handle this one, don't you?

CHAPEL

The Movie Doctors' chapel is open to all. In your **time of need**, we provide a space for candles and serenity where you can think warm thoughts without fearing any oppressive patriarchal theology. Here we discuss the **'After-Life Options'**, the songs that could accompany your loved one's departure and the vexed issue of the death of commissioned soundtracks. There's fresh fruit and pot-pourri in small bowls to sweeten the mood. Come on in and sit down. **We're here to help**.

A CHAPTER TOO FAR

Is There Movie Life After Death?

Occasionally the Movie Doctors are asked to step outside their area of expertise. Strictly speaking, we try to limit ourselves to earthly matters; to heal and tend to the sick through the power of movies. But sometimes we are asked about *what happens next*. If 'an unfortunate event' has been experienced, *where do you go?* Over the years, you might have noticed that some people feel quite strongly about this sort of thing. It is not our job to add to that ferment. Indeed we should state publicly we think all ideas and beliefs in this area are of equal value (even if they aren't). Whatever you believe, you'll find something below to support it. No awkwardness, just reinforcement.

What you believe
THIS IS IT GUYS, THERE IS NOTHING ELSE

What you watch
CONTACT *(1997)*

Top-drawer sci-fi co-written by the eminent astronomer, cosmologist and author Carl Sagan. Jodie Foster is the astrophysicist searching for extra-terrestrial life, Matthew McConaughey (before he needed a McConaissance) is the spiritual guru hoping to spend some quality exploration time with Jodie. She says stuff like: 'So what's more likely? That an all-powerful, mysterious God created the Universe, and then decided not to give a single proof his existence? Or that He simply doesn't exist at all, and that we created Him, so that we wouldn't have to feel so small and alone?' She goes on to travel in space and meet aliens (probably) but this is a quality atheistic title.

What you believe
HEAVEN IS FOR REAL

What you watch
HEAVEN IS FOR REAL *(2014)*

Greg Kinnear leads this 'based on a true story' drama as Todd Burpo, a pastor and father to Colton and Cassie. After a visit to a spider sanctuary which you sense isn't going to conclude happily, Colton ends up having emergency surgery for appendicitis, during which he has a near-death experience. He tells his parents that he has met Jesus (white robes and a purple sash) and been given a tour around Heaven. They are about to discount this as the hallucinations of a sick child when he says he met his 'other sister' in Heaven, the one his mother miscarried many years ago. As they had never told their son about this, they

(and you) become convinced that maybe he did visit Heaven after all. Unbelievers never got past the name Colton Burpo.

What you believe
THE RAPTURE WILL COME AND THE FOUR HORSEMEN OF THE APOCALYPSE SHALL SMITE THE UNWASHED ETC.

What you watch
THE RAPTURE *(1991)*

Written and directed by Michael Tolkin (co-writing credit, please, for St John the Divine), and starring Mimi Rogers and David Duchovny, it turns out that all that stuff in the Book of Revelations is totally and utterly true The end is no longer nigh, the end is totally now and, so as to be as clear as possible, is announced with a trumpet. Folk get raptured all over the place but Mimi is angry with God for killing David so decides to stay in purgatory for ever (see Canvey Island, p.29).

What you believe
REINCARNATION

What you watch
CLOUD ATLAS *(2012)*

The cinema loves reincarnation. This is because all movie bosses know that just because something has died, doesn't mean it can't come back again. More theologically, David Mitchell's book was roundly declared to be brilliant but unfilmable,

but if anyone can do reincarnation it'll be the Wachowskis. Here we have six stories, a vast cast and the message that we are all connected and that every good or bad deed shapes our future (Michael Bay – be afraid, be very afraid). The movie also features the appearance of Hugh Grant playing six different characters, five more than he has played in the rest of his career.

What you believe
NOT QUITE SURE BUT I'VE DONE MY BEST GIVEN THE CIRCUMSTANCES . . .

What you watch
DEFENDING YOUR LIFE *(1991)*

The tag line for this Albert Brooks/Meryl Streep comedy demands inclusion here. 'The First True Story About What Happens When You Die' shows us the perils of trying to alter the CDs in your car while driving. Just because you can't bear to hear the opening bars of '(Everything I Do) I Do It for You' again is no reason to drive headlong into a truck.

Anyway Albert is not quite in Heaven but Judgement City, which is a bit like a celestial Holiday Inn where he has to account for his time on earth. This all comes as a bit of a shock, compounded by the requirement that he has to wear white robes with a cream cummerbund. Fortunately Meryl Streep has to wear them too, so naturally they fall in love and find the calorie-free food gives them all the energy they need.

HOSPITAL RADIO

The Death List

A young Dr Mayo worked in hospital radio back in those vinyl days. There are many songs that have featured on popular movie soundtracks that you will not hear via the ward-supplied headphones, as they have been deemed 'unhelpful'. This is because they are too miserable, mention disease or death, or go on about your loved one being in the arms of another. Consider all of these banned:

DON'T FEAR THE REAPER
HALLOWEEN *(1978)*

A SPOONFUL OF SUGAR
MARY POPPINS *(1964)*

TAKE MY BREATH AWAY
TOP GUN *(1986)*

THE TROLLEY SONG
MEET ME IN ST LOUIS *(1944)*

I'VE GOT YOU UNDER MY SKIN
BORN TO DANCE *(1936)*

BLOOD HANDS
INSURGENT *(2015)*

DEAD MAN WALKIN'
DEAD MAN WALKING *(1995)*

MY HEART WILL GO ON
TITANIC *(1997)*

I NEED TO WAKE UP
AN INCONVENIENT TRUTH *(2006)*

STAYIN' ALIVE
SATURDAY NIGHT FEVER *(1977)*

I'M CHECKIN' OUT
POSTCARDS FROM THE EDGE *(1990)*

ANOTHER ONE BITES THE DUST
IRON MAN 2 *(2010)*

ALL COUNTRY MUSIC

ORGAN DONATION

A Clinical Examination

In the spring of 2015, the Royal Albert Hall played host to a unique performance of Christopher Nolan's *Interstellar*, complete with a live musical score performed by a sixty-piece orchestra. While the Movie Doctors' chapel may be blessed with only a Bontempi electronic organ, composer Hans Zimmer made powerful use of the Albert Hall's Grand Organ, upon which Roger Sayer played the movie's thunderous theme. If you thought *Interstellar* sounded good in cinemas (the reason it's one of our cures for tinnitus – see p.50), then hearing it accompanied by the second-largest pipe organ in the United Kingdom was genuinely out of this world.

The *Interstellar* concert was just the latest in a string of live score performances to which audiences have been flocking in recent years. One of the highlights of 2014 was a live rendition of Mica Levi's unearthly music for *Under the Skin*, played by a 25-piece orchestra at the Royal Festival Hall to accompany Jonathan Glazer's creepily unsettling sci-fi oddity. Earlier that same year, Jonny Greenwood joined the London Contemporary Orchestra at the Roundhouse for a performance of his electrifying score for *There Will Be Blood* (2007). 'How could I ever cynically have wondered whether a live orchestra would sound noticeably much different to the soundtrack being played on some speakers?' wrote the *Independent*'s spellbound reviewer, concluding breathlessly that 'It's magnificent.'

Accepting that a live score can add an extra dimension to a movie is one thing, but the Movie Doctors have always been fascinated by the peculiar prospect of transplanting an entirely new score onto a movie. A few years ago, the British rock band 65daysofstatic composed and performed original music for Douglas Trumbull's seminal 1970s sci-fi gem *Silent Running*, stressing that their efforts were in no way a criticism of the existing score, but rather an intriguing 'alternative'. Having earned his cinematic spurs conjuring mind-bending visual effects for *2001*, Trumbull had always envisaged *Silent Running* as an antidote to the emotional sterility of Kubrick's masterpiece. An unashamedly sentimental piece about one man's struggle to save the last of the Earth's forests, this tear-jerking treat boasts a lush orchestral score by Peter Schickele (better known as musical satirist 'P.D.Q. Bach'), and two lyrical vocal performances from folkie legend Joan Baez. Originally released on collectable

green vinyl, the soundtrack has long been a cult favourite, beloved of fans of the movie, which has grown in critical stature in the decades since its first release. But in an age in which DVD and Blu-ray offer viewers the chance to isolate and, if they wish, remove the musical score from a film at will, 65daysofstatic decided to take a very different bash at the movie, creating a grungier, noisier accompaniment which throws new light on the film's bittersweet action.

Originally developed for live performance, the 65daysofstatic soundtrack was recorded with the blessing of Trumbull, who confessed that while it wasn't really his 'thing', he was delighted that they were attempting to do something new and inventive with his forty-something-year-old film. Although *Silent Running* has never been officially issued with the new 65DOS music, at the time of writing there's a rescored version of the film available on YouTube for anyone interested in checking it out.

The amputation and transplanting of musical scores is, in fact, a surprisingly common experience. Since music tends to be the last thing added to a film, it is also the element with which producers feel most inclined to fiddle when a movie starts to look like it's not engaging with its target audience. Classic examples of film scores which have been variously commissioned, written or recorded, and then either rejected or bowdlerised/ 'augmented' include:

- Oscar Straus's score for *The Thief of Bagdad* (1940)
- John Barry's score for *Promise Her Anything* (1960)
- Bernard Herrmann's score for *Torn Curtain* (1966)
- Alex North's score for *2001: A Space Odyssey* (1968)
- Jimmy Webb's score for *Love Story* (1970)
- Jimmy Page's score for *Lucifer Rising* (1972)
- Philip Lambro's score for *Chinatown* (1974)

- David Bowie's score for *The Man Who Fell to Earth* (1976)
- Franco Mannino's score for *Caligula* (1979)
- Carl Davis's score for *Five Days One Summer* (1982)
- Dominic Muldowney's score for *1984* (1984)
- Jerry Goldsmith's score for *Legend* (1985)
- Maurice Jarre's score for *The River Wild* (1994)
- Mark Isham's score for *Waterworld* (1995)
- Ennio Morricone's score for *What Dreams May Come* (1998)
- Gabriel Yared's score for *Troy* (2004)
- Howard Shore's score for *King Kong* (2005)
- Jon Brion's score for *The Fighter* (2010)

And that's just the tip of the iceberg ...

Perhaps the most celebrated of the cases cited above is that of Alex North and his dumped music for *2001: A Space Odyssey*. According to legend, *Spartacus* composer North was enlisted by Stanley Kubrick to score *2001*, and he duly wrote and recorded music to accompany the film's groundbreaking visuals. Kubrick, however, had started to have other ideas. 'However good our best film composers may be,' he told cineaste Michel Ciment years later, 'they are not a Beethoven, a Mozart, or a Brahms.' Describing how he would often use pre-existing recordings as 'temp tracks' for cutting his films (a common practice), Kubrick explained that, 'I engaged the services of a distinguished film composer to write the score. Although he and I went over the picture very carefully, and he listened to these temporary tracks (Strauss, Ligeti, Khachaturian) and agreed that they worked fine ... he nevertheless wrote and recorded a score which could not have been more alien to the music we had listened to, and much more serious than that, a score which, in my opinion, was completely inadequate for the film.'

Convinced that North's work simply wasn't up to scratch, the notoriously perfectionist Kubrick decided to attempt to clear the rights to the now-iconic temp tracks (with which he had clearly fallen in love) but apparently neglected to inform North of his decision. 'With the premiere looming up,' Kubrick told Ciment, 'I had no time left even to think about another score being written, and had I not been able to use the music I had already selected for the temporary tracks, I don't know what I would have done.'

And so it was that Alex North attended the New York premiere of *2001: A Space Odyssey* fully expecting to hear his score, only to be greeted with the sounds of 'Also sprach Zarathustra' and 'Lux Aeterna', which have since become inseparable from the film.

2001: A Space Odyssey – Track Listing

1. 'Also sprach Zarathustra' – Richard Strauss
2. 'Requiem for Soprano, Mezzo-Soprano, 2 Mixed Choirs and Orchestra' – György Ligeti
3. 'Lux Aeterna' – György Ligeti
4. 'The Blue Danube' – Johann Strauss II
5. 'Gayane Ballet Suite' (Adagio) – Aram Khachaturian
6. 'Atmosphères' – György Ligeti

Apparently North was 'devastated' – unsurprisingly so. 'What can I say?' he mused later. 'It was a great, frustrating experience, and despite the mixed reaction to the music, I think the Victorian approach with the mid-European overtones was just not in keeping with the brilliant concept of Clarke and Kubrick.'

Although the master tapes for North's score were kept for decades at Anvil Studios in England, they were eventually wiped, leaving the mono recordings held by the North family as the only record of his work. But in 1993, Jerry Goldsmith (no stranger to the 'dumped' score himself – his

orchestral score for *Legend* was famously replaced by some youth-friendly Tangerine Dream techno in the US) produced and conducted a recording of North's entire *2001* score which was released to great acclaim on CD by soundtrack stalwarts Varèse Sarabande. In 2007, Intrada Records issued the original 1968 North recordings, featuring nine tracks from the score (conducted by Henry Brant) and 'precise cue points' which would allow enthusiasts to sync the music up to a DVD or Blu-ray of the film and see for themselves what Kubrick rejected.

'There is no doubt that *2001* would have been better if Kubrick had used North's music,' wrote Kevin Mulhall in his sleeve notes for the Jerry Goldsmith re-recording. 'Even if one likes the choices Kubrick made for certain individual scenes, the eclectic group of classical composers employed by the director . . . resulted in a disturbing melange of sounds and styles overall.'

Five years after North's infamous falling-out with Kubrick, composer Lalo Schifrin would find himself locking heads in a similar manner with *Exorcist* director William Friedkin. Like *2001*, the finished score for *The Exorcist* consists largely of excerpts from pre-existing material, a patchwork of cues by Krzysztof Penderecki, Hans Werner Henze, George Crumb and (perhaps most famously) Mike Oldfield. Yet Friedkin had initially planned on using original music, and approached not one but two legendary composers to sound them out about working on the picture.

His first port of call was Bernard Herrmann, who had scored such classics as Orson Welles's *Citizen Kane* (1941) and Alfred Hitchcock's *Psycho* (1960), and who was arguably the most well-respected film composer in the business. Friedkin and Herrmann discussed the music for *The Exorcist*; on this matter, both are agreed. What happened next, however, is a classic case of He said/She said. According to Friedkin, Herrmann liked what

he saw, and believed that he could produce some excellently fitting music using a much-loved pipe organ located in St Giles' Church, London. Apparently, recording in London was a deal-breaker for Herrmann, who was convinced that the acoustics at this particular church in Cripplegate would be perfect for the movie. Friedkin was distinctly uneasy about the idea of letting Herrmann run wild with a massive organ thousands of miles away from where he was mixing the movie, and politely told the composer that it was a no-go.

That's Friedkin's version of events. Herrmann tells a very different story. According to the composer, he didn't like the film at all and really didn't want anything to do with it. The situation was made worse by the fact that Friedkin (who had very clear ideas about the soundtrack for *The Exorcist*) started suggesting that he would like to share a 'co-composer and musical director' credit. Finally, when the director told Herrmann that he wanted him to do a score 'better than the one you wrote for *Citizen Kane*', Herrmann is alleged to have replied tartly: 'Well, you should've made a better picture than *Citizen Kane* then!'

And that was the end of that.

Having drawn a blank with Herrmann, Friedkin turned next to Lalo Schifrin, another giant in the world of film music. Again, accounts differ as to how the two came to blows. Friedkin insists that he told Schifrin to write a score which would be the aural equivalent of 'a cold hand on the back of the neck'– something which would subtly provoke unease in the audience. As per the director, Schifrin assured him that he knew exactly what he meant, and went off to write and record some appropriately chilling material. What he came up with, with the aid of a large orchestra, was a 'big scary wall of sound', the shrieking, stabbing jolts of which can still be heard in a very early trailer for *The Exorcist*. Friedkin was appalled and promptly ditched Schifrin's score, recordings of which (from October/November 1973) survive and were included in a CD accompanying the film's twenty-fifth anniversary DVD re-release. According to one story, Friedkin actually grabbed the master tape of Schifrin's music and hurled it out into the parking lot, with words to the effect: 'Get this fucking shit out of my movie!'

Schifrin, naturally, tells a rather different story. According to the composer, Friedkin engaged him to write the music for the trailer, which scared the bejeezus out of audiences, causing them to rush to the nearest toilet and vomit. (The Movie Doctors would like to point out that while film-related vomiting is not serious, it can be contagious.) 'The trailer was terrific,' he recalled, 'but the mix of those frightening scenes and my music, which was also a very difficult and heavy score, scared the audiences away.' According to Schifrin, Warners were so alarmed by reactions to the trailer that they told Friedkin to instruct his composer to 'write a less dramatic and softer score. But Friedkin didn't tell me what they said. I'm sure he did it deliberately. In the past we had an incident, caused by other reasons, and I think he wanted vengeance. This is my theory.' Thus, Schifrin continued to score the film 'in the same vein as that of the trailer', only to have his completed work hurled into a parking lot by a director who, according to the composer, had basically set him up.

Schifrin's story makes little sense; the idea that a film-maker rushing to complete a movie with a 26 December release date would deliberately allow a composer to write and record an entirely ill-fitting score in November just to get his own back over some long-forgotten spat is surely the stuff of sheer invention. Yet the tangible sense of hurt which the composer's words evoke reminds us that having your score removed can be a painful procedure for which there is no efficient anaesthetic; the musician just has to bite the bullet and bear it.

Not all musical transplant operations are quite so traumatic. In 2014, BBC Radio 1 DJ Zane Lowe oversaw the rescoring of Nicolas Winding Refn's *Drive* (see also p.236) for exclusive broadcast on BBC

Three. Refn's violent, existential thriller had won plaudits for its iconic original soundtrack by Chris Martinez, a late-in-the-day replacement for Johnny Jewel (whose songs feature in the film). Bizarrely, early screeners of *Drive* actually credited David Lynch's long-time collaborator Angelo Badalamenti as composer, although the film-makers insist that this was merely a 'holding credit' on a version which actually used temp tracks by Brian Eno. But by the time Refn's movie premiered at the Cannes Film Festival in May 2011 (where it picked up the award for Best Director) Martinez was definitely in the musical driving seat, his name featuring prominently in the glowing reviews which the film attracted in the weeks and months which followed.

Unsurprisingly, the announcement that Radio 1 were to rescore the film with new tracks by the likes of The 1975, Laura Mvula, Bring Me the Horizon, Chvrches, Bastille, Foals, Banks, Baauer, Jon Hopkins, and SBTRKT was not met with universal delight. A typical online article published in the wake of a Radio 1 press release led with the headline 'The BBC Let Zane Lowe Re-Score *Drive* and We Have Absolutely No Idea Why', and began with the words 'Well, this sounds like a horrible idea …' Several high-profile commentators followed suit, with large sections of the music press dismissing the rescoring (sight unseen) as a preposterous act of egomania by Lowe, even when it was revealed that the DJ had the full backing of director Refn, who had both approved and endorsed the project.

When *Drive* aired on BBC Three on 30 October 2014, its broadcast was accompanied by a blizzard of Twitter responses commenting in real time on each new musical choice. Opinions on the rescoring were divided, with many viewers arguing that Lowe's version lacked the depth and subtlety of the original. Others, however, disagreed, finding Lowe's efforts imaginative and inventive, and praising Radio 1 for their use of up-and-coming artists, many of whom the station had championed from the outset. Most importantly, the screening provoked a proverbial heated debate about the role of music in *Drive* in particular, and modern cinema in general, with many of the most insightful and excitable comments coming from younger viewers who wrote extensive online screeds about the merits (or otherwise) of this audaciously televised live organ transplant.

Intriguingly, this most modern experiment actually takes us right back to the birth of cinema, and the days when silent movies would be accompanied by live musicians, many (if not most) of whom were making it up as they went along. Literally. Although some early feature films were distributed with sheet music which was intended to accompany the on-screen action, cinema in the days before the arrival of sound recording was bandit country when it came to soundtracks. From the lone pianists merrily improvising to whatever was on screen to the local bands who would be enlisted to play a selection of fitting favourites while the celluloid action unspooled, music in movies was a moveable feast. Indeed, audiences would specifically seek out cinemas in which the musicians provided the kind of music they wanted to hear, choosing for themselves how best to experience the wonders of this newly emergent art form.

Today, film enthusiasts can sit at home with their PCs and DVDs merrily mashing up and remixing film scores in the comfort of their living room. Like those addled Pink Floyd obsessives who used to spend hours replaying their vinyl copies of *Dark Side of the Moon* while watching *The Wizard of Oz* on VHS ('man, it's incredible, it's like the whole thing really matches up . . .'), audiences have increasingly taken the musical direction of movies into their own hands, with often surprising results.

Whether the patient (cinema itself) will survive this kind of home surgery, or wind up crying in the Movie Doctors' chapel, remains to be seen. Watch this space.

OUTPATIENTS' CLINIC

If you have to go to hospital, then a **short visit** is preferable – and the same goes for the cinema (see 'Excessive Length', p.216). So here is our guide to our **favourite** '**operating theatres**', and also some films that will make you **feel better**, if you can't summon the energy to leave your sickbed. There's also some parental guidance for you stay-at-home ne'er do wells . . .

NURSE, THE SCREENS!

The Movie Doctors' Favourite 'Hospitals'

THE PHOENIX, EAST FINCHLEY, LONDON

One of the UK's oldest and most revered cinemas, this is where Dr K spent his formative years, enjoying late-night screenings of *The Crazies*, *Eraserhead*, *The Devils* and, of course, *The Exorcist*. Sublime!

www.phoenixcinema.co.uk

SCREEN ON THE GREEN, ISLINGTON, LONDON

Nice flapjack.

www.everymancinema.com/venues/
screen-on-the-green

THE (OLD) ODEON, HOLLOWAY, LONDON

When it was still an ashtray, the curtains were stained and you got chased by drug dealers.

www.odeon.co.uk/cinemas/
holloway/97

BFI IMAX, WATERLOO, LONDON

Biggest screen, loudest speakers.
Deep joy.

www.odeon.co.uk/bfi_imax

THE PLAZA, TRURO, CORNWALL

A beautiful independent cinema
where 35mm projection still thrives
alongside digital, Doom Bar is served
in the lobby, and both staff and
clientele are true film lovers.
www.wtwcinemas.co.uk/truro-the-
plaza-cinema

THE ELECTRIC, BIRMINGHAM

A little gem of a theatre whose
rich history dates back to 1909,
and which has flourished since a
thorough 2004 renovation.
www.theelectric.co.uk

WATERSHED, BRISTOL

The perfect place to enjoy an
eclectically programmed movie and
then have an intense discussion about it
afterwards in the lively restaurant/bar.
www.watershed.co.uk

THE REX, BERKHAMSTED

Lovingly restored, this art deco jewel prides itself on offering the finest viewing experience, with a mission to 'remind us what we have long stopped expecting from public buildings'.
www.therexberkhamsted.com

WARWICK UNIVERSITY FILM SOC

Weird, sweet smell most of the time.
www.filmsoc.warwick.ac.uk

THE DOME, WORTHING

From the time when smokers had to sit on the left. Boy, that helped.
www.domecinema.co.uk

HYDE PARK PICTURE HOUSE, LEEDS

Billed as 'the cosiest in Leeds', this grand cinema – first opened back in 1914 – oozes old-school charm from the stalls to the balcony.
www.hydeparkpicturehouse.co.uk

GLASGOW FILM THEATRE, GLASGOW

A programme of international classics and contemporary art house fare keeps the loyal GFT audience entertained, educated and entranced.

www.glasgowfilm.org/theatre

MAREEL, SHETLAND

Shetland's only purpose-built cinema screens can be found in this stunning modern building overlooking the waters of Lerwick. Miranda Richardson has been seen dancing a reel in the bar.

www.mareel.org

QFT, BELFAST

Few places can match the vibrant atmosphere of Northern Ireland's best-loved cinema, which prides itself on projecting both digital and celluloid with equal dexterity.

www.queensfilmtheatre.com

PRESCRIPTION MEDICATION

Movies to Aid Your Recovery

So there you are, all tucked up at home and feeling rather sorry for yourself. You'd rather be at work/rest/play but instead you are flat on your back with a pile of shallow magazines, a honey and lemon drink and a sack of potions. The magazines are full of healthy athletic folk, the honey and lemon is cold and congealed and, as The Verve have taught us, the drugs don't work. All the so-called remedies are making you feel worse about yourself.

If you're a guy you've probably let everyone know just how ill you are, but somehow you're still not getting the sympathy you deserve. If the Movie Doctors can't make a house call and our emergency helpline is busy, here's what we advise. Get your laptop or stagger to the sofa and turn on your DVD player. Watch one or all of these movies. They have been hand-picked to make you feel better about yourself. You are a beautiful person (apart from when you aren't). You deserve the positive rays which have been scientifically proven to radiate from these films.

THE LORD OF THE RINGS TRILOGY:
THE FELLOWSHIP OF THE RING *(2001)*
THE TWO TOWERS *(2002)*
THE RETURN OF THE KING *(2003)*

What better place to start than Middle Earth? The combined running time (depending on which version has been dispensed) is a minute over *twelve hours*. That's right. It's so long you'll be able to measure your improvement film by film. *The Fellowship of the Ring* – at death's door. *The Two Towers* – propped up, taking solids, wearing clothes. *The Return of the King* – drinking beer, gone shopping. You probably feel as though you have spent a week being forged in the fires of Mount Doom with only the Dark Lord Sauron for company, so there is also great comfort to be taken from watching someone who looks and sounds worse than you. Gollum is our ministering angel here.

Deathly white, stick thin and with a bad case of bronchopneumonia, everything about him is worse than you.

While you might need a ring to live to 'eleventy-ten' as Bilbo Baggins proclaims, Peter Jackson's masterpiece should get you through to the weekend. **WARNING** Just because hobbits and wizards smoke copious amount of Old Tobey weed doesn't mean that you can. You might be able to blow smoke rings like galleons, but you also might get impaled by an orc.

THE PRINCESS BRIDE (1987)

The ancients looked for a panacea to cure all ills. The Cahuilla Indian people of the Colorado Desert believed the red sap of the elephant tree could make everyone better. The Movie Doctors prefer to prescribe this gem from director Rob Reiner. If all the films we've already listed aren't working for you, then here's our banker. If it's all hurting too much, here comes the epidural.

The Princess Bride is the ultimate feel-good, get-better movie (apart from the bit when Westley dies – what were you thinking, William Goldman?). What you need when you are under the weather is someone to read you a story, and that's precisely what this movie does. Not only is it a classic fairy tale (apart from the hero dying bit) but it takes the form of a kindly grandpa (Peter Falk) *actually* reading an *actual* story to an *actual* sick child (Fred Savage). The young boy may be faking it (Are you sure *you* aren't? Not just a little bit?) but he is astute enough to stop the story with a plaintive 'Is there going to be lots of kissing?' The accurate answer here is 'Never mind the kissing, check out the Rodents of Unusual Size.'

We can prescribe this movie for all ages for the following medically sound reasons:

- It's properly funny. 'Life is pain. Anyone who says differently is selling you something.'
- It's a proper adventure with only mild torture.
- You can say 'as you wish' a lot and drive everyone crazy.
- It's that bloke from *Homeland* (Mandy Patinkin) who plays the master swordsman. 'My name is Inigo Montoya. You killed my father. Prepare to die.'
- Buttercup is the best name for a princess, ever.
- The Dread Pirate Roberts is the best name for a sea-based baddie, ever.
- While you are still poorly, you can use Billy Crystal's line that you have been 'only mostly dead'.
- The movie visits the Pit of Despair and scales the Cliffs of Insanity so you don't have to.
- Mark Knopfler's fabulous soundtrack will remind you that while you have the fever, an eighties super-absorbent red sweatband will save you many forehead-wiping hours.
- It's only ninety-eight minutes long.

THE ROAD (2009)

Not everyone's choice. It is true that this terrifying drama, starring Viggo Mortensen as 'The Man', and Kodi Smit-McPhee as 'The Boy', is about as grim as a post-apocalyptic story can be (none of them tend to be that cheerful). It is true that the world is grey and getting greyer, that all warmth has gone and cannibalistic hordes roam every street. But on the plus side Viggo has a gun. He might only have two bullets – one for him and one for his boy if the hungry ones get too close – but that should be enough. Plus they have a shopping trolley and they have a plan: head south. As plans go, it's not that inspiring, but as the north isn't looking too attractive right now, it sort of works.

Why are we prescribing this movie drenched in fear and despair? The reason is this. However rubbish you are feeling right now, everyone in *The Road* is feeling *so* much worse. There are no duvets in *The Road*.

GEORGE OF THE JUNGLE *(1997)*

We only have two things to say. 1) Seeing a Tarzan-like man swing at full speed into a vast tree trunk is funny. Every time. 2) An elephant that thinks it's a dog is funny. All the time. Watch twice a day till better.

GREASE *(1978)* AND DIRTY DANCING *(1987)*
DOUBLE BILL

In the world of the stupid, there exists something referred to as 'a guilty pleasure'. This is manifestly ridiculous. Style bullies always try to ruin your life, and they invented this phrase. Trust us when we say there is no such thing as a guilty pleasure. There is stuff you like and there is stuff that you don't. And that is it. As Graham Norton says in his seminal work *The Life and Loves of a He Devil*, 'Unless your pleasure is bear baiting or watching snuff movies,

then save your guilt for something that deserves it.'

Grease will boost your immunity and *Dirty Dancing* will bring colour to your pallid flesh. Once you've decided you don't have to wear pyjamas all day, these films will tempt you with the physical thrill of pink dresses, leather jackets and tight-fitting black singlets. As you try to look normal again, enjoy Danny dressing softer and Sandy dressing harder in *Grease* (much like Van Morrison and Cliff Richard did for 'Whenever God Shines His Light'. Van was Sandy, Cliff was Danny. Or maybe the other way round). *Dirty Dancing* may have what Roger Ebert called an 'Idiot Plot', but sometimes you can let the clichés pull you through and the stock characters act as useful props. If these two toe-tappers have worked their magic, you can always go for the daring treble. *Strictly Ballroom* (1992) may have spawned the omnipresent *Strictly Come Dancing*, but this gem will make Len Goodman and chums seem like Pan's People. You might be a stranger to the lure of the sequinned matador shirt, but here you will watch the Pan-Pacific Grand Prix Amateur Championships and *need* to be part of the magic. Deep inside you know that when you are well, you will think that all this was some kind of strange, drug-induced hallucination, and that ballroom dancers are as weird as magicians, but for now let's flex, flick and follow through with the man in tight pants.

PATIENT
TRANSPORT

We hope that your particular complaint has been addressed and you are now ready to **face the outside world**. We want you to take away this prescription which we think of as our ***deus ex machina*** (the *machina* in question preferably being a projector). On it you'll find two movies that will cure absolutely anything. Guaranteed. Watch them whenever you feel up, watch them when you feel down. In fact, watch them every week until **everything about the world improves**. As it will do.

PHARMACY STAMP	AGE	TITLE, FORENAME, SURNAME & ADDRESS

1983 -03- 29
MIST ON THE MOUNTAINS
FERNESS · CDG
B363

AGE

32

TITLE, FORENAME, SURNAME & ADDRESS

Mac
23 The Rocks
Ferness
Scotland

NHS NUMBER   **47-97-12-03-BF**

ENDORSEMENTS

DOSAGE Ideally, this should be taken at least once a year; studies show that people who have ingested *Local Hero* on an annual basis since it first came onto the market in 1983 are happier, healthier, and generally more whimsical than those using other, similar treatments. It can be taken in a number of formats: on film in a cinema; on VHS, DVD or Blu-ray in the home; or as a digitally downloadable soundtrack album while on the move. If symptoms persist, you can try taking the air on the sandy beaches around Camusdarach, sipping a forty-year-old malt in Banff, or making a call from the phone box in Pennan – all of which have magical healing qualities.

SIGNATURE OF PRESCRIBER   *Dr Kermode*

DATE   *29/3/83*

TEN REASONS WHY LOCAL HERO
WILL CURE ALL YOUR ILLS

1 It's a story that tells us true happiness doesn't come from owning a Porsche 930 Turbo, while reminding us that 'you can't get four or five winter lambs into the back of a Maserati'.

2 It was described by writer/director Bill Forsyth as '*Brigadoon* meets *Apocalypse Now*' – arguably the best movie pitch ever.

3 It has a score by Mark Knopfler so beautiful it could cause the sick to rise from their beds and walk.

4 It tells us to be kind to rabbits (especially those with a name, particularly those with *two* names) while offering a handy recipe for *casserole de lapin*.

5 It features the endlessly quotable epithet; 'Are there two g's in "Bugger Off"?'

6 It boasts a love story between Jenny Seagrove as a mermaid and Peter Capaldi as a young linguist who will, in time, become a Time Lord.

7 It's one of the very rare cases of a movie whose ending wasn't ruined by Hollywood. Having been offered several million dollars to shoot a new ending in which Mac *stays* in Scotland, Forsyth appeased the studio with an out-take of the now iconic phone box, arguing that it would prove just as uplifting *and* save them loads of money. The rest is history...

8 It's Fulton Mackay's finest hour.

9 It features a drunken Russian sea captain singing 'Even the Lone Star State Gets Lonesome' – once heard, never forgotten.

10 Honestly, if watching *Local Hero* doesn't make you feel better, you're already dead.

SYMPHONY
NO.5
15-02-1985
SALZBURG
AUSTRIA

AGE

224

TITLE, FORENAME, SURNAME & ADDRESS

Wolfgang Amadeus Mozart
Vogelweiderstraße 63
Salzburg
Austria

NHS NUMBER **47-97-12-03-BF**

ENDORSEMENTS

DOSAGE To be taken daily. It is safe to take alongside your *Local Hero* medication. You may inhale or apply externally, and it will still be safe to drink alcohol or drive machinery. The following points are taken from the patient information leaflet.

SIGNATURE OF PRESCRIBER *Dr Mayo*

DATE **15/2/85**

ELEVEN WAYS THAT AMADEUS WILL MAKE YOU HAPPIER, NICER AND EVERYTHING

1 Nipples of Venus. Maybe the greatest movie snack of all time. Constanze Mozart goes to Salieri desperate for a smoky bacon crisp or something of that nature. Her feckless husband has failed to put money in the kitty again so, in desperation, she turns to the great court composer for a salty treat. But it turns out that he doesn't do savoury. Instead Old Sal (as we have come to know him) offers Mrs Mozart the most astonishingly calorific, crème-laden, heaped pile of fancies since Private Godfrey's sister Dolly made more upside-down cakes than the verger could manage for the Walmington-on-Sea church fête. These are the Nipples of Venus, and jolly good they look too, in a Mary Berry kind of way. Even Paul Hollywood would smile knowingly at the classic pastry and innuendo combo.

2 For DVD Director's Cut viewers there is a special bonus. Much to Salieri's surprise (and ours), Mrs M. decides to take her top off as a means of payment. This of course makes the cost of purchasing any Nipples of Venus a bit of a daunting task for the rest of us. We're not sure that your deli counter manager will be quite ready for this unorthodox means of payment for services. ('I can't give you your doughnuts for that, Mr Jones.')

3 The greatest music evs. End of. Mozart's hits have been scientifically proved to *make you more intelligent*. It's not just unborn babies who absorb the IQ-enhancing sonic waves. It works on all of us. One dose of *Eine kleine Nachtmusik* and you're at GCSE Maths Grade A. A repeat prescription of the *Marriage of Figaro* and you're at Ph.D. in Horror Fiction level. And an intravenous drip of the *Requiem Mass* could get you into Harvard. Even the Wombles did the *Minuetto Allegretto* and you don't want to mess with Uncle Bulgaria. The mere presence of the soundtrack in your CD collection marks you out as *special* (but not in that way).

4 Fancy dress is rarely proper for grown-ups, but if the offer is to go to an eighteenth-century Viennese masked ball, even the Movie Doctors might be tempted. The ball scenes in *Amadeus* (Nipples of Venus aplenty) are so *irresistible* and *sumptuous* that even the most dour, browbeaten hack will leap for joy and ask the Duchess of Salzburg for a fling around the circuit.

5 Wigs and face powder. Who knew you could rock both? Don't let ridicule get in the way of simple pleasure. Make sure you get the right product – don't scrimp! – Hungarian Super-Fine Dust Paint is a classic. We can assure you that when it's time to wind down, the Movie Doctors can be found be-wigged and be-powdered, trying on their latest pantaloon purchases.

6 You might have used the cinema as a babysitting service when going to see assorted inappropriate 12As. You may well have mocked *The Pokemon Movie* in spite of it being your nipper's favourite film. And you possibly told them about *Walkabout* way too soon after seeing *The Railway Children*. But! You are no way near as bad as Leopoldo Mozart. We highlight some bad parents for you on p.136; well here's one more for you. Watch *Amadeus* and feel instantly better about your parenting skills. Have you dragged your child around Europe to perform in front of royalty? No, you haven't. Have you made disparaging comments about your daughter-in-law's housekeeping skills? Probably not (though you might have been tempted). Have you tormented your prodigy to the extent that he writes an opera featuring a murdered father carrying his sin to hell just after you've died? Thought not.

7 None of us is looking as fabulous as we once were. Even the Movie Doctors don't wear their leather trousers quite as often as they used to. But none of us has ever looked as bad as F. Murray Abraham in his opening scene with the luckless Father Vogler. Called to hear the court composer's confession in a local asylum, Vogler is fixed with the most terrifying stare that any insane, withered, suicidal, bloody-tongued former musician has ever managed. Study Salieri in this shot and take comfort; your skin will never be this battered, your eyes never this tiny, your hair never this crazy (unless you're John Pilger). You're a looker, you really are.

8 *Amadeus* will make you feel better about your furniture. Every single piece of wood that is sat on, leant against or asked in any way to be wood-like, creaks and squeaks as though it is about to give way under the sheer weight of the padded stockings and flouncy lace. There's not a single decent piece of MDF anywhere to be seen.

9 Music criticism. Courtesy of the emperor (played by Jeffrey Jones but bearing an uncanny resemblance to Graham Chapman) we get the classic line 'too many notes'. Originally attributed to the monarch's sister Marie Antoinette, suggesting her musical ear was as sharp as her cake-based generosity, this line is delivered to Mozart after the first performance of *The Abduction from the Seraglio* and he doesn't take it too well. But the old emperor is on to something. Some music does indeed have too many notes (as opposed to, say, skiffle, which barely has any notes at all). It's the moment when the tune goes all noodly, the bit where the producer should have said, 'We need to lose this bit, Eric.' Franz Josef was right. Just cut a few notes. There it is.

10 Are you envious of the Queen? No, because she is not like us. Are you jealous of the President of the USA? No, because he has nuclear weapons. In the same way, we watch *Amadeus*, we love the tunes, respect the genius, maybe order some velvet britches for church on Sunday, but *we do not want to be him*. We are grateful for our lot and our place in life.

11 *Amadeus* is a movie with Simon Callow in it but not Simon Callow's bottom. This is both a surprise and a blessing. And so . . . we emerge from *Amadeus*, happier, nicer and everything.

OUT OF HOURS

The Movie Doctors' Clinic is open

MONDAY TO FRIDAY, 9 A.M. – 5 P.M.

Need help with a modern life or movie dilemma?
Emergency consultations and screenings are available on request.

To arrange a consultation outside the
standard opening times please contact:

f THEMOVIEDOCTORS 🐦 @MOVIEDOCTORS

INDEX

IMAGE PERMISSIONS

All images (except pp.111, 112, 113, 275 , 300-303), are from the archives of The Kobal Collection, a library dedicated to preserving the history of motion picture stills, posters and ephemera.

Accident & Emergency

p. 14 *The Expendables 3* (2014), Nu Image/Millennium Films/Lionsgate

p. 16 *Swing Time* (1936), RKO

p. 19 *The Blues Brothers* (1980), Universal Pictures

p. 21 *Die Hard With a Vengeance* (1995), Cinergi Pictures/20th Century Fox

Pharmacy

p. 27 *Angela's Ashes* (1999), Paramount Pictures/Universal Pictures/Scott Rudin Productions/David Appleby

p. 30 *Mamma Mia!* (2008), Universal Pictures/Relativity Media/Littlestar/Playtone

p. 33 *Groundhog Day* (1993), Columbia Pictures/Louis Goldman

p. 35 *Casablanca* (1942), Warner Bros/Jack Woods

p. 40 *Blade Runner* (1982), Ladd Company/Warner Bros

p. 46 *The Music Box* (1932), Hal Roach/MGM; *The General* (1926), United Artists/Buster Keaton Prods

p. 47 *Young Frankenstein* (1974), 20th Century Fox; *Annie Hall* (1977), Rollins-Joffe/United Artists

Ear, Nose & Throat

p. 51 *School of Rock* (2003), Paramount/Scott Rudin Productions/MFP/New Century/SOR Productions/Andrew Schwartz

p. 60 *Little Shop of Horrors* (1986), Warner Bros/The Geffen Company presents A Frank Oz Film

Sleep Clinic

p. 65 *The Piano* (1993), Jan Chapman Prods/CIBY 2000/Miramax

p. 69 *A Nightmare on Elm Street* (1984), New Line

Psychiatry

p. 73 *The Cabinet of Dr. Caligari* (1920), Decla-Bioscop

p. 74 *Back to the Future* (1985), Amblin Entertainment/Universal Pictures; *The Silence of the Lambs* (1991), Orion Pictures/Ken Regan; *MASH* (1970), 20th Century Fox/Aspen

p. 75 *Carry on Screaming* (1966), StudioCanal Films Ltd; *Behind the Candelabra* (2013), HBO Films; *One Flew Over the Cuckoo's Nest* (1975), United Artists/Fantasy Films

p. 79 *The Rocky Horror Picture Show* (1975), 20th Century Fox/Michael White Productions

p. 82 *The Big Lebowski* (1998), Polygram/Working Title Films/Merrick Morton

p. 87 *It* (1990), Lorimar TV/Warner Bros. TV

Geriatrics

p. 245 *Driving Miss Daisy* (1989), Warner Bros/The Zanuck Company

p. 246 *The Godfather* (1972), Paramount Pictures

p. 253 *The Best Exotic Marigold Hotel* (2012), Blueprint Pictures/20th Century Fox

Transplants

p. 258 *Face/Off* (1997), Paramount Pictures/Touchstone Pictures

p. 262 *The Wizard of Oz* (1939), MGM

p. 264 *Mrs Doubtfire* (1993), 20th Century Fox/Blue Wolf

Morgue

p. 275 *Bambi* (1942), Disney courtesy of the Cinema Museum, London

p. 276 *Bonnie and Clyde* (1967), Warner Bros/Seven Arts/Tatira-Hiller Productions

Chapel

p. 287 *Heaven is for Real* (2014), Tristar Pictures/Roth Films/Screen Gems

p. 291 *2001: A Space Odyssey* (1968), MGM/Stanley Kubrick Productions

p. 294 *The Exorcist* (1973), Warner Bros/Hoya Productions

Outpatients' Clinic

p. 300 The Phoenix, East Finchley, London © Maurita van Droogenbroeck; The (Old) Odeon, Holloway, London, courtesy of Cinema Theatre Association Archive

p. 301 BFI IMAX, Waterloo, London as proudly presented by ODEON; The Plaza, Truro, Cornwall © Jonathon Jacobs; Watershed, Bristol © Toby Farrow

p. 302 The Rex, Berkhamsted © Jacqui Adams; Warwick University Film Soc © Chloë Pugh; The Dome, Worthing © gary.levett@ntlworld.com; Hyde Park Picture House, Leeds © Ollie Jenkins

p. 303 Glasgow Film Theatre, Glasgow © Neil Thomas Douglas

p. 307 *Grease* (1978), Paramount/RSO

Patient Transport

p. 310 *Local Hero* (1983), Enigma/Goldcrest

p. 312 *Amadeus* (1984), Saul Zaentz Company

ACKNOWLEDGEMENTS

The Movie Doctors would like to thank

The entire, lovely team at Canongate, in particular Jenny Lord without whose patience, determination, diplomacy and general editorial excellence you would not now be holding a copy of this book.

Hedda Archbold at HLA, not only for her all round efficiency and guidance, but also her keen eye for a damn fine movie still.

Sam Copeland at RCW, the thinking writer's agent of choice.

Martin and Simon Toseland, for providing the glue which held the disparate Doctors' ramblings together.

Dave Norris, for keeping the Movie Doctors in the right ratio; and Julie Edwards for keeping Dave Norris in the right ratio.

Tim Clifford, for once again proving himself the connoisseur's choice in the index department.

Kim Newman, for running a rigorous cinematic eye over the manuscript.

Rafaela Romaya, and the team at Hüman After All, for making this book look much more handsome than the people who wrote it.

Finally, thanks to our families, for their love and encouragement, and for generally putting up with two grouchy old men who can be so much less fun in real life.